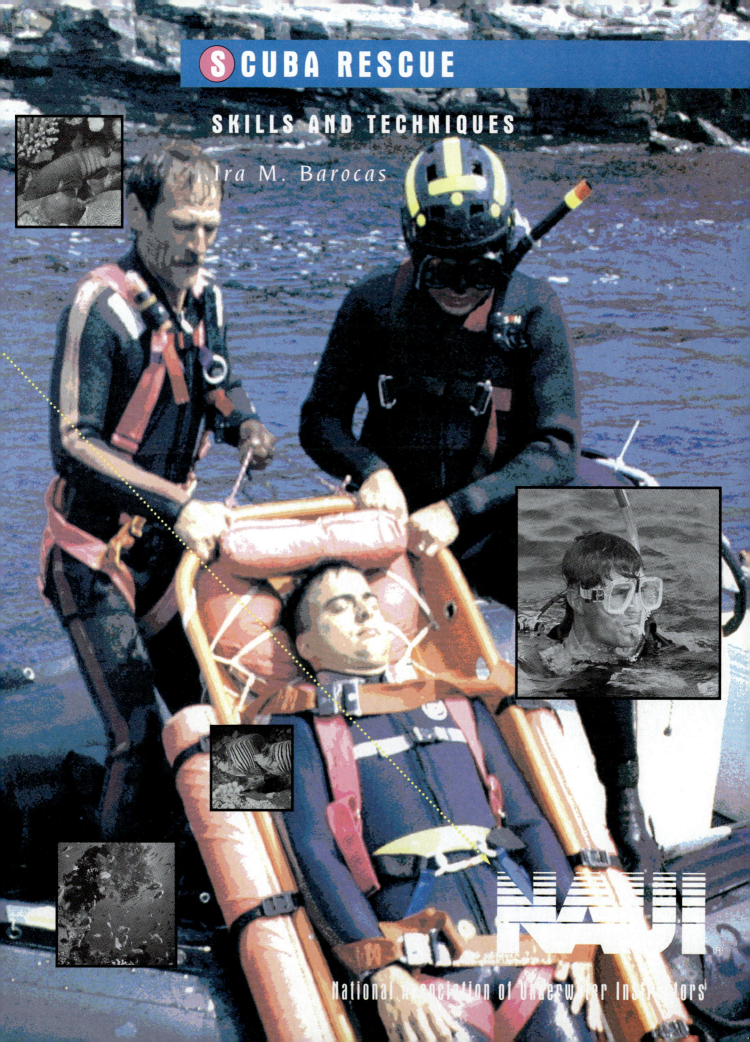

Mosby Lifeline
Dedicated to Publishing Excellence

A Times Mirror Company

Publisher: *David T. Culverwell*
Editor-in-Chief: *Richard A. Weimer*
Editor: *Eric Duchinsky*
Senior Developmental Editor: *Cecilia F. Reilly*
Developmental Editor: *Julie Bauer*
Assistant Editor: *Carla Goldberg*
Project Manager: *Chris Baumle*
Senior Production Editor: *Shannon Canty*
Electronic Publishing: *Chris Robinson*
Manufacturing Manager: *Theresa Fuchs*
Design Manager: *Nancy McDonald*
Cover Design/Chapter Openers: *Sheriff-Krebs Design*

Copyright © 1995 by the National Association of Underwater Instructors (NAUI)

All rights reserved. No part of this publication may be reproduced, stored in a retrieval system, or transmitted, in any form or by any means, electronic, mechanical, photocopying, recording, or otherwise, without prior written permission from the publisher.

Permission to photocopy or reproduce solely for internal or personal use is permitted for libraries or other users registered with the Copyright Clearance Center, provided that the base fee of $4.00 per chapter plus $.10 per page is paid directly to the Copyright Clearance Center, 27 Congress Street, Salem, MA 01970. This consent does not extend to other kinds of copying, such as copying for general distribution, for advertising or promotional purposes, for creating new collected works, or for resale.

Printed in the United States of America

Composition by: Mosby Electronic Production
Printing/Binding by: W.C. Brown

Mosby-Year Book, Inc.
11830 Westline Industrial Drive
St. Louis, MO 63146

International Standard Book Number 0815162863
95 96 97 98 99/9 8 7 6 5 4 3 2 1

NOTE

Text boxes, used throughout the book to help the reader and instructor focus on key information, are color-coded as follows:

 purple bordered boxes stress information

 yellow bordered boxes denote precautions

 red bordered boxes indicate possible danger

REVIEWERS

The following NAUI members participated in the review of this text:

Steve Barsky
Gordon Boivin
Cory Briggs
Jim Corry
Tony D'Andrea
Bret Gilliam
Walt "Butch" Hendrick
Jim Hicks
Sam Jackson
Mike Joyce
Jed Livingstone
Joe Mokry
Pat O'Donovan
Jack Pauli
Scott Raish
Andrea Zaferes

WARNING

Scuba diving is an adventure activity with inherent risks of serious personal injury or death. Good training and good equipment can minimize those risks, but there are no guarantees that these risks can be completely eliminated. The code of the responsible diver states that:

You must accept responsibility for your own actions and safety during every dive.

You must dive within the limits of your ability and training.

Evaluate the conditions before every dive, assuring that they fit your personal capabilities.

Be familiar with and check all equipment before and during every dive.

Know your buddy's as well as your own ability level.

CREDITS

Cover Photography
Bret Gilliam-courtesy of Ocean Tech, Four by Five, Tony Stone Images, FPG International, and The Bettmann Archive

Interior Photography
The Bettmann Archive, all other interior photography by Bret Gilliam-courtesy of Ocean Tech

Illustration
Ben Clemens-Millennium Design

Contents

Scuba Rescue: Skills and Techniques

CHAPTER 1
ACCIDENT PREVENTION
2

CHAPTER 2
SELF-RELIANCE AND THE BUDDY SYSTEM
18

CHAPTER 3
WHAT CAUSES DIVING ACCIDENTS?
32

CHAPTER 4
RECOGNIZING AND RESPONDING TO STRESS AND DISTRESS
60

CHAPTER 5
EMERGENCY ASCENT PROCEDURES
74

CHAPTER 6
TOWING, ASSISTING, AND SURFACE RESCUE
90

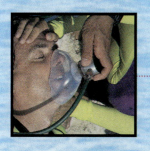

CHAPTER 7
DECOMPRESSION ILLNESS AND DIVING INJURIES
118

CHAPTER 8
ACCIDENT MANAGEMENT
154

APPENDIX A
SAFETY IS NO ACCIDENT
173

APPENDIX B
BLOOD-BORNE PATHOGENS
175

APPENDIX C
CHANGES TO NAUI STANDARDS AND PROCEDURES 1994
176

APPENDIX D
NAUI ACCIDENT REPORT FORM
178

APPENDIX E
DIVING INCIDENT REPORT FORM
179

SCUBA RESCUE

CHAPTER ONE

ACCIDENT PREVENTION

Challenging, adventurous, exciting—scuba diving is all this and more! As any diver knows, there are few outdoor recreational activities that can match scuba for sheer exhilaration. There are surely no other easily accessible leisure activities that allow people to visit another world: the underwater environment. Properly equipped and prepared, appropriately trained divers share literally hundreds of thousands of successful dives every year. People freely enjoy scuba during any season, diving everywhere from high mountain lakes to tropical reefs. Divers participate in underwater photography or videography, spearfishing or collecting, and some relish exploring shipwrecks or even underwater caves.

Yet for all its pleasure and variety, recreational scuba is a serious, equipment-intensive activity that requires physical fitness, extensive training, and informed judgment. Although they may be easy to learn, *all underwater and in-water pastimes pose risk*. Errors or accidents underwater, though fortunately quite rare, can result in serious injury, permanent disability, or death. NAUI's members believe that even one such incident is too many.

As certified diving professionals, NAUI leaders work diligently to eliminate accidents by making dive training more effective and participation more pleasurable as they develop new divers, teach specialty skills to certified divers, or conduct recreational dives. But recreational diving is a dynamic, shared activity that always includes some risk. One diver's problem can jeopardize others, from an individual's buddy to other members of a diving group. Thus, *the responsibility for preventing accidents belongs to every diver*.

To help divers meet this responsibility, NAUI's members encourage participants to fully understand, prepare for, and continuously evaluate the risks of every dive. By using and expanding their knowledge, maintaining and developing their fitness and water skills, including rescue skills, and personally judging and accepting the risks of each dive they make, all divers can help to prevent or limit the effects of any mishaps that may occur.

Reducing diving's inherent risks begins with frankly assessing your own fitness to make any dive, then reasonably appraising the fitness of your buddy, and, finally, gauging the fitness and abilities of other participants as they may concern you.

A DIVING MEDICAL EXAMINATION

Fitness for diving depends first on overall physical health, particularly the healthy function of the respiratory and circulatory systems. Sound lungs, heart, and blood vessels are crucial for divers. A problem in any of these areas may temporarily or permanently disqualify a person from diving.

Recognizing this, NAUI requires its members to have all diving students submit a completed NAUI Medical Form before beginning in-water instruction (Fig. 1-1). Past conditions that may have a continuing effect and current health are both evaluated to help ensure that a student can enjoy the course without undue risk. While prospective students are encouraged to undergo a medical examination with a knowledgeable diving physician to complete the form, all divers and their physicians can use the NAUI Medical Form as a useful guide for reevaluating fitness for diving. Periodic assessment will help

> **KNOWLEDGE, ABILITY, and VIGILANCE are the essence of preventing accidents!**

make sure that any conditions or developing medical problems will be dealt with promptly, preventing them from becoming the cause of a diving accident. Most NAUI members can recommend several local practitioners familiar with the unique physical demands of diving. Other sources of information on qualified doctors include the Undersea and Hyperbaric Medical Society (UHMS) and the Divers Alert Network (DAN).

CONTRAINDICATIONS TO UNDERWATER ACTIVITIES

Doctors use the term *contraindication* to describe conditions that are incompatible with the demands of an activity. Physical circumstances such as a chronic lung problem or disability or psychological issues like severe claustrophobia compromise the goal of accident-free diving.

Contraindications fall into three broad categories.

Absolute Contraindications

Absolute contraindications to underwater activity include Chronic Obstructive Pulmonary Disorders (COPD), any respiratory (breathing) and pulmonary (lung) disabilities, seizure disorders, insulin-dependent diabetes, diagnosed heart disease, and pregnancy. Individuals with these conditions should never dive, despite the advice or clearance of physicians who may not be completely aware of the physical processes and stresses of diving. While NAUI respects the opinions of all medical professionals, specialists in *diving* medicine support the view that conditions that may cause fits of coughing underwater, disrupt breathing, or lead to sudden incapacitation or unconsciousness totally disqualify persons from recreational diving.

> **ABSOLUTE CONTRAINDICATIONS are conditions that totally exclude an individual from diving now or at any foreseeable time in the future.**

Fig. 1-1: The NAUI Medical Form.

NATIONAL ASSOCIATION OF UNDERWATER INSTRUCTORS
POST OFFICE BOX 14650, MONTCLAIR, CALIFORNIA 91763-1150

MEDICAL HISTORY FORM

Before your medical examination by the physician, this entire side and the top of the reverse side are to be completed. Be prepared to discuss any abnormalities or problems with your physician.

Check the appropriate blank if you have ever had any of the following apply to you, and explain under remarks, indicating the number.

- ___ 1. Electrocardiogram
- ___ 2. Mental or emotional problems
- ___ 3. Operation or illness
- ___ 4. Hospitalized
- ___ 5. Serious Injury
- ___ 6. Physical handicap
- ___ 7. Regular medication
- ___ 8. Allergies, including drugs
- ___ 9. Frequent colds or sore throat
- ___ 10. Severe or frequent headaches
- ___ 11. Rejected from any activity for medical reasons
- ___ 12. Hay fever
- ___ 13. Sinus trouble
- ___ 14. Motion sickness
- ___ 15. Claustrophobia
- ___ 16. Contact lenses
- ___ 17. Ear or hearing problems
- ___ 18. Alcohol problems
- ___ 19. Dental plates
- ___ 20. Trouble equalizing pressure
- ___ 21. Dizziness or fainting
- ___ 22. Epilepsy
- ___ 23. Heart trouble
- ___ 24. Asthma
- ___ 25. Tuberculosis
- ___ 26. Respiratory problems
- ___ 27. Persistent cough
- ___ 28. Diabetes
- ___ 29. Chest pain
- ___ 30. Use of street drugs
- ___ 31. Over 40 years old
- ___ 32. Pregnant
- ___ 33. Medication
- ___ 34. Bronchitis
- ___ 35. High blood pressure
- ___ 36. Any medical problem not listed

PRINT OR TYPE REMARKS: _____

_____

_____

_____

Date of chest x-ray _____

IF STUDENT IS A MINOR, BOTH PARENTS OR GUARDIANS MUST SIGN THIS FORM.

Date of previous medical examination _____

Parent/Guardian Signature _____ Date _____

Student Signature _____ Date _____

Parent/Guardian Signature _____ Date _____

Legal Name (for certification or records) _____

Nickname (for informal course use) _____ Social Security/PIN No. _____

Home Address _____ City _____ State _____ Zip _____

Birthdate _____ Age _____ Sex _____ Home Phone _____

Occupation _____ Company _____

Course applied for: _____ City _____

In case of emergency, contact:

Name _____ Relationship _____ Phone _____

Doctor _____ Day Phone _____ Night Phone _____

Medical Insurance Co. _____ Policy No. _____ Phone _____

How did you learn of this course? _____

88-0074

7/88
Item No. 117

Asthma

Asthma, the common term for the symptoms of "reactive airway disease," is a condition that disrupts normal inhalation and exhalation. It has many possible causes, from allergic reactions to airborne particles like dust, mold, and spores, to the breathing of cold air or exertion. Its effect is the inability to catch one's breath or exhale properly.

During an asthma attack, a sufferer may cough excessively or choke, dramatically increasing the risk of lung overexpansion injury underwater. Airways literally swell and may close with the same outcome. A severe asthmatic attack can lead also to passing out as a result of lack of oxygen to the brain (hypoxia). Any of these events can be fatal underwater or can lead to panicked flight to the surface.

Though the likelihood of asthma attacks may be reduced with medication, some asthma medications are themselves contraindications to diving, detracting from divers' ability to concentrate or causing other undesirable physical and mental effects. Worse, some people with asthma consider their use of medication equivalent to being cured. They may deny that they have the disease even to themselves and ignore its effects, eventually becoming victims underwater.

Emphysema

Emphysema is a condition characterized by progressive loss of lung elasticity. The resulting damage to lung tissue's normal capacity and ability to exchange gas with the circulatory system prevents participation in any strenuous physical activity, certainly diving.

Like asthmatics, emphysema sufferers may be unable to catch their breath, a potentially fatal condition underwater. The emphysemic's damaged lungs frequently have weak spots that may rupture under normal diving conditions and patches that can inadvertently trap air. Either problem can result in life-threatening lung overexpansion injuries while scuba diving.

Tuberculosis (TB)

Tuberculosis (TB), once commonly known as *consumption*, is a contagious, degenerative disease of lung tissue, caused by exposure to airborne bacteria. Victims suffer from greatly reduced lung function—the result of damage to lung tissue from the infection. Although once believed all but eradicated, TB is again reaching epidemic proportions in some parts of the world, including some major US cities. Drug-resistant forms also are developing.

It is doubtful that anyone with advanced TB would want to dive, since even simple activity could leave an affected individual weak and breathless. However, early stages of the disease may be hard to detect without a specific examination. Divers who may have been exposed can discuss the risk with their physicians and may choose to be tested for the illness. Anyone diagnosed with active disease should not dive.

Epilepsy

Epilepsy is the generic name for a group of neurological conditions that may cause seizures, generally without warning. Seizure underwater is almost certain to result in death by drowning. Though many epileptics control the disease through medication and ongoing medical care, even the remote possibility of unconsciousness or complete loss of control underwater presents an unacceptably high risk to the epileptic and any companions that may respond to aid the stricken diver.

Diabetes

Medication-dependent diabetics must use doses of insulin to maintain the delicate chemical balance of their blood sugar level. This balance easily can be disrupted by the increased physical stresses of exercising underwater. With too little insulin, the brain does not receive its needed nourishment, leading to diabetic coma. With too much insulin, or even the diabetic's failure to eat enough to offset the normal medication, insulin shock leading to unconsciousness can develop.

In either case, the risk to the diver, the buddy, and the group or leader is unacceptable. Unfortunately, many people with diabetes refuse to accept this fact and, like some asthmatics, equate medication with cure. Some conceal their condition, and others convince well-meaning companions of its minor effect on them.

Heart Disease

Heart disease can range from mild, exercise-induced angina to nearly full blockage of one or more cardiac blood vessels, leading to damage to the heart muscle itself. Whatever the range of illness or symptoms, participation in underwater activity is unwise. The inability to deal with strenuous physical demands disqualifies individuals with heart disease for diving.

A problem can arise when the disease goes unnoticed, progressively reducing ability over time until a heart attack occurs seemingly without warning. Underwater, such attacks usually result in death by drowning. Having regular medical checkups that include cholesterol and exercise stress testing, eating nutritiously, and maintaining a regular exercise program can reduce the likelihood of heart disease even in predisposed individuals.

The same measures can lessen its effects if one has the disease. Despite these precautions, a diagnosis of serious heart disease is an absolute contraindication to diving.

Pregnancy

Though pregnancy is obviously temporary, it is considered an absolute contraindication to diving. Under no circumstances should women who are, or may be, pregnant scuba dive. Doing so exposes their unborn children to unknown danger. There are no valid studies of the offspring of divers who participate while pregnant, and (understandably) no volunteers willing to risk their children's well-being to gather such data. Animal studies of the effects of increased pressure on an embryo's development suggest possible adverse effects in the later stages of pregnancy.

Temporary Contraindications

Any diver can become temporarily unfit to dive. This may be caused by an illness or injury, medication for a seemingly unrelated condition, motion sickness, or the effects of alcohol or "recreational drugs." Whatever the temporary reason, until it is completely gone, scuba diving should be avoided.

Respiratory Infections, Colds, Coughs, and Earaches

Just a routine cough or "summer" cold can cause changes in the lungs that impair normal gas exchange. These changes, excessive mucus or actual tissue damage, persist long after the person feels better. It is obviously much smarter to wait until a cold or sore throat is completely gone, a period of about 2 weeks after symptoms have ended, than to dive as soon as one stops sneezing or coughing and risk injury.

More severe upper respiratory infections like bronchitis or pneumonia can cause long-term damage to lung tissue. These diseases can be extremely debilitating for some time afterwards. The full recovery period depends on the age, general health, and fitness of patients, as well as how long and how seriously they are ill. In any case, resuming diving is best preceded by a complete diving physical to ensure that there are no lingering ill effects.

A severe ear infection or any illness or injury that affects the mechanisms or paths that help equalize internal pressure in the ears, sinuses, or other air spaces is also probably best evaluated by a diving physician. These problems include facial injuries like a broken nose or jaw and illnesses such as sinus infection or earache. The inability to equalize is extremely painful, stress-producing, and can cause serious permanent damage to the internal and middle ear, which can lead to partial or complete deafness and affect normal balance and motion.

Doubts about whether clearing problems exist are easily resolved by "testing" the clearing procedure before entering the water and clearing "early and often" throughout descent.

Medications

The use of prescription medications may preclude diving for two reasons. Some medicines can adversely affect the vital physical systems of a diver underwater—the lungs, heart, and circulatory systems—though presenting no such problems on the surface. In other cases, the stresses of being underwater, from physical exertion to higher atmospheric pressure, can alter the effects of a drug. Pressure can either increase (potentiate) or decrease (attenuate) any medication's strength.

Few doctors consider the side effects and increased risks prescribed drugs may cause underwater unless they know a patient may be diving. All divers are urged to tell their physicians of their participation and discuss whether any medications they routinely take may be a problem underwater. Doctors may have an alternative medicine or may suggest not taking some medicine on diving days.

Non-prescription Drugs

Some divers take a variety of non-prescription drugs regularly. These drugs may be taken to relieve many kinds of discomfort, from sinus pain to headaches to backaches. Despite their generally low dosage and over-the-counter availability, such medications may be a problem for a diver for the same reasons some prescription medications are. Any drugs that carry a warning about drowsiness or possible effects on the circulatory system, blood pressure, heart rate, and so on, are probably best avoided, or at least discussed with a diving physician.

Other divers routinely or occasionally use decongestants or antihistamines to help enable them to equalize pressure. NAUI strongly condemns this practice. Diving is a recreational activity. No person *must* dive, any more than one must

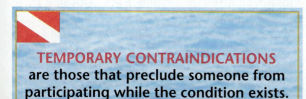

TEMPORARY CONTRAINDICATIONS are those that preclude someone from participating while the condition exists.

play golf or go to the movies. Diving is a leisure-time choice. Taking medication to ensure the ability to participate is foolish and unreasonable.

Even a casual use of decongestants subjects a person to unacceptably increased risk when diving. If the drug wears off underwater, the condition it was supposed to help will often return more forcefully. Swollen and irritated airways or sinuses can make normal equalization impossible, and pressurized air may be trapped in blocked passageways, making ascent extremely painful.

Worse, many over-the-counter medications can become addictive with habitual use. Proper systemic functioning may decrease when the body is chronically affected by drugs. Ever-larger doses may be required for normal function. Any drug dependency can have serious physical and emotional consequences apart from its danger in diving.

Motion Sickness (Seasickness)

Though few people realize it, avoiding seasickness or, if ill, avoiding diving, can be a significant means of preventing diving accidents. Motion sickness, whatever the cause, detracts from a diver's ability to concentrate or perform even simple, well-learned skills. Becoming ill underwater can cause a diver to choke or eject the mouthpiece as a result of retching. At the least, the spasms associated with vomiting are equivalent to holding one's breath, a gravely dangerous practice underwater. Vomiting also leads to serious dehydration, an important contributing factor in decompression sickness (DCS).

There are a number of medications available to deal with common motion sickness, but unfortunately many of these are ineffective for some individuals. Others may be unsuitable for divers because of the side effects they carry, like dry mouth, blurred vision, or lethargy. There are also folk and alternative remedies for seasickness, varying from ginger shavings to accupressure. Again, *some* may *sometimes* work for *some* people. In any case, it is smart to try any seasickness medication before going diving to ensure that you can at least tolerate it. Most motion sickness medications are ineffective once you are ill.

Since common motion sickness seems caused by the difference between what individuals feel (motion) and what they see (a stable, unmoving environment like the enclosed interior space on a boat), bringing these distinct cues into line may help. Mariners often advise ill persons to "watch the horizon," urging them to stay on deck. (This advice may also have a hidden agenda: at least the crew's quarters and belowdecks passenger spaces remain unspoiled.) Others tell you to always have something to eat or, if you are beginning to feel ill, have a swim or snorkel. Still others suggest the opposite! Most victims agree that once illness sets in, it is difficult to cure until you are back on land. Seriously ill persons should avoid diving until they feel better.

Substance Abuse

For many people, one of the greatest attractions to recreational diving is its social component. Participating in scuba is a wholesome, shared activity with a group of like-minded friends and provides a rich source of new acquaintances. Unfortunately, for some people a social situation is an excuse or justification for drinking too much alcohol or using "recreational drugs." Others may use tobacco excessively under the same circumstances, while perhaps never or rarely smoking at other times ("I only smoke when I'm . . ."). Whatever the reasons, these practices are incompatible with reducing diving risk.

Alcohol and drugs affect physical processes like heart rate and blood pressure and detract from mental acuity. Nitrogen narcosis, an indirect effect of pressure present in every dive, can enhance the already-negative effects of these substances on the body and mind. Diving under the influence of alcohol or drugs is stupid. Allowing a person who appears impaired to dive unchallenged is irresponsible. Though people have the right to do as they please within the law, condoning drinking and diving is out of the question for a diving leader especially if another diver will depend on an impaired person as a buddy.

Most dive operators and boat captains have strict policies concerning alcohol and even more rigid rules regarding drugs aboard. In most parts of the world, the threat of serious fines, forfeiture of licenses, or confiscation of vessels still makes boat owners, captains, and crews responsible for ensuring that their boats, personnel, and passengers are free of illegal substances. Finding anyone aboard with contraband is usually cause to cancel a diving excursion.

Tobacco contains nicotine, a toxic substance, as well as many other compounds that have serious effects on the health of smokers and possibly on those around them. Whatever the opposing positions of the cigarette industry, or the stridency of various anti-smoking advocates, the Food and Drug Administration has required health warning labels on tobacco products for many years. Warnings emphasize users' greatly increased risks of heart disease, lung cancer, and emphysema. Surprisingly, many divers still smoke, though the lung changes that even occasional smoking causes can increase a person's risk of decompression illness.

Realizing that one is impaired from substance abuse is, however, quite difficult under some circumstances. Whether from embarrassment, peer pressure, ignorance, or substance-induced belligerence, the decision not to participate in a specific activity is often hard for the affected person to make. Other members of the group, particularly diving leaders or those in positions of authority, may have to help this person understand why diving is a poor choice at the moment.

Relative Contraindications

Every individual is unique. How a specific physical or medical condition affects an individual's fitness to dive is equally unique. The category of relative contraindications recognizes that ability is not necessarily a clear issue. By requiring a complete medical assessment by a diving physician in some situations, NAUI hopes to make diving more accessible to those who might otherwise (wrongly) be assumed unable to dive and thus enjoy the underwater world. The goal of preventing diving accidents requires that any medical recommendations for limited, adapted, or modified participation finally must be judged by qualified NAUI members. Questions should be referred in writing to the Training Department at NAUI Headquarters.

Heart Ailments

Though serious heart disease is an absolute contraindication to diving, some mild problems, such as "heart murmur," may be acceptable risks. Participation would depend upon the written recommendation of a qualified diving physician who has personally conducted a thorough examination of the individual. Assessment would include an exercise stress test to help ensure that strenuous activity is unlikely to cause debilitating effects underwater and a complete review of any recommended medications for side effects that might occur while diving.

> **RELATIVE CONTRAINDICATIONS** are those that require a complete medical assessment by a diving physician, who may advise against participation, or recommend modified or adapted participation.

Hypertension

Hypertension (high blood pressure) often can go undetected until it kills an unsuspecting victim. Other persons with hypertension can experience symptoms similar to those of decompression illness, such as headaches, blurred vision, and ringing in the ears, making early recognition and treatment at a dive site less likely. Yet many individuals with hypertension are on drug therapy that completely controls the problem.

Persons under treatment for hypertension are urged to discuss the wisdom of diving with their personal physicians and to have a complete diving medical examination done by a qualified physician.

Physical Disabilities

Physical disabilities can range from loss or malfunction of limbs or organs to loss of any of the senses, or even obesity. Disabilities can result from trauma leading to permanent injury, chronic disease such as multiple sclerosis, or a temporary injury like a broken bone. Disabling problems can also exist in combinations. Whatever the actual circumstances, only a qualified diving physician can evaluate a person's ability to dive without undue risk.

There are also many divers and diving leaders who are members of organizations that seek to include individuals who might not otherwise have the opportunity to dive. Some groups, like the Handicapped Scuba Association (HSA), seek to help diving facility operators adapt areas and equipment better to accommodate persons with disabilities. HSA and other groups also train divers and leaders in the special techniques necessary to enable disabled persons to dive.

Although NAUI applauds and generally supports these efforts, there are other considerations. Among these are the unique natures of diving maladies, some of which depend on normal sensation and feeling for recognition. For instance, an individual who is paralyzed because of spinal cord injury may have no sensation in a significant portion of the body. As a result, this person would be unable to discern characteristic pain, numbness, or tingling associated with decompression sickness. Unnoticed and, as a result, untreated, the illness could progress and result in more serious permanent damage or death—outcomes that might be avoided with timely therapy. Disabled persons seeking instruction or divers who become disabled and wish to continue participation must be individually evaluated by a diving physician.

NAUI members and interested divers are encouraged to consult with the Training Department at NAUI Headquarters for further guidance regarding these issues.

Mental Illness

The variety of symptoms and manifestations covered under the umbrella of "mental illness" is astounding. How they relate to acceptable diving risk is, however, quite restrictive. Individuals taking medications for mental illness should not be diving without the approval of a knowledgeable psychiatrist, diving physician, and psychopharmacologist. Individuals formerly diagnosed with, or previously confined for, mental illness are encouraged to discuss their participation in diving with their physicians. They should receive written clearance before entering instruction or before returning to the activity if they were previously certified for diving.

Whether you are a recreational diver or professional diving leader, it is important to be observant of those with whom you dive. If a person's actions or idiosyncrasies seem to indicate a lack of touch with reality, you have good reason not to accept that person as a dive buddy or companion. Your lack of confidence in your buddy's fitness to dive will affect your comfort and peace of mind, and will ultimately detract from your enjoyment. Using good judgment beforehand will help prevent problems underwater.

DIVING FITNESS

Even sound individuals, otherwise fit to dive, can be a bad choice for dive buddies if they have poor water skills or are out of shape. Maintaining diving fitness takes continuing effort to refine diving skills and to develop key physical traits such as strength, aerobic endurance, and flexibility.

Training And Continuing Education

Ability to perform in the water is based on practice and coaching. NAUI expects its members to maintain a high level of preparedness for diving by participating in a formal program of continuing education. It is a requirement for maintaining active professional status. Though there are no activity requirements for retaining recreational diving certification, all divers would do well to continue their own diving development by participating in continuing dive training, working to refine their diving skills, and maintaining ability and fitness.

Participating in professional, carefully monitored dive training, like that provided by qualified NAUI instructors, is one of the most effective methods available to prevent diving accidents (Fig. 1-2). Dive training is a multifaceted learning experience. It concentrates nearly equally on increasing a student's knowledge, developing judgment, enhancing fitness, and imparting specialized skills. No single component is more important than another in training successful, competent divers.

Taking part in a NAUI *Scuba Rescue Diver* or *Advanced Scuba Rescue Diver* course provides a good example of the benefit of continuing education. Students in either program build new diving skills onto the base of skills already learned and increase and review diving knowledge. At the same time, students work hard, challenging and enhancing physical abilities as they learn and practice skills under the watchful eyes of a professional NAUI instructor and staff.

Reading diving publications, such as periodicals and professional journals like *Sources*, the popular diving magazines, and this text, is another method of increasing your diving knowledge and subsequently your ability. Scuba diving is a dynamic, evolving leisure activity, and keeping current with new developments, techniques, and skills will better prepare you for its demands.

Going Diving

Recreational diving itself is a good way to maintain the level of fitness and ability you need to prevent diving accidents (Fig. 1-3). NAUI leaders regard every dive as a "training dive" in the sense that all underwater experience teaches something new or reinforces previously acquired skills and techniques. Adopting this attitude can help you prevent accidents and profit from every dive.

Fig. 1-2. Professional training and continuing education help prevent accidents.

**Practice
MINIMAL IMPACT WATER SKILLS!
Maintain Buoyancy Control
Streamline Your Equipment
Kick Carefully and Efficiently**

By setting aside some time to practice a basic skill with a buddy, like mask clearing or sharing air under controlled circumstances, you will benefit in better preparation and more command and confidence while diving. Supporting NAUI's commitment to improving the diving environment by concentrating on and practicing Minimal Impact Water Skills is another means of increasing your diving ability.

On the other hand, infrequent diving will dull your skills. Depending on the individual diver and past experience, periods between dives as brief as 4 or 5 months may require refreshing critical diving skills and reviewing fundamental knowledge before resuming active participation. Many NAUI facilities and other dive shops have "refresher courses" to provide divers an opportunity to review dive planning and basic knowledge and practice diving skills with an instructor in a confined water environment.

Keeping Fit

Besides taking diving courses and enjoying diving, participating in a routine exercise program is an excellent means of preventing diving accidents. A diver's fitness program is most useful when aimed at developing strength, endurance, and flexibility—the results of repeated hard work, though it can be disguised as play.

Participating in competitive sports, aerobic activities, or leisure pursuits like skiing or dancing, helps increase your diving fitness. A good fitness program also includes time to relax, and a healthful, balanced diet. Exercising yields rewards far beyond the enjoyment of recreational diving. It improves your appearance, energy, and self-esteem—benefits for diving and for life.

PLANNING AND PREPARATION

Preventing a diving accident begins long before anyone gets into the water. It starts with the planning and preparation that go into enjoying every dive. After thorough training, the amount of time

Fig. 1-3. Diving frequently will help maintain your skills.

that a diver spends considering diving variables like when, where, how, and, most importantly *what if. . .?* is the wisest investment divers can make to ensure that everyone enjoys a good time.

Know Before You Go

There are many sources of information about specific dive sites but none generally so accurate and reliable as a fellow diver whom you know and trust. Whether that person is a diving leader or another recreational enthusiast, first-hand experience is invaluable. Local diving groups and clubs also usually maintain a database of local and remote sites that their members have visited. The camaraderie of divers usually makes this information available just for the asking.

The diving press regularly reviews popular dive sites at destinations all over the world. Most divers subscribe to one or more diving publications, and they are available from public libraries. Though some published reports can be opti-

**THINGS TO THINK ABOUT
ON EVERY DIVE:

Site Selection and Alternatives;
Environmental Conditions and Weather;
Transportation, Planning the Dive's
Depth, Duration, and Activity;
Equipment Requirements; Companions
and Buddy Pairing; Preparing for
Contingencies and Emergencies.**

mistic, they also can be quite informative and provide valuable information on local conditions, travel recommendations, and the like. Reading them certainly provides many divers with the inspiration, if not the means, for foreign travel in pursuit of great diving.

Dive shops in the areas where you anticipate going are also ready mines of diving information. If they are contacted by phone or mail in advance, most operators are happy to discuss their locales with a visiting diver and potential customer for their goods and services. Tourist agencies and travel retailers are other good sources of information about an intended destination. Even a visit to your local library or bookstore can be part of the research that goes into planning a successful dive.

Personal Dive Gear and Specialized Equipment

Good dive equipment is fundamental to preventing accidents, though for most divers, carrying their gear is the least favorite part of the pastime! Sheer weight aside, without appropriate, functional specialized equipment, scuba diving would not exist. Even though all divers know this, observing how some people treat their gear can make anyone wonder!

Besides routine rinsing and cleaning after each diving excursion, regular preventive maintenance of life support systems, including regulators and cylinders, dry suits, and buoyancy control devices is excellent "dive insurance" (Fig. 1-4). The care you give your equipment by sending it, at recommended intervals, to a professional technician certified by the manufacturer will usually pay off in successfully completed dives unplagued by breakdowns. It is an excellent source of peace of mind, as well.

All dive equipment contributes to "life support" underwater. As a diver, pay attention to your basic personal gear in the same way that a professional would. Mask, fins, snorkel, dive tool, weight system (from belts to integrated weights), exposure suit, and dive accessories should be stored according to the manufacturer's recommendations.

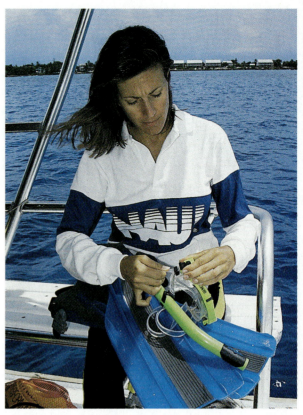

Fig. 1-4. Keeping all your gear neat and organized will help you prepare better for every dive.

Remember that rubber dive gear is harmed by prolonged exposure to ultraviolet light, ozone, hydrocarbon oils and greases. It not only will save you the money of replacement, but it also will help ensure that your gear stays functional and useful for its intended purpose: helping you enjoy your time underwater!

Whatever service and care you give your equipment, no predive preparation is complete without a thorough check of all items that will be used. Using a checklist to ensure systematic examination of all required items, a wise diver will go through each piece carefully, checking buckles, straps, valves, and function to avoid nasty surprises at a dive site or, worse, underwater. Assembling a kit of useful spares is often an exercise in entry-level training. Having a complete kit on hand to be able to deal with the inevitable, annoying mask- or fin-strap tearing can often make the difference between sitting out or enjoying a dive.

Going through the equipment you need beforehand, knowing that it is properly serviced and working well, will help you enjoy much greater confidence underwater. These practices, especially when combined with a good, pre-entry buddy check of gear function and placement before every dive, will help eliminate another, albeit infrequent, cause of diving accidents.

TEST YOUR REGULATOR for function at least every 6 months. Have it bench-tested, serviced, and tuned by a manufacturer-qualified technician at least annually.

Specialized Equipment

All dives require considerably more gear than just personal equipment. From floats, flags, and lines to specialty items such as line reels, underwater lights, or collecting bags, successful dives depend on appropriate, and functional, gear. How much and what kind of extra equipment you will need depends on the situation. Diving instructors, for instance, must identify the site for a training group. This typically means setting up floats and flags, rigging various dive lines, identifying and securing a staging area and entry/exit point, and so on. But a team of divers conducting a shore dive on its own has similar needs. Common sense and experience will help you determine what is necessary for your diving activities. In any case, it will certainly be more than just your personal dive equipment!

First Aid Kits and Oxygen

Assembling and maintaining an appropriate first aid kit that may include oxygen administration equipment is another facet of being prepared for a diving or dive-site emergency. Such kits can be elaborate, complete portable medical facilities or a simple collection of essential items. The complexity of the kit will depend on your diving activities and your qualifications and ability to administer aid (Fig. 1-5).

Fig. 1-5. What you need to carry will depend on your diving activities.

If all your diving takes place from well-equipped, commercial dive vessels, your first aid kit might be a simple collection of assorted adhesive bandages, antiseptics, and basic tools like scissors and tweezers available at a drugstore. Since virtually all these boats carry well-stocked, professional-level first aid kits, oxygen administration equipment, and trained care providers, carrying your own would be superfluous.

On the other hand, if you are traveling to dive in a remote area, or on your own with a buddy or group of companions, or if you are working as a dive leader, you may need to assemble a more extensive medical kit. Besides more medical and first aid items, you will probably want to secure or have access to a ready source of oxygen, the primary first aid treatment for many diving illnesses. If so, you also will need to become familiar with the local rules governing the administration of oxygen as a first aid for diving maladies, complying with applicable requirements for training and licensing.

Dive Planning

Every diver knows the importance of planning to trouble-free diving, yet many dive plans leave out some key elements. Essentially predicting how a specific dive will unfold, good planning considers the question "what if it doesn't?" Contingency factors, such as knowing how much to reduce bottom time if divers inadvertently go deeper than planned, and how much air will be necessary for a controlled ascent at the recommended rate from the planned depth and reasonably beyond it, are important additions to basic planning.

The most useful dive planning also includes the divers—their goals, training, experience, and ability. Although planning strictly according to the NAUI Dive Tables (Fig. 1-6) will keep the dive within the recommended no-decompression time and depth limits, considering the people making the dive and the activities planned will add reality to the numbers. These factors can make a planned site a poor choice on a particular day because of weather or water conditions.

For instance, a dive to 60 feet in warm, clear water with newly certified, relatively inexperienced companions is different from a 60-foot dive with the same group in surge, kelp, or cold, turbid water. The same is true for divers trying out some new skills, such as underwater photography. Though less dramatic than the difference between temperate and tropical water, the extra attention that will be given to new equipment or tasks should be considered in advance, particularly when planning air consumption.

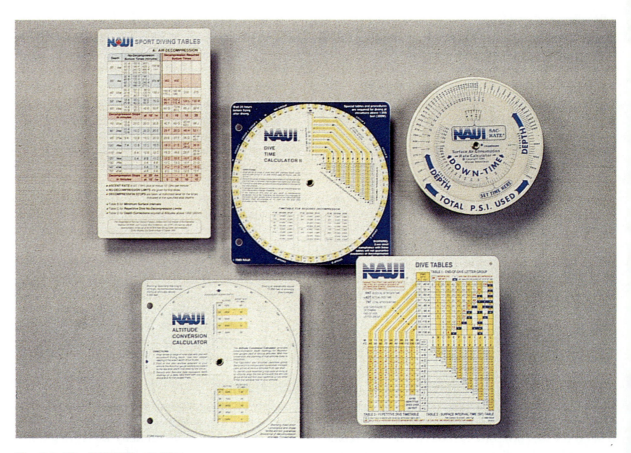

Fig. 1-6. The NAUI Dive Tables.

Emergency Planning

Though careful planning will help reduce the likelihood of diving emergencies, no amount of planning can totally eliminate the chance of a diving illness, accident, or other injury at a dive site. For this reason, emergency planning is part of every diving event.

Preliminary plans include knowing what sources of emergency aid are available at your dive site and being prepared to contact them quickly. Depending on the location, there are a number of possible aid providers that can respond to divers' problems. These include the local Emergency Medical Service (EMS), operating independently or under the jurisdiction of the local fire, police or sheriff's department, all of which may also provide emergency services. It can be the National Park Service if you are diving in or around a national park, or the United States Coast Guard if you are diving in U.S. navigable waters. Other sources are the state police, highway patrol or local marine police, the local Red Cross or Volunteer Ambulance Service, or even the United States Navy if you are diving near a naval base. Nearly every diving area in the world will have similar services available. Information on other emergency service providers in an area can be gathered in advance by contacting local dive shops or through the non-emergency number of the Diver's Alert Network (DAN).

Having the sources at hand in your dive kit is only the first step. Being able to reach them is another matter entirely. Diving takes place offshore. Whether you are in sight of land or not, being even a short distance away from land complicates contacting and receiving any help you may need. Inland or ocean diving can be equally remote and equally far from emergency care.

Contacting suitable aid and receiving it quickly becomes progressively more difficult as the site becomes more remote. Getting help in exotic dive locales may require foreign language fluency or access to an interpreter.

Aboard boats, marine VHF radio is the primary means of communication in coastal waters within about 20 miles (32 km) of land if you are using a full-power (25 watts) radio, or within 3 to 5 miles (5–8 km) of land or in sight of other vessels if you are using a less powerful handheld unit (Fig. 1-7). Outside this range, communication with land-based aid depends on higher power, single side band transceivers.

Close inshore near populous areas, shore diving or inland, cellular telephone service or a handy public phone often can be as convenient and useful as a home telephone in summoning emergency aid. If available, record emergency services contact numbers in indelible ink in an easily accessed spot like the inside cover of your first aid kit. Coins can be stored compactly in a small plastic film canister. In some inland diving areas, those near highways particularly, citizen's band (CB) radio can be very useful in summoning aid, but depending on them for help when you are in distress on the water is unwise.

Fig. 1-7. Emergency communication from a boat usually depends on marine band radios.

CHAPTER TWO

SELF-RELIANCE AND THE BUDDY SYSTEM

Recreational diving is a shared activity. Successful, enjoyable dives require cooperation between independently capable divers (Fig. 2-1). Divers usually organize themselves as buddies—mutually dependent teams. Most of the time a buddy team is made up of two divers, but in some kinds of diving, teams of three or four are used. Regardless of team size, how large the overall group, or the type of diving, the buddy system of interdependence is at the core.

In NAUI's view, all divers' first responsibilities are to themselves. Divers are then responsible to their buddies insofar as they are able to help them without incurring excessive risk. Diving leaders are responsible for defining their role and level of supervision for all the people with whom they work, but no diving leader could possibly be in a better position to help every diver than each diver's buddy. As a result, even recreational diving professionals depend on the buddy system, on teams of self-reliant divers, to manage a group, to prevent accidents, and to deal initially with most problems.

If you were asked to design a "perfect dive buddy," what are some of the traits you would choose? Competent, well-trained, observant, careful, mature, confident, dependable, organized, disciplined, skilled, well-equipped, experienced—it is likely that your list would include some, if not all, of these attributes, and others too (Fig. 2-2). As a diver, you have learned that these qualities are highly desirable in your buddies. Unfortunately, you likely have learned this by dealing with buddies that lack many of these characteristics! It is also probable that, at times, your buddies may have found you lacking some of these same qualities. People are not perfect all the time, no matter how hard they may try to be. But understanding how to be a good diving buddy, and trying to be one, are fundamental to preventing diving accidents.

Above all, a good dive buddy is a self-reliant diver, someone on whom you can depend if you need assistance. Becoming a good dive buddy is a process of developing diving abilities, judgment, and self-reliance. By cultivating in yourself the qualities you would choose in your "perfect buddy," you will become better able to avoid diving problems. Training, such as you receive in this course, also will help you anticipate and deal with problems and increase your ability to aid your dive buddy if the need arises.

ALTERNATE AIR SOURCES

Though it happens extremely rarely, an out-of-air emergency is probably the first thing that comes to people's minds when they hear the phrase "diving accident." This may be due to the belated development of the submersible pressure gauge (SPG) and the wide use of "reserve air" J-valve cylinders. Without an SPG, recreational diving pioneers routinely ran out of air (hopefully only once!) on every dive. Whatever the original reason for the perception, it is certainly true that being underwater and unable to breathe is a frightening and dangerous situation.

Extremely reliable for their intended uses, modern regulators rarely fail, and if they should they are usually designed to free-flow rather than stop working. But poor planning, inattentive diving, or some mishap can still leave a diver low on air or without enough air to make a normal ascent. In these instances, your buddy's alternate air source and air-sharing technique are crucial to preventing an incident from turning into a diving accident or injury. Though some divers view alternate air sources and extra gear as unnecessary and rarely practice air-sharing techniques after their initial certification training, a "perfect buddy" obviously would be able to help in this type of emergency. There are many choices available to you both.

Fig. 2-1. A buddy team is made up of independently competent divers.

Fig. 2-2. Perfect buddies are self-sufficient.

The Alternate Second Stage

Commonly referred to as an "octopus" regulator, an alternate second stage comes in two main configurations. The first is an extended low-pressure hose (ideally from 48 to 60 inches (122–152 cm)) connected to a spare port on a normal first stage and equipped with its own second stage (Fig. 2-3). The long hose enables the receiver (donee) to maintain a comfortable position in close contact with the air provider (donor).

A more recent development places the alternate second stage on the donor's buoyancy compensator (BC). Combining the second stage with the low-pressure inflation device (Fig. 2-4) provides a reduction in hoses. The donor's primary second stage, which is normally breathed from, is given to the donee.

As with any innovation, there are advocates and critics, but the underlying issue is the effectiveness of the method of sharing air from the same cylinder under the stress of an emergency. Most out-of-air emergencies come at the end of a dive made by both divers. Unequal consumption rates throughout the dive leaves one buddy low on, or even out of, air. But the other diver also has a greatly depleted air supply; the bulk of air has been consumed during the dive. Sharing the remaining air under these circumstances can result in two diving casualties if both divers breathe the remaining cylinder empty.

Fig. 2-3. An "octopus" second stage attached in the center of the diver's chest is the most common air sharing set-up.

Another consideration is that most recreational diving regulators are designed and tuned to support a single diver throughout the recommended range of diving depths. When two agitated divers are simultaneously drawing air through a common first stage, they may defeat the equipment's ability to deliver a consistent supply of air. This is especially true at deeper depths when larger volumes of air are being drawn.

Yet another weakness in this type of system can develop because of *Charles' Law*. As all divers know, when gas is compressed its temperature goes up. (This phenomenon is well illustrated every time a scuba cylinder is filled, unless pressure is increased very slowly.) When it is released from pressure, the gas and surrounding hardware, including the valve and cylinder, become cooler. When two divers are breathing from the same cylinder, both being served by the first stage, a relatively large amount of air is being uncompressed quickly. This much air can rapidly chill the water within the first stage to the freezing point, rendering the first stage inoperable. Though much more likely to happen in temperate or cold water diving, freezing can occur in relatively warm water given sufficient volumes of air.

An Alternate Air Source

The difference between an alternate second stage and an alternate air source is profound. Instead of two divers using the remainder of one diver's air supply, a second source of air, preferably another appropriately-sized cylinder with a separate first and second stage and its own SPG, is available to support the buddy team's return to the surface. This system, often called *redundant scuba*, can have one of several possible configurations.

Fig. 2-4. An alternate second stage attached to a BC low-pressure inflator.

Pony Bottles

Pony bottles are air cylinders with less capacity than the smallest normal scuba cylinder, but they have more than enough volume to support a diver's controlled ascent to the surface at the recommended rate from any recreational diving depths. Averaging 15 cubic feet (429 L) in compressed gas volume, these cylinders may be attached either to the primary scuba cylinder, to the backpack, or to the BC's cylinder retaining band; or they may be held in a dedicated sleeve-type pocket in the BC.

Equipped with its own complete regulator and a submersible pressure gauge, a pony rig is an excellent back-up system, eliminating personal equipment failure as a source of mishap and dealing effectively with a buddy's need for air in an emergency (Figs. 2-5 and 2-6). If it is easily detachable underwater, such as when carried in a specially designed BC, it can be handed to a needy diver in an emergency. If the pony rig is attached to the donor's main air cylinder, either second stage can be retained or given to the donee.

Multiple Scuba Cylinders

Some divers use multiple air cylinders on every dive (Fig. 2-7). For divers generally engaging in deeper dives, sometimes beyond the recommended depths of recreational diving, having double-the-normal-capacity of air available on every dive may seem like an excellent back-up system for dealing with a buddy's need. However, this may not be true, particularly if both cylinders are connected to a single first stage through a manifold bar so that both cylinders give air throughout the dive.

Though there is much more initial capacity (as with other alternate second-stage systems), if one does run out of air, that diver is dependent on the other diver's also-depleted supply. If a mandatory decompression stop was part of the dive plan, as in technical diving, then both divers once again are faced with needing to use an air supply

Fig. 2-6. Adding a pressure gauge to a pony bottle relieves doubt about remaining air.

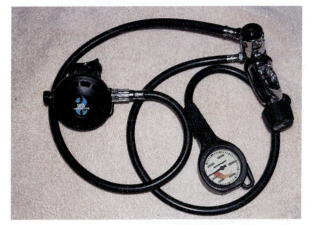

Fig. 2-5. A pony bottle with its own regulator is a redundant scuba back-up system.

Fig. 2-7. A double cylinder rig with an extra long, high-visibility hose, second stage regulator for sharing air.

planned for one. Because both divers are breathing from the same cylinder, there is risk of "overbreathing" or freezing the single first stage.

On the other hand, multiple full-size cylinders connected to separate air delivery systems that each have independent first and second stages and their own SPGs have all the advantages of a pony set-up. They will, however, be heavier and less easily transported out of the water and should be used only when the double-sized air supply is not necessary for the diving activity planned. Recognizing the value of an appropriately sized, redundant scuba back-up, experienced divers who need the extra air of multiple cylinders to make the dives they enjoy will almost always carry a complete pony rig.

Tiny Tanks

Some divers depend on a small, integral air cylinder and mouthpiece as a spare source of air in an out-of-air diving emergency. Though popular, and commanding a relatively high price for itself and a number of accessories, this device may have too little air capacity to help a diver except at relatively shallow depths. On the other hand, having even a few breaths of air readily available at any depth can help forestall air hunger and give divers crucial moments to respond more effectively to an out-of-air emergency.

Fig. 2-8. Regular practice under controlled conditions is the only way to ensure your ability to use any back-up system.

Divers who elect to buy and carry these devices are cautioned to regularly rehearse handling and using them underwater with their dive buddies under controlled conditions (Fig. 2-8). The relatively small size, the danger of possibly dropping the device, and other handling problems that can arise under the stressful conditions of an emergency make thorough practice mandatory. In any case, using a small integrated cylinder and mouthpiece as the primary or only tool for dealing with an out-of-air emergency is not recommended.

Predive Buddy Activities

Time spent preparing is generally rewarded by an enjoyable dive. This is especially true of time spent preparing and planning with a dive buddy. Frequent buddies work well together and often are ready to enter the water at a dive site well in advance of the rest of the group. Their experience and comfort with each other is evident. But diving with an unfamiliar buddy can be disconcerting, even stressful, unless the newly acquainted divers make sure that they are coordinated on a number of essential points.

Maintaining a checklist of items and procedures to go over with a new buddy on diving vacations or local excursions is an excellent idea. Doing so will help new buddies work together like old friends and will reduce the chances for mishaps caused by confusion or lack of coordination. You may construct such a checklist as part of this course, on your own, or with a customary dive buddy.

The most common cause of divers not enjoying their time together underwater is the problem that develops when buddies are not making the same dive! Your first clue about your buddy's intentions should not be when you are reaching for some extra piece of gear, like a camera or collecting bag, just before descent. Nor should you be surprised after the descent when your buddy begins swimming off in the opposite direction you intended to follow. In fact, the most satisfying diving has no surprises, except the surprising beauty of the underwater realm. When buddies take the time to communicate and coordinate their intentions and underwater procedures before gearing up, thoroughly checking their own and each other's equipment before entering the water, they are most likely to share an enjoyable dive.

Planning the Dive

Every successful dive's plan includes depth, time, and air consumption planning and a coordinated activity goal (Fig. 2-9). Using NAUI Dive Tables, a dive computer, or some other accepted

QUESTIONS FOR EVERY DIVE:

1. Do I understand and accept the risks this dive entails?
2. Am I enthusiastic, physically able, and adequately trained to make this dive?
3. Is my buddy also completely ready?
4. Are we properly equipped for this dive?
5. Do we completely understand our plan, and have we planned for emergencies?

means, every diver is responsible for planning depth and time exposures to minimize the risk of decompression illness. NAUI recommends that a precautionary stop of three minutes at a depth of 15 feet (5 m) be included in every dive. An appropriate air reserve for this and other contingencies should be included in air consumption calculations. (Complete information on air consumption calculations is included in the NAUI text *Advanced Diving: Technology and Techniques*.) Buddies planning individually can use each other as a check for accuracy. Checking planning also helps ensure that there is no confusion about the parameters of the dive, including the minimum amount of air needed to make a controlled ascent that includes the precautionary stop.

Fig. 2-9. Planning before diving pays off in enjoyment underwater.

It also is recommended that contingency plans be included in case the planned depth, time, or both are exceeded. Divers are strongly urged to make sure that depth or time violations do not place them in a situation requiring mandatory decompression. This is avoided easily by carefully monitoring depth and time and controlling buoyancy throughout the dive.

Coordinating the Activity

Though buddies are equal, most dives proceed more efficiently when one member of the team is designated its leader by mutual agreement. On a day of multiple dives, the buddies may take turns leading; however, experience or some other factor may dictate that one diver consistently act as buddy team leader. Under the best circumstances, each diver in a buddy team will be self-reliant and capable of either leading or following. Whatever the case, defining this relationship in advance will minimize the chances of confusion underwater.

Discussing the goals of the dive, which might be to practice and fine-tune buoyancy control, to find and explore some underwater feature, or to take photographs, will help the buddy team shape the dive to achieve the goals. The team leader acts on the basis of the dive's goals in cooperation with the buddy. For instance, the team leader initially will signal the dive's significant events—descent, direction and activities, ascent and precautionary stop—but the dive will proceed only after the other team member agrees. Each member of the team tracks depth and time throughout the dive and shares remaining air information at regular intervals (Fig. 2-10).

The team leader also helps maintain position underwater after agreeing in advance what arrangement to assume. Regardless of the designated leader, it is a good idea to have the slower swimmer slightly ahead. This lessens the possibility of separation underwater. If it is diving as part of a larger group, such as from a charter boat, the team should know where in the group it will remain, particularly on a guided dive.

Mutual Gear Checks

Though divers routinely check their own equipment, the special relationship of mutual dependence between buddies makes careful coordination of gear location and familiarity with your buddy's gear function (especially the alternate air source!) essential to good preparation. Equipment checks, especially after the cylinder and regulator are assembled and everything is donned before entering the water, are among the

Fig. 2-10. Coordinating with a buddy continues throughout any dive.

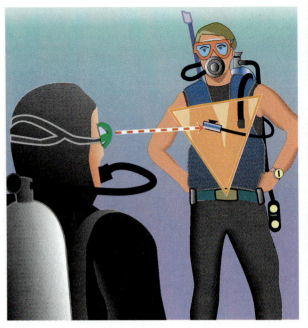

Fig. 2-11. Make sure your buddy knows where to look for your alternate second stage.

most important services buddies can perform for each other and an excellent method of preventing accidents.

Placement of the alternate second stage is especially important. NAUI recommends that divers attach their alternate second stages in the triangle, with its base at the center of the chest and its apex at the navel, so that a needy diver may readily locate it underwater (Fig. 2–11). Some divers wrap the hose in high-visibility covering, and others may use a brightly colored face on the alternate second stage itself. The lack of color at depth may make decorative effects only marginally useful. Uniform placement and buddies' mutual familiarity with each other's equipment are far more important.

Wherever in the preferred area the alternate second stage or alternate air source is located, it should be easy to retrieve the mouthpiece with a simple tug. A hook and loop-type fastener, which may dramatically increase holding power when wet, or some other clever design is often less useful than a simple rubber loop, such as a snorkel keeper. With one end threaded onto the BC and the other around the mouthpiece of the alternate second stage, a sharp tug on the hose or second stage will release it instantly for use.

Other important features to examine are the general appearance of the gear, its apparent age, and its complexity. If your buddy is neat and organized about dive gear, and it is up to date, serviceable, complete, and well cared for, chances are you may have found a good dive buddy.

Before entering the water, two equipment features merit particular attention. These are the release function and placement of your buddy's weight belt or weight system and the placement of any dive tools or accessories carried. NAUI recommends that all divers should be completely familiar with the most efficient method of jettisoning their own and their buddy's weight belts or integrated weight systems on every dive (Fig. 2-12).

In addition, any dive tools, knives, or other items such as lights or cameras carried or worn should be placed so that they cannot possibly interfere with jettisoning ballast. This usually means wearing dive knives on the inside of the calf (Fig. 2-13) or on the backpack or BC shoulder strap and carrying extra gear on quick-release clips, usually on the BC. Attaching extra, possibly expensive items, such as a camera on a lanyard, to a weight belt is not recommended because it may cause a diver to hesitate to drop the weight

> Know how to don, adjust, take off, and operate your buddy's equipment as well as you know your own!

CHAPTER 2   SELF-RELIANCE AND THE BUDDY SYSTEM

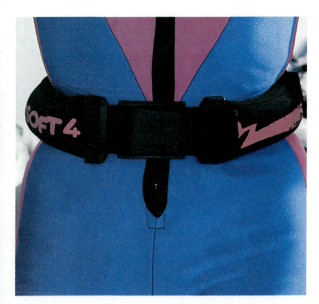

Fig. 2-12. Know how to drop your own and your buddy's weight on every dive. Practice this skill regularly.

in an emergency, or it may cause the item to catch on the diver, defeating the purpose of the emergency maneuver.

Signals

Communication is a basic requirement of any coordinated activity. Underwater, and at a distance on the surface, hand signals serve this purpose. In low visibility water or at night, tactile signals, line-pull signals, or underwater light signals may be used. In any case, unless signals are reviewed and their meaning clearly understood in advance, they will be useless.

The most effective diving signals are simple to make and unmistakable. All divers should recognize the OK signal and the signals customarily used to communicate direction, ascent, descent, depth, air pressure, time, difficulty clearing, discomfort such as cold or pain, hazards, danger, and distress. Other important signals to review are those that concern emergencies, such as "low on air" or "out of air." Examples of standard diving signals are included in the NAUI text *Adventures in Scuba Diving*.

Planning for Emergencies

No dive plan is complete until it considers how to deal with the problems that may occur. While there are any number of emergency situations to consider, buddies are chiefly concerned with two: separation and the need to share air. Discussing and agreeing on procedures to follow can prevent serious distress and injury.

Fig. 2-13. A dive knife on the outside of the calf can catch a dropped weight belt. Make sure that you can always drop your own and your buddy's weights effectively.

SEPARATION UNDERWATER:

1. STOP, stabilize, check air and depth, and orient yourself.
2. LOOK up, down, and around for about 1 minute.
3. ASCEND at the recommended rate, and establish buoyancy at the surface.
4. GET HELP if your buddy doesn't join you on the surface after a short time.

Separation Underwater

Divers become separated for many reasons: from uncoordinated plans, to poor water visibility and lack of consistent observation. The reason is less important than dealing with the problem swiftly and effectively before it escalates into a more serious, even dangerous, incident. Timely, coordinated action is the key to dealing with separation. NAUI recommends that all divers review this procedure with their buddies as part of their predive planning. NAUI leaders include reference to it in their group briefings, to help divers focus on its importance.

As soon as a diver realizes that separation has occurred, the following steps are recommended (Fig. 2-14):

1. Stop where you are, stabilize buoyancy, and check your remaining air supply, depth, and time. Note your position by some underwater feature, if possible, and how long it has been since you last saw your buddy.
2. For a short time, approximately 1 minute, look up, down, and around you slowly for signs of your buddy or other divers within your immediate vicinity. If you are in close proximity to other divers or a diving leader, signal them that your buddy is missing.
3. If you do not see your buddy after looking completely around (unless otherwise instructed by someone leading the dive group), make a controlled ascent directly to the surface at the recommended rate. Upon reaching the surface, establish buoyancy. Most of the time your separated buddy will meet you on the surface shortly, generally within 2 or 3 minutes. You will likely be signaled by the activity leader if you are participating in a group dive. That person will undoubtedly ask if you are OK and will ask where your buddy is. If you do not respond, the leader and other divers will assume that you are in distress and probably will initiate a surface rescue. This can waste time that would otherwise be spent searching for your buddy so, unless you need help, be sure to signal that you are OK and waiting for your buddy.
4. In the unlikely event that your buddy does not surface after a short time, notify whoever is in charge that a diver is lost underwater and activate emergency service providers.

If your buddy follows the same procedure, and if you both are consistently monitoring each other's positions, the team almost always will reunite on the surface. If there is insufficient air and time to comfortably continue the dive, return as a buddy team to your exit point. If you agree to redescend, spend a moment on the surface discussing what went wrong and planning how to avoid it next time.

Note that dives made with a surface interval of less than 10 minutes to the same or a lesser depth are considered one dive. Their bottom times should be added when consulting the NAUI Dive Tables. Divers should be aware that there may be slightly increased risk of decompression sickness as a result of missing the precautionary stop. This risk may be further increased if divers decide to continue the dive after reuniting on the surface. If the separated divers do continue the dive, the final ascent should certainly include the recommended precautionary stop.

Sharing Air Procedures

How a buddy team chooses to share air will depend on the training the divers have received and the kind of equipment they have. (Whether they will need to do so, however, depends primarily on how well they planned the dive, including their air consumption, and how well they monitored remaining air throughout the dive.) There are really only two techniques for sharing air: buddy breathing, and using an alternate second stage or redundant-scuba air source. While either method can be effective for well-trained, calm divers, in a real emergency, having a second regulator available to yourself without the need to relinquish it even momentarily is a great comfort. Regardless, buddy breathing has saved many lives and is an important diving skill to master and practice under the supervision of an instructor in confined water.

Buddy Breathing Buddy breathing was long the only accepted method for dealing with an out-of-air emergency and is still highly regarded among many experienced divers as the least cumbersome, most universal method for sharing air. NAUI recommends the following procedure for buddy breathing.

1. The needy diver signals the buddy that air is needed.
2. The donor takes a normal breath and passes the regulator to the donee, grasping the hose at the swivel joint between the mouthpiece and hose so that access to the purge button is not blocked. The donor retains control of the regulator, exhaling slowly while the donee breathes from the shared regulator.
3. The donee takes two normal breaths and then relinquishes the regulator to the donor to breathe while exhaling the second breath. The donor takes two breaths and passes the regulator back while slowly exhaling the second.

CHAPTER 2   SELF-RELIANCE AND THE BUDDY SYSTEM

Stop where you are as soon as you see your buddy is missing.

"Where did my buddy go?"

Look around in three dimensions (up, down, side to side).

Wait for about 1 minute.

Make a controlled ascent.

Re-unite at the surface.

"If you hadn't shown up, I would have had to signal the boat!"

Redecending.

Fig. 2-14. Lost buddy procedure.

4. When synchronized after the first round of passes, the donor signals the donee to begin the ascent and the divers continue to pass the regulator between themselves as they swim directly to the surface, venting their buoyancy control devices as necessary to help control their ascent rate.

5. Immediately upon surfacing, the divers establish buoyancy and return to the exit point, or, if necessary, signal for aid.

It is important that divers maintain eye and physical contact throughout the ascent as a means of ensuring calm, rational behavior (Fig. 2-15). Without frequent dry-land drills and supervised practice under controlled conditions, preferably with your customary dive buddy, buddy breathing can be a difficult skill to perform when faced with the stress of a real emergency.

Sharing Air With Alternate Second Stage   The clear advantage of both divers having consistent access to air

Fig. 2-15. Hold on firmly and maintain eye contact throughout a shared air ascent.

throughout the event is that there is less possibility of inadvertently holding one's breath during the ascent. Better control also is possible, since divers are able to breath at their own rates throughout. Either reason is a compelling argument for appropriate equipment. NAUI recommends that all divers have an alternate second stage and requires that all students be so equipped. As previously noted, a redundant-scuba back-up system like a pony bottle with separate regulator and SPG is generally the most versatile method for dealing with out-of-air emergencies. The following procedure is recommended:

1. The needy diver signals the buddy that air is needed, or the diver takes the alternate second stage and commences to breathe from it.
2. The donor takes hold of the donee's shoulder strap, BC, or arm with the right hand, and the donee does likewise to the donor.
3. The donor signals the donee to begin the ascent, and the donee responds.
4. The divers swim directly to the surface, holding on to each other with their right hands and venting air from the BC with their left hands as necessary to control their bouyancy and maintain the recommended ascent rate.
5. Immediately upon surfacing, the divers establish buoyancy and return to the exit point, or, if necessary, signal for aid.

In any case, divers who have made an emergency ascent should notify the person in charge of the activity. At the least, divers who make an emergency ascent usually will miss the precautionary stop. It is likely that they will have ascended more quickly than recommended. The incident also may have occurred on a repetitive dive. Any and all of these factors increase the risk of decompression sickness. As a result, an immediate brief neurological assessment, as discussed in Chapter Seven, is mandatory regardless of the lack of obvious signs or symptoms of decompression illness (DCI). The same is true for divers not participating in a professionally organized dive. Individuals who have made an emergency ascent by any means are strongly urged to monitor themselves and their buddies carefully for any ill effects and to refrain from diving for at least 24 hours or until they have been thoroughly examined by a qualified diving doctor.

Following recommended procedures will help divers become "perfect buddies" and in the process help them become confident and self-reliant. Coordinating efforts in this manner, spending time on the surface to work out an accurate, mutually acceptable plan that covers the diving activity, contingencies, and emergency procedures, and making sure to check and double-check equipment will enable buddies to work well together underwater. It also will yield dividends in successful, enjoyable dives for all participants. Neglecting these essential planning elements often will produce unfortunate results. A rushed introduction followed by a quick entry into the water usually leaves at least one team member feeling uncomfortable and ill-prepared and places all participating divers at increased risk.

In an **OUT-OF-AIR EMERGENCY**, your alternate second stage can save a diver's life. Make sure it is easily accessible and ready to be used.

Removing the rubber exhaust port can reduce the chance that a needy diver will mistakenly try to breathe from it instead of the mouthpiece.

CHAPTER THREE

Examined in retrospect, most diving accidents seem to have obvious causes like insufficient planning, poor skills, or lack of judgment when divers are confronted with adverse environmental conditions or a contraindication to diving. People who dive infrequently may have accidents when they forget important procedures or options they once knew. Experienced divers may grow careless and complacent. Some accidents can be attributed to sudden injuries or illness. A few are caused by equipment malfunction. And sometimes any number of minor problems can combine to overwhelm even a well-trained, well-prepared diver's ability to cope.

The causes of some other diving accidents are less open to analysis. A diving illness may strike a diver on a carefully planned, well-executed dive, yet divers who have violated recommended depth and time limits or ignored other usual procedures apparently suffer no ill effects.

Despite the unique circumstances of any accident, there are some problems and situations that experience has shown to be part of many diving mishaps. By learning to recognize, properly evaluate, prevent, or deal with these, you can lower significantly the possibility of being involved in a diving accident.

EQUIPMENT PROBLEMS

Unless you have gills, going underwater for any length of time and returning to the surface unharmed depends on the proper use of specialized equipment. Should this equipment fail, which is generally caused by misuse or neglect, serious injury can result. Though most equipment failure is easily prevented by regular maintenance and careful inspection before every dive, it is prudent to learn to deal with the unexpected breakdown.

Mask Loss

Losing your mask underwater, whether through a strap or buckle failure or by having it accidentally dislodged, is an annoying surprise. Vision is suddenly blurred. Closing your eyes makes finding your mask nearly impossible. Pinching your nose to prevent water from entering and holding it closed is uncomfortable at best. On the other hand, maintaining, through regular practice, the basic certification skill of breathing comfortably from a regulator without a mask on makes losing one's mask underwater a minor problem.

In practice, most masks are lost upon entry. A buddy team may volunteer to descend and search for it, but if it cannot be found quickly or be replaced with a spare, leaving the water is recommended. During a dive, especially if you are close to the bottom, your mask is probably right at your feet or close by, so descending and feeling for it may quickly solve your problem. Your buddy may even hand it to you before you have a chance to look for it yourself! If not, cupping your hands around your eyes while tilting your head slightly downward will trap some of your exhaled air, creating a "lens" from a bubble of air that will allow you to look around for your mask.

Water pressure will hold the mask on even if the strap is broken, so long as you do not exhale through your nose. Normal mask-clearing procedures will also work, but of course the mask must be held on while you do these. In any case, once you find it, a normal ascent is possible. Carrying a spare rubber strap or a large rubber band in your BC pocket helps avoid delay or a canceled dive because of mask strap failure.

Fin Loss

Swimming with scuba gear but without fins can be difficult, especially when the diver is wearing booties. Leg cramps are likely because of the increased strain of propelling yourself with one leg. Fortunately, surfacing with only one fin is easy; simply assume a vertical ascent position, begin to kick, and carefully release air from the BC, paying close attention to maintaining an appropriate ascent rate and controlling buoyancy. Some divers, in order to prevent having to terminate a dive because of a broken fin strap, keep an extra one in their BC pockets. Most divers, however, prevent the problem by examining their straps before diving, changing any that seem at all worn before entering the water.

Buoyancy Compensators (BCs)

Though they are apparently simple air bags, BCs can still develop problems. These usually are related to sudden loss or increase in buoyancy. Avoiding problems is a matter of maintaining the BC according to the manufacturer's recommendations, and having the valves, low pressure inflator mechanism and bladder checked by an authorized technician at least annually (Fig. 3-1). Such maintenance is particularly important if your BC carries an alternate second stage as part of its low pressure inflation mechanism. This is another second stage regulator (life support device) that needs regular professional inspection and servicing.

VIRTUALLY ALL EQUIPMENT PROBLEMS CAN BE PREVENTED THROUGH:

1. Proper use, storage, handling, and periodic professional maintenance according to the manufacturer's directions.
2. Careful inspection and mutual buddy checks before every dive.
3. Thorough rinsing and cleaning after each use.

Fig. 3-1. Rinse equipment thoroughly after every dive.

Except for equipment malfunctions, making sure of proper fit and strap adjustment and that the cylinder is securely fastened at the appropriate height in the backpack will ensure proper BC function.

Buoyancy Failure

If you are properly weighted and adjusted to achieve buoyancy on the surface at the end of your dive, loss of BC lift is not a source of great concern. On the other hand, if you are tired on the surface and dependent on the BCs buoyancy to rest comfortably, lack of lift is serious. Looking down to make sure that the area beneath you is clear and immediately dropping weights is the recommended procedure. It also is possible that the empty cylinder and attached regulator(s) and gauges, or other equipment, can cause you to sink if the BC bladder fails. If so, drop this equipment as well. Your exposure suit very likely will maintain you on the surface if you are unencumbered by any additional equipment.

Getting out of the water with a BC that may be filled with water because of a tear or valve failure also can be difficult. The weight of the water can make climbing a ladder, or even standing up in shallow water, extremely difficult. Back injury can result. It may be necessary to shed your cylinder and BC in the water, then lift or drag the rig out slowly while it drains.

Low Pressure Inflator Problems

Low pressure inflation mechanisms can fail, but all BCs may be orally inflated. A more common problem occurs when the inflator slowly leaks air into the bladder, increasing buoyancy through the dive. In this case, an unwary diver can be brought rapidly to the surface. This can be avoided by making sure that low pressure inflator mechanisms are functioning properly before each dive and carefully monitoring depth throughout any dive.

If the inflation mechanism is leaking, divers will notice the BC filling and can vent air accordingly to maintain appropriate buoyancy throughout the dive. Remaining air should be diligently monitored, though most slow leaks will have a negligible effect on air consumption.

Removing the low pressure inflator from the BC is not recommended unless the valve fails completely or the actuating mechanism becomes stuck causing the low pressure inflator to free flow into the BC. In that case, the inflator hose must be disconnected to prevent an uncontrolled buoyant ascent. Disconnecting the mechanism underwater may be difficult while wearing gloves. Cold water divers are urged to practice this technique with their own equipment on dry land to ensure their ability. Disconnecting the low pressure inflator will usually stop the freeflow, and the dive can continue with the diver maintaining buoyancy by inflating the BC orally, if necessary. If removing the inflator hose from the BC does not stop the freeflow, a controlled, direct ascent to the surface at the appropriate rate is advised. A major air leak of this nature can empty the cylinder in a few minutes depending on how much air remained when the problem occurred.

Malfunctioning low pressure inflators should be serviced or replaced at the first opportunity.

Exposure Suits

Problems with exposure suits are rare, so long as they fit properly and are well maintained. Designed primarily to protect divers from cold, most exposure suits, and particularly some dry suits, also provide additional buoyancy. In all cases, exposure suits are indispensable to diver comfort and help reduce risks associated with chilling.

Leaks and Tears

Snagging an exposure suit underwater can tear it, leading to leaks. In a wet suit or dry suit, such leaks will expose the diver to cold that can warrant terminating the dive. This is avoided most easily by diving carefully, particularly in turbid water around sharp objects such as wrecks or underwater debris.

Improper Fit

Wet suits depend on good fit to maintain their environmental protection (Fig. 3-2). If they are too large, water will flow freely through the suit, ren-

Fig. 3-2. Exposure suits depend on proper fit to keep you comfortable.

dering it much less effective for conserving diver heat. The resulting discomfort likely will force the diver to abort the dive, but even if you are not compelled by cold to leave the water, it is still wise to do so to avoid becoming hypothermic.

If it is too small, a wet suit will be constrictive, retarding normal circulation and hampering effective respiration. Either of these possibilities can be dangerous. Normal circulation is crucial to maintaining the body's thermal balance and assuring adequate gas exchange between bodily fluid and tissues. If this exchange is disrupted by an ill-fitting suit, decompression illness is more likely.

If adequate respiration is prevented by a suit that fits too tightly, the labor of breathing can increase dramatically. Effective ventilation will also be prevented. This combination of extra breathing effort and inadequate ventilation can lead quickly to carbon dioxide excess, resulting in the inability to catch your breath, possibly triggering panic (see Chapter Six). Fortunately, such negative consequences are easily avoided by wearing an appropriately sized suit whenever you are diving. (Many divers discover that their wet suits have "shrunk" when first trying them on after a long interval. Whether this is from weight gain or the age of the rubber, recutting or a new suit may be considered.) Trying on rental suits until you find one that fits properly is highly recommended.

Dry suit wearers are not immune to the negative effects of poor fit. If neck and wrist seals are loose, water will enter the suit compromising its thermal protection and buoyancy. If the seals are too tight, proper circulation is hampered. Neck seals are especially important since air accumulates in the upper portion of the suit whenever the diver is vertical, generally during descent, ascent, and while making a precautionary stop. Overly tight-fitting neck seals can result in excessive pressure on the throat, windpipe, carotid artery, and tissues surrounding the Eustachian tube. This constriction can have a negative effect on breathing ability and circulation. In particular, the carotid sinus, a pressure-sensitive nerve net that helps to regulate blood pressure and heart rate, can be stimulated by a constricting exposure-suit neck seal or dive hood—resulting in dizziness, disorientation, or fainting.

Dry Suits

Dry suits enable divers to comfortably enjoy waters that would make most divers in wet suits shiver. Depending on the increased insulating properties of air, they can have some of the same difficulties discussed with buoyancy compensators. The following brief review is only for informational purposes. NAUI recommends that all users seek additional dry suit training. Such training would include confined water exercises to ensure a diver's ability to deal with common dry suit problems and emergency procedures before using a dry suit in open water.

Puncture or Seal Failure. Dry suits that are punctured, or have wrist or neck seals torn underwater, leak air, lose buoyancy, and admit cold water. NAUI recommends using an appropriate buoyancy compensator with a dry suit at all times and immediately aborting any dive in which the suit loses its insulating ability.

In addition, a punctured or torn dry suit can fill with water in the same way that a BC can. Unlike a BC, however, which can be relatively easily shed and handled out of the water, a dry suit full of water may be impossible to remove while you are in the water and, while being worn, may make it impossible to get out of the water without aid! Exiting the water anywhere but on a calm, gently graded beach front in a dry suit full of water is unlikely. Additional help will be needed and should be planned for.

Valve Failure. Most dry suits depend on either manual or automatic (pressure-activated) valves to vent air during ascent. Proper function of these valves is crucial. If the pressure relief valve is inoperable, uncontrolled buoyant ascent can result. This can be prevented by checking gear carefully before each dive and maintaining the suit according to the manufacturer's recommendations. If the valve fails to vent underwater, the diver can

> Dry suit valves must be regularly serviced. Store your dry suit carefully to prevent damage to the valves or suit.

usually vent large amounts of air quickly through the wrist or neck seal, preventing an uncontrolled, rapid ascent. This maneuver is usually part of recommended dry suit user training, and is best practiced by all wearers to ensure proficiency.

Dry suit valves also can be damaged through improper care and storage, as well as by the careless donning of a BC over the suit. Like other dive equipment, dry suit valves are best rinsed thoroughly after every dive and serviced and stored according to the manufacturer's recommendations. Avoiding external damage to the valve and valve stem while donning other gear takes practice.

If the inflation mechanism leaks air into the suit, intermittent venting may be employed to control buoyancy. As in the case of BC leaks, air consumption should be carefully monitored. In case of freeflow, disconnecting the inflator hose (a maneuver that is best practiced while wearing customarily used gloves or mittens) is recommended. A direct ascent to the surface, venting air as appropriate, then should be made, using the BC to establish buoyancy at the surface.

Trim Problems. The air inside a dry suit may migrate to any part of the suit depending on the diver's position in the water. Too much air in the suit can cause problems. If you are upright, air will flow to the upper chest and neck area, causing the same discomfort and difficulties as an overly tight neck seal. If the air migrates to the feet, the diver may become buoyant upside down and ascend uncontrollably to the surface in this position. Fins may be lost in the process as the foot areas of the suit expand rapidly, making recovery to a normal position even more difficult.

Learning to deal with these events underwater is part of recommended dry suit training. Many dry suit divers also use "finkeepers," strong rubber straps in addition to the fin's normal strap, to prevent fin loss caused by suit expansion. Using ankle weights and redistributing ballast to either a chest harness or shoulder-supported belt also can help control diver trim.

Over–weighting. Fear of being too buoyant leads some divers to over-weight themselves needlessly, rather than learning to use only enough air in the suit to maintain comfort. (Over-weighting is not solely a problem for dry suit users!) This practice can lead to various accidents, from back problems and strains associated with poor posture and heavy gear to inability to cope with a loss of buoyancy if the suit should fail. It is recommended that dry suit users learn the unique characteristics of their suits and wear the least amount of weight that will allow them to maintain appropriate buoyancy throughout any dive. U*sing large amounts of air to offset a lot of lead is a battle that the diver will eventually lose.*

Depth, Time, or Air Consumption Problems. Dry suits are comfortable. They may be so comfortable that divers sometimes inadvertently or intentionally exceed their planned depth and time limits. This can result in an increased risk of decompression sickness and the possibility of running out of air. Also there seems to be an increased susceptibility to nitrogen narcosis and a statistically higher-than-usual risk of decompression illness among dry suit wearers. Either of these may be due to the types of diving that dry suit wearers engage in, such as deeper, longer dives, or the effects of cold water diving on inert gas uptake. In any case, wearing a dry suit does not reduce the need for conservative, careful dive planning and following recommended practices.

Weight Systems

Most divers use lead weight to overcome their natural buoyancy and the additional buoyancy of exposure suits. Worn on a weight belt, as part of an integrated system that includes the backpack and BC, or on the ankles, this ballast is a normal part of diving. Problems ensue when the weight is either excessive or inadequate, or cannot be easily jettisoned in an emergency.

Proper weighting, including the amount and location of ballast, is crucial to diver comfort and ability. Too much weight makes the diver work excessively hard underwater. Too little weight makes maintaining appropriate buoyancy impossible. Having all the weight concentrated in front of or behind the diver will affect trim and make swimming difficult.

NAUI recommends that divers should use the minimum amount of weight necessary to be neutrally buoyant, floating at about eye level at the surface, in full gear with an empty buoyancy compensator at the end of their dives. Weight should be distributed to allow the diver to easily change and maintain body position (trim) underwater at will. Buddies are urged to check each other's buoyancy and weighting to achieve this condition before descent. Divers are advised to record weighting information in their logbooks to make equipping themselves for future dives under the

> Adjust your **WEIGHT BELT** or **BALLAST** system for "weightless" diving! Record how much weight you need for different environments and equipment configurations in your log-book.

same conditions easier. Useful information will include the thickness and type of exposure suit and water type (fresh or salt).

Many instructors recommend that weight belts be worn so that the release can be operated with the right hand, standardizing the placement so that all divers will know where to look for and how to release another diver's weight belt. Others suggest that the weight release be worn so that the diver can operate it with "the strong hand," be that left or right. In any case, NAUI urges all divers to ensure that however weight is worn, it can be easily and swiftly discarded with a simple one-hand release maneuver if the need arises. This maneuver should be practiced on dry land until it is second nature. All divers are urged to check their own and their buddy's weight releases, and to be completely familiar with the location and operation of both divers' weight systems before every dive.

Regulators

Diving regulators are rugged and reliable, but no mechanical apparatus is totally foolproof. Making certain that your primary life support gear is completely functional and well cared for is one of the best ways to avoid underwater problems.

Water Leaks

A rubber mouthpiece may tear or become dislodged, or the diaphragm can become damaged or misplaced, allowing water to leak into the air chamber. In either case, the diver is presented with water in addition to the expected air. If this water is inhaled, coughing or choking will undoubtedly ensue, very possibly leading to greater problems.

Water entering through a torn mouthpiece will continue to trouble a diver until the mouthpiece is replaced. It may be possible to switch to an alternate second stage (octopus) to continue the dive, but doing so reduces your available emergency options. Under most circumstances, surfacing by making a controlled direct ascent, and quickly replacing the mouthpiece, is preferred. Having a spare mouthpiece and tie-wrap readily available is recommended.

If the mouthpiece is lost, you may continue to breathe from the second stage with no mouthpiece by making a seal around the orifice with your lips. However, this is uncomfortable and requires that you hold the second stage in place manually. It is possible to switch to the alternate second stage and make a controlled direct ascent to the surface to replace the mouthpiece.

Underwater, dealing with water in the second stage, not caused by a damaged mouthpiece, is an exercise in control. The needed skill can be acquired only through practice, such as breathing past residual water in a snorkel, a skill taught in basic certification classes. If there is no alternate second stage available, take shallow, cautious inhalations, keeping the mouthpiece at a slightly downward angle, usually with your chin tucked. This position will allow the air to rise over the water in the second stage. Ascend directly to the surface at the recommended rate, breathing carefully and continually as described. Your buddy should be made aware of the problem and be prepared to share air or render other aid, if necessary.

If equipped with a back-up second stage (octopus or redundant scuba), switch mouthpieces and breathe from the alternate second stage, and sharply tap the primary second stage against your palm once or twice. Operate the purge button momentarily to flush out the interior of the primary second stage. If the problem is due to displacement of the purge diaphragm, this procedure should remedy it. Cautiously attempt to breathe from the primary second stage again. If it is not functioning normally, replace it again with your alternate second stage. Terminate the dive, with your buddy, by making a normal ascent to the surface at the recommended rate, including an appropriate precautionary stop while breathing from the alternate second stage.

Malfunction

Regulators can malfunction in two ways: providing too much air or providing too little air. The former is far preferable, but in either case, terminating the dive is the recommended course of action.

Freeflow. Though unusual, a second stage may begin to free-flow, delivering a large volume of air without demand. This can happen at the surface or underwater. On the surface, a regulator freeflow can usually be stopped by tapping the second stage sharply against the palm once or twice. If this does not stop the flow, the regulator should be removed from service, adjusted by a manufacturer-certified technician, and bench-tested before being used again.

Sometimes a second stage will free-flow if dropped into the water with the purge button pointed down. This freeflow is caused by the sensitivity of the second stage demand setting. In an effort to make the regulator "easy to breathe," the adjustment is set quite finely. Inverting the second stage so that the mouthpiece points down and water fills the chamber will usually stop this (Fig. 3-3).

A freeflow underwater can empty a full, 80-cubic-foot (2286 L) scuba cylinder in under 9 minutes. It is important to deal quickly with this problem. If a couple of sharp raps of the second stage on the palm (exhaling while the regulator is out of one's mouth or breathing from an alternate second stage as detailed above) do not work and depressing the purge button for a second or two does not correct it, make a direct, controlled ascent, breathing from the alternate second stage, if available. If the second stage in freeflow is your only choice, replace the mouthpiece, inhaling cautiously and exhaling normally throughout the ascent. Monitor the remaining amount of air throughout, adjusting the rate of ascent accordingly to ensure reaching the surface with air.

Fig. 3-3. Inverting a second stage will usually stop freeflow. Exhale continuously while the regulator is out of your mouth.

Too High a Demand Setting. A regulator with too high a demand setting (hard-breathing) can make diving miserable. Each breath is labored and fatiguing. Fortunately, this seldom occurs. Having your regulator serviced at the recommended intervals, at least annually, by a manufacturer-certified technician ensures easy breathing.

A problem can arise, however, when you rent or borrow dive gear. Always test the breathing effort and function of a regulator before leaving the shop by placing it on a source of compressed air and breathing from it. Reject any regulator that you find uncomfortable for any reason. Under most circumstances, using borrowed dive equipment is not recommended.

If it begins to become difficult for you to breathe from a regulator underwater, it is possible that you are running out of air. Although it should never happen, at the beginning of a dive this may mean that the cylinder was not turned on or was incompletely turned on. Immediately signal your buddy that you are low on air, and check the SPG to determine if this is the case. If it is empty, signal your buddy that you need to share air and commence the air-sharing procedure agreed upon before beginning the dive. If the cylinder is not completely turned on, the SPG needle (or digital display) will move (change) with each inhalation effort. In that case, inhale and exhale slowly while opening the valve completely. If you are unable to reach the valve comfortably, signal your buddy to assist you.

If breathing becomes hard at the end of the dive, if the SPG indicates there is air and the cylinder is completely turned on, the gauge may be malfunctioning. In this case you may in fact be low on, or out of, air. Immediately signal your buddy that you need to share air, commencing the air-sharing procedure agreed upon before the dive.

At other times in the dive, any sudden change in breathing effort from the regulator is best dealt with on the surface. Immediately terminate the dive by making a controlled, direct ascent to the surface at the recommended rate. The buddy should be ready to render any assistance necessary, including sharing air, until both divers exit the water.

Lock-up or Freezing. Regulator first-stage failure is extremely rare in modern gear used according to the manufacturer's recommendations. If it happens, however, a diver must immediately initiate an appropriate out-of-air ascent to the surface with or without a buddy's aid. The possibility of this failure, albeit remote, is another good reason for being personally equipped with a redundant scuba back-up system.

Hose and SPG Failure. Low pressure hoses connecting the first stage of the regulator to breathing second stages, low pressure inflators or dry suit valves can fail. The high pressure hose connected to a submersible pressure gauge, or the gauge itself, also may fail. These problems are best prevented by careful handling, thorough inspection before every dive, and regular replacement and servicing at manufacturer's recommended intervals. Never lift or drag cylinders by hoses, or tightly twist or knot hoses. Inspect hoses for cracking, discoloration or loss of suppleness. Replace any worn hoses immediately. Before every dive, inspect the pressure relief plug of your SPG, usually located on the back of the gauge. This small rubber plug keeps water out of the gauge's interior, a condition that will lead to internal corrosion of the gauge that can result in inaccurate readings and possible failure. If the plug is missing, have the gauge serviced before diving with it.

Most hose and SPG failures happen on the surface when the cylinder is first turned on. Failures most often occur at the joint between the rubber hose and the metal end fitting that is screwed into the first stage. This joint is usually covered by a rubber or plastic sleeve applied to protect the joint from bending stress. Divers are advised to check this area for signs of corrosion or wear at the joint by sliding the sleeve down the hose. Do so before any diving trip or at least annually, and immediately have worn hose replaced.

In addition, NAUI recommends that all hoses attached to the first stage be gathered up and controlled as the cylinder is opened. The face of the SPG should be held against the cylinder, pointing away from the diver and any other persons in the area, while the air is slowly turned completely on. By following these precautions, unexpected failures of any of the hoses or the gauge itself are unlikely to cause injury.

Low-pressure hose failures underwater can be handled by making a direct, controlled ascent to the surface. Monitor remaining air supply to ensure reaching the surface with air, adjusting the ascent rate if necessary. High pressure hose or SPG failure underwater requires the same response: immediate, controlled direct ascent. In this case, however, there is an increased chance of injury because the pressure being released is substantially greater, approaching the working pressure of the cylinder. The end of any failed hose, especially a high pressure hose, can whip around and cause injury. It may be possible to catch the hose, but time should not be wasted trying to do so underwater.

ENVIRONMENTAL HAZARDS

However beautiful and engaging, all scuba diving takes place in an extremely hostile environment for land–dwelling, air-breathing mammals like people. Besides requiring specialized life support equipment (dive gear) and protective clothing (wet suits and dry suits), there are hazards peculiar to the water environment or to the activity itself. In fresh or salt water, at sea level or altitude, in remote areas or at popular beaches, divers must consider how these factors will affect their enjoyment (Fig. 3-4).

Many of these hazards, such as water current or water visibility can change in a moment. They may be difficult to predict and are certainly impossible to control. As a result, dealing with all environmental factors requires sound judgment and caution. Successfully meeting the challenges presented by the environment can sometimes mean postponing an activity or choosing an alternate site.

Cold Water or Weather

Virtually all diving can be said to take place in cold water, because *any* water more than 3° F (-16° C) colder than normal skin temperature, 93° F (34° C), will eventually chill an inactive, unprotected diver. Even small alterations in internal temperature can have a large effect on your physical abilities and mental processes. These effects can go unnoticed for a time, then may progress rapidly to serious incapacity. This insidious progression makes cold especially hazardous to scuba diving, an activity that requires dexterity, alertness, and judgment.

In addition, cold increases the solubility of a gas. A chilled diver will absorb more nitrogen than a diver who maintains normal temperature during a dive. Recognizing this, NAUI recommends using the next-greater time interval on the NAUI Dive Tables for determining the amount of residual nitrogen (Letter Group) on any dive in which a diver feels cold. NAUI also recommends terminating any dive when shivering, the first symptom of severe chilling, begins.

Fig. 3-4. Carefully assessing environmental conditions before entering the water and throughout the dive will reduce your risks.

Chilling

Chilling is the first stage of the process that culminates in hypothermia, a life-threatening loss of body heat. Characterized by a feeling of uncomfortable cold, it can strike any person after even moderate exposure to cold water and can occur despite wearing exposure protection. Signs of chilling include blue lips and mild shivering. These are difficult to observe underwater, so divers are urged to monitor their comfort level throughout all dives.

Chilling is a cumulative condition, persisting between dives and recurring with greater intensity much more quickly on repetitive dives. Although you may feel rewarmed during surface intervals, particularly if you are sunbathing or in a well-heated area, it takes a relatively long time, sometimes up to a full day or more, to regain lost internal heat. Just how long will depend on the diver's unique physiology, including sex, body composition, age, and general health. Some people chill easily, but all people will chill given long or repeated exposures (multiple dives) in cold water without extended surface intervals to rewarm and adequate exposure protection.

Reviewing the signal for feeling cold underwater and agreeing in advance to end any dive if a member of a buddy team is chilled will prevent harmful effects of chilling. Accommodating the limitations of your exposure protection and diving within your thermal comfort zone will make diving more enjoyable and will help reduce dive accidents.

Hypothermia

Hypothermia is a life-threatening condition that results from a progressive decrease in core temperature. It is characterized by severe, uncontrollable shivering, decreasing dexterity and coordination, increasingly muddled thinking, unresponsiveness, and unconsciousness. Early onset phases of hypothermia begin with a core temperature drop of as little as 1° or 2° F (0.6° C)! Because hypothermic divers cannot control their movements and cannot think rationally they are in grave danger underwater. Unfortunately, neither they nor their buddies may realize the problem before it is too late: therefore avoiding hypothermia is imperative. Divers who engage in cold water diving, or specialties like ice-diving, are urged to guard against hypothermia by careful self-monitoring and conservative decision-making and dive-planning.

Regulator Freeze-up

Though unlikely under normal diving conditions, diving in very cold water (<50° F) (10° C) increases the possibility of water freezing in the first stage of the regulator. Freezing can occur when high volumes of air are rapidly uncompressed from cylinder storage pressure (2250 (155 bar) to 3000+ (207 bar) psi) to the relatively low pressure of the second stage (approximately 150 (10 bar) psi), such as when you are working hard underwater or drawing even normal breaths at deeper depths. Purging a second stage for more than 5 or 6 seconds in colder water, especially at depth, or on the surface if air temperatures are low, such as when ice-diving, can freeze some regulators. Two divers sharing air via an alternate second stage (octopus) on a single first stage in cold water can also cause a freeze-up.

Besides avoiding the situations mentioned, not over-filling cylinders beyond their rated capacity, thereby increasing the initial pressure differential, is a wise practice. Using a redundant scuba system that includes a separate first and second stage, either on a Y-valve (Fig. 3-5), or with multiple cylinders or a pony bottle, is another effective means of managing freeze-up emergencies, especially in colder water. NAUI recommends that divers be appropriately equipped for any diving activities they plan and familiar with the appropriate procedures for any unusual hazards they may represent.

Hot Weather

Ironically, though most diving takes place in cold water, the weather is generally warm! This makes dressing for diving a hot-weather activity that can have serious effects on a diver's ability and health. Like chilling, overheating is a progressively more debilitating condition. Exposure to heat, strong sunlight, and high humidity, especially when dealing with heavy gear or wearing an exposure suit, can lead to problems before the dive begins or underwater.

Fig. 3-5. A Y-valve allows a cold water diver to use two separate first stages to reduce the effect of regulator freeze-up.

Dehydration

Depletion of the body's fluid, dehydration, is a serious health condition. It is particularly so in diving since normal fluid balance is one of the assumptions upon which all dive tables are based. Dehydrated divers are at significantly greater risk of decompression sickness because the diminished amount of bodily fluid becomes more rapidly saturated with inert gas, and can also hold less gas in solution as ambient pressure decreases during ascent. This combination of higher saturation and more rapid off-gassing invalidates normal calculations according to accepted no-decompression limits.

Divers can unknowingly become dehydrated a number of ways, many of them usual parts of a diving excursion. Compressed breathing air is dry and cold, requiring body moisture to humidify and warm it. Travel is dehydrating because of exposure to dry air-conditioning, lower-than-normal atmospheric pressure (on aircraft), and less convenient opportunity to drink plenty of water. Caffeinated, carbonated, and sugar-laden drinks like coffee, iced teas or colas, and acidic fruit juices such as orange or grapefruit also draw water from the tissues. Alcohol consumption seriously dehydrates. (Most of the ill effects of a common "hangover" are due to dehydration.)

Drinking lots of water along with juices rich in pulp such as papaya, guava, or pear nectar, whether you are feeling thirsty or not, will stave off dehydration. A good rule of thumb is to drink at least two to three cups of water per hour on any diving day, more if the day is uncomfortably warm (Fig. 3-6). Doing so, and monitoring yourself for frequent, clear, and copious fluid elimination (urination), will ensure that you are properly hydrated for diving. Note that dehydration is possible in any weather or season, though it is more likely in hot climates.

Heat Exhaustion

Heat exhaustion is the debilitating stress caused by a rise in the body's internal temperature. It can come from strenuous exercise in high temperature environments, such as when lugging air cylinders and dive gear across a black-topped parking lot, wearing exposure suits too long while out of the water, or other factors common to a recreational dive trip. Decongestants or aspirin, alcohol, or caffeinated beverages can all contribute to heat exhaustion by increasing the likelihood of dehydration.

Divers who suffer heat exhaustion feel uncomfortably hot and fatigued and usually sweat profusely, which contributes to dehydration. They

Fig. 3-6. Dehydration can cause real problems. Don't wait for thirst. Drink plenty of water before and between dives.

may be erratic and light-headed and pale. Muscle cramps, headache, nausea, and disorientation can result. Or they may ignore warning signs and symptoms, just as a hypothermic diver might, until they are totally incapacitated. In any case, heat exhaustion places divers at increased risk when they enter the water. Sudden immersion in temperate water, even if the diver is wearing exposure protection, can cause severe thermal imbalance and circulatory distress.

Heat Stroke/Hyperthermia

Heat stroke (hyperthermia) is the final phase of heat exhaustion, in which the body's core temperature rises to the point where purposeful activity is no longer possible and unconsciousness ensues. It is the second leading cause of athletic deaths. Heat stroke is a danger whenever there is a combination of high temperature and heavy exertion. These conditions are met before or after any hot-weather dives in temperate waters when heavy wet suits or dry suits are worn while transporting equipment or during long surface intervals.

The progress from heat exhaustion to hyperthermia can be rapid without intervention. An uncomfortably warm and formerly sweating diver may suddenly faint. The diver's skin will be hot and dry, and breathing will be rapid and shallow as in panting. *Hyperthermia is a life-threatening condi-*

tion *that requires immediate medical attention.* Victims should be removed at once from hot areas and direct sunlight, covered lightly, and monitored constantly for vital signs while awaiting evacuation by emergency medical services. Sponge bathing with cool, tepid water to reduce body temperature can help. Life support may become necessary. If the victim is conscious, water may be given in small amounts.

General Underwater Environmental Hazards

Underwater activities present divers with physical and mental challenges other than temperature-related problems. A diver best can meet these challenges through foresight and preparation, training, and judgment.

Depth, Density, and Nitrogen Narcosis

Many wonderful recreational dive sites abut steep drop-offs well beyond usually recommended depths. Great dives may be made on sheer walls that rise from an abyss to within comfortable reach of the surface. Worthy sites may lie just a few feet or meters beyond recommended recreational dive depths. Surroundings like these can represent a hazard to the unwary or foolhardy, unprepared diver.

Though depth limits are controversial, even the most avid technical diver would advise caution, meticulous planning, additional training, and specialized equipment and support as prerequisites for deeper diving even within usually recommended limits. Air consumption increases proportionally with depth. Breathing effort can increase noticeably at deeper depths, causing fatigue and possible carbon dioxide retention as divers labor. Nitrogen narcosis progressively more seriously alters perception, emotional state, and physical ability. Intensified nitrogen absorption at deeper depths can increase the possibility of decompression sickness. Convulsion, as a result of Central Nervous System Oxygen Toxicity, is another possible outcome of deeper, prolonged exposures. For all these reasons, the margin for error, small on any deeper dive, is reduced if not completely eliminated when you venture towards and beyond the limits.

These negative possibilities can be almost completely prevented by confining diving to the middle range of recommended depths or shallower, practicing buoyancy control, and monitoring your own and your buddy's air consumption and condition. Effects of nitrogen narcosis vanish completely when you ascend only a few feet. Oxygen toxicity in particular is virtually impossible during typical recreational exposures on compressed air.

NAUI urges all divers to monitor depth and practice buoyancy control on any dives where maximum depths can be inadvertently exceeded, and to practice sound, conservative dive planning for all underwater activities.

Visibility

Enjoying time underwater is primarily a visual activity. Observing in person the fantastic array of creatures and terrain is at the core of most divers' desire to participate—as the burgeoning growth of underwater photography and videography attests.

Yet underwater visibility is as changeable as the rest of underwater experience, extending from literally hundreds of feet to less than inches, sometimes within a moment! Such variation is particularly prevalent in cave- and wreck-diving, activities that require extra training, equipment, and preparation, but underwater visibility can change dramatically on almost any dive. Sudden loss of visibility can be disorienting, even dangerous, unless a diver is prepared to deal with it or wisely chooses to avoid diving where or when it may happen. Diving in poor visibility (under 5 feet (1.5 m)), or limited visibility (under 10 feet (3 m)) is possible, but requires extra caution and preparation to avoid or deal with buddy separation.

Silt and Mud. Silt, accumulated fine sediment settled on the bottom, or mud can rapidly cloud good visibility. Avoiding the problem is easy if one practices Minimal Impact Diving Skills. By maintaining good buoyancy, finning carefully, and keeping all gear streamlined instead of dragging, a diver will not stir up the bottom matter and reduce visibility. This is particularly important when diving around underwater wreck sites or other obstructions where the combination of low visibility and sharp or entangling objects can be especially dangerous. Underwater dive lights are not helpful in this situation because the floating cloud will not allow penetration, reflecting light back into the diver's eyes (backscatter). Guidelines and compasses also may be necessary since usual visual navigation may be disrupted.

It is often possible, if the bottom is badly stirred up by a diver ahead, or by some accidental

---

If you don't like the way it looks,

DON'T DIVE!

Visibility will often improve while you wait.

brush against something, to find better visibility by simply rising a few feet above the cloud. Divers are also cautioned to remain in close proximity to their buddies in any conditions where visibility may alter suddenly.

Suspended Material and Run-Off. Sometimes water is turbid because of suspended material. This may be the result of unsettled weather or surf stirring up relatively shallow bottoms. Or it may be due to rain, snow-melt, irrigation, river incursion (or some combination) that carries soil and other debris into the water. Whatever the cause, the water will be thick with fine, floating material, and diving may not be wise.

At other times, this matter may only occupy a band within the top layer of the water column. Fine diving can often be found beneath the layer, though ambient light from above will be blocked. Precautionary stops are also likely to take place in the area of least visibility, and disorientation can be a factor.

"Blooms" and Pollution. In areas where agriculture or high population density lies adjacent to diving environments, fertilizers, household chemicals and wastewater can pollute the water with large amounts of nitrogen-based chemicals and other matter. The influx of these chemicals and materials can increase dramatically the growth rate of algae and other microorganisms. Apart from the negative effect on animal and plant life resulting from the oxygen depletion these creatures cause, there is a tremendous reduction in visibility throughout the water column.

Recreational diving under such conditions is not recommended. To be sure, there is an increased risk associated with the poor visibility that results, however this may be the least worrisome element. The pollution that caused the runaway growth is an even more serious concern and can represent a significant health risk to divers.

Entanglement and Debris

Divers may become entangled in natural or man–made obstructions (Fig. 3-7). In either case, extrication generally is easy if the individuals remain calm and act deliberately. In kelp or other dense marine vegetation, good buddy practices, such as staying within touching distance or contact, and diving with streamlined gear, will help divers avoid the problem. Kelp also will snap easily. A diver who bends and breaks restraining strands, rather than struggling, will be freed quickly. On the surface, pushing kelp downward and gliding over helps avoid its catching on cylinder valves or regulator first stages, as it will if divers swim face-up.

Fig. 3-7. Some diving activities are unusually hazardous. Never dive beyond the limits of your training and ability.

Entanglement is also a hazard in and around most wrecks and many reefs. The rich ecosystem that attracts fish and divers also invites surface fishing with either nets or lines and hooks. Abandoned fishing tackle can still trap fish and divers. Many experienced wreck divers carry strong, blunt-tipped shears, like those used by paramedics, as an extra dive tool to facilitate cutting themselves free. Others choose to carry two or more knives, ensuring that at least one tool can be reached easily with either hand if the diver becomes entangled. Besides lines and hooks, partially intact wrecks also may have precarious interior or exterior structures that can trap or injure divers. NAUI recommends that all divers intent on exploring around or penetrating underwater wrecks receive training in the special techniques and equipment required.

Many excellent dive sites are simply the accumulation of years of debris. Attracting a great variety of marine life, these sites often contain sharp edges that can cut flesh or exposure suits. As well as causing immediate pain, such cuts may easily become infected. Practicing Minimal Impact Diving Skills, buoyancy control, streamlining, and proper finning will help divers avoid bumping into or brushing against objects that can cause injury.

Fresh Water

Freshwater diving has much to offer inland divers, from beautiful rock formations and underwater terrain to interesting aquatic life and, in some areas, spectacularly clear water. With all its attractions, however, there are unique hazards.

Buoyancy

Less dense, fresh water provides less buoyancy. Divers who regularly dive in saltwater environments will not need their usual amounts of weight in fresh water. Using the same weight belt as one would for an ocean dive will result in being over-weighted and require extra effort to maintain buoyancy. NAUI recommends that all divers adjust their buoyancy according to their needs on each dive. (Consult NAUI's *Advanced Diving: Technology and Techniques* for suggested methods.) Recording weighting information in your logbook will facilitate gearing up for different environments.

Thermoclines

Unlike tidal waters, enclosed freshwater sites like lakes, ponds, or quarries may have little internal water movement except for seasonal events like thaws or upwellings. Other freshwater sites are continually fed by cold underground springs. Dramatic thermoclines are often the result. Wise divers prepare for this by wearing appropriate exposure protection on every dive, especially when exploring a new freshwater site.

If the surface water and air temperature make wearing hoods and gloves uncomfortable, donning these items in the water just before descent is possible. Leaving wet suit zippers open during the descent until the thermocline is reached is another good technique divers can use to remain comfortable and efficient without risking either shocking cold water immersion or overheating.

Altitude

Altitude diving is a special activity requiring additional training. Sea-level dive tables and most dive computers are insufficient tools for planning dives at altitude. Dives at altitude are based on the concept of Equivalent Depth. In order to plan and execute dives within the recommended limits of exposure, such as those presented in the NAUI Dive Tables, altitude divers must account for the decreased ambient air pressure at which they begin and the altered on- and off-gassing they also will experience because of altitude. Divers who ignore this face increased risk of decompression illness, ironically in an environment that may be especially remote from timely treatment. With appropriate training, however, altitude diving is an enjoyable facet of recreational scuba.

Rivers

Inland or estuarine, river diving is an exciting pastime. Often conducted by drift-diving, or live-boating techniques, rivers present many challenges to divers. There may be strong currents, marginal visibility, pleasure and commercial boat traffic and other hazards to contend with; however, it is still a rewarding and fascinating underwater activity.

Current

Current is the chief factor to consider on most river dives. Like altitude diving, river diving in strong current is a specialized activity for which NAUI recommends additional training and orientation. Experienced river divers have developed many unique techniques to make participation less risky. Among these are the considerable logistical and rigging aspects of successful dives in swiftly flowing rivers.

Obstructions

Many river dives also will have obstructions, ranging from discarded automobiles and other debris, to objects like pipelines, dams, outfalls or fishing weirs. These all present hazards that should be carefully weighed when choosing a site and operational area for any river dive. The possibility of gear loss, entanglement, and the danger of moving quickly past sharp debris underscore the need for professional supervision in rivers until you are thoroughly experienced.

Outfalls. The discharge ends of sewer lines, storm drains, or other pipelines are often attractive dive sites, though they may represent great hazards to divers. Although fish life may thrive, divers can become ill. Worse, divers can be surprised by increased water flow or suction. Some outfalls may have grates or gates on their ends, seemingly inviting exploration. Unfortunately, such devices are often remotely operated, making entry, or even peering in while holding on, dangerous. Should the gate be closed, a diver can be trapped or injured. If not totally avoiding such areas, experienced river divers research the appropriate contact sources beforehand, notifying them of planned diving in the vicinity, thereby opening a ready line of communication to help prevent mishaps. Local divers and NAUI facilities are excellent sources of information.

Dams. Many rivers are blocked by dams built either for conservation or energy production purposes. Dams may be constructed to help regulate a river's flow around areas of homes or farms, guid-

CHAPTER 3   WHAT CAUSES DIVING ACCIDENTS?

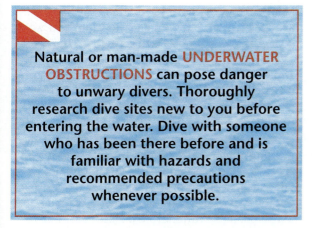

Natural or man-made UNDERWATER OBSTRUCTIONS can pose danger to unwary divers. Thoroughly research dive sites new to you before entering the water. Dive with someone who has been there before and is familiar with hazards and recommended precautions whenever possible.

ing it on a preferred course. These obstructions can provide interesting river and basin diving, but they also can be extremely dangerous.

Low-head dams, so-called because they are often little more than a slightly raised lip from bank to bank without a traditional spillway, are particularly dangerous for divers or swimmers. The water flow creates a churning circular current that can hold a diver against the face of the dam. Escape may be possible beneath the back-flowing current, but other hazards, like rubble or fencing, can make escape impossible. Rescue from a boat or river bank may be feasible, but is extremely hazardous to aid-providers. Appropriate planning would identify these features as areas to avoid (Fig. 3-8).

Weirs. Some rivers are abundant sources of fish, making them interesting diving sites. But these areas also attract recreational and commercial fishing that can include trapping grates, or weirs, set partially across swiftly flowing streams. These may be invisible from the surface, the only indication being an unusual eddy or flow pattern common to any underwater obstruction. A drift-diving excursion could lead a diver into one of these underwater grates, resulting in entanglement or injury. In a strong water flow, a suddenly-stopped diver's mask, fins, even regulator, may be dislodged and lost. Extrication may be possible, but identifying and planning to avoid such hazardous areas is preferred.

Oceans

Most recreational diving takes place in coastal areas. Consequently, most diving accidents occur in the ocean. Though this can be attributed to the sheer weight of statistics, some accidents are caused by unique features of oceanic environment.

Current

Ocean currents may be either global, vast flowing rivers within the ocean itself like the Gulf Stream. They may be tidal, daily ebbing and flowing according to a fairly predictable timetable. Or they may be geographic, caused by local terrain and conditions. All must be accounted for in dive planning and execution.

Fig. 3-8. Freshwater diving can have unique hazards. Research new areas thoroughly.

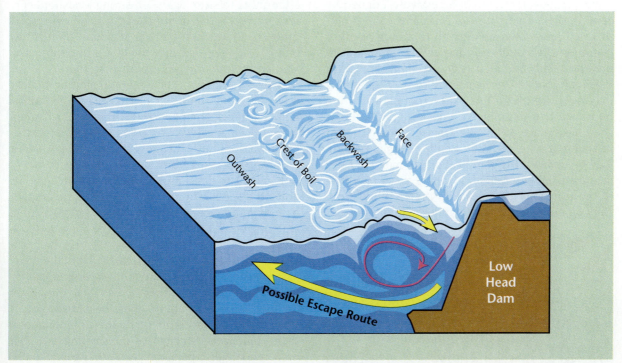

In areas subject to relatively stable geographic currents or strong tidal currents, drift-diving or liveboating often are the best choices. These allow divers to cover large distances almost effortlessly, as in river diving, but require a great deal of logistical support and planning. Typically, however, divers are faced with moderate current on almost every ocean dive.

Tidal Currents. Ranging from flow rates of only a few to as much as hundreds of feet per minute, tidal current (in excess of about 50 feet per minute (15 m/min)) can be a reason to postpone a planned dive or change the site to a more protected area. Strong currents can quickly overwhelm even a strong diver. This is particularly true at the end of a dive when a diver may be tired. The feeling of being out of control caught in a current can lead to panic. In addition, being swept out of sight of the exit point or boat can be a prescription for disaster. Fortunately, such events can be avoided with good planning.

Tidal currents reverse flow approximately twice daily. T*ide T*ables and *Current Charts* provide divers and other water users with a good estimate of the times and locations of least flow (slack water). These publications can be used to minimize the effects of current on any dive. Predictions may, however, differ from reality, and reliably judging current by looking at the water is impossible. Current below the surface may also differ markedly from surface flow. Because of this, divers are advised to check current upon descent by observing indicators like the direction in which underwater plant life may be leaning.

If feeling overpowered or excessively fatigued by current, divers are urged to relax and calm themselves. Underwater, holding on to a rock or other feature of the bottom and just taking a moment to breathe calmly and relax is an excellent method of regaining control. Once calm and rested, continuing may be possible. If not, surfacing, establishing buoyancy, and signalling for aid is recommended.

At the surface, swimming against a strong current in scuba gear, especially if fighting wind as well, may be difficult. The combination can make the surface especially turbulent. Planning dives to return to the exit point underwater is preferable. If sufficient air supply is available, redescending to a less disturbed part of the water column, which may also have less current and certainly no wind, and working back to the exit point is often a good choice.

NAUI recommends careful assessment of the predicted and actual tidal current before commencing, and throughout, any ocean dive, as means of preventing diving accidents.

Geographic Currents. Some formations of shoreline create strong currents that can imperil divers, particularly on beach dives. These areas are generally known, but the conditions may develop undetected over time, or only be in effect in certain kinds of weather, specific seasons, or states of tide. Whatever the reason, these currents are no less hazardous.

Rip Current. Rips are currents that develop offshore where a break in the terrain channels and accelerates out-flowing water from a (usually) steep beach front (Fig. 3-9). A diver or swimmer seeking to return to the beach may be prevented by such a flow and, very likely, driven out to sea by it.

Dealing effectively with a rip current requires that a diver relax and literally "go with the flow," which will generally weaken as it moves offshore. Rather than uselessly fighting the current and exhausting yourself, swimming perpendicular to the rip current even as it takes you away will take you out of the flow. Once free of the localized current, the diver can swim in towards shore. Rip currents are well-illustrated in NAUI's *Academic Video Series*.

Longshore Currents. These currents run parallel to the shoreline and are created by strong wave action (Fig. 3-10). A longshore current can quickly carry divers far from their planned exit point, and attempting to swim against a strong longshore current to regain the desired exit will be tiring and probably futile. Swimming at an angle towards the beach, however, usually will allow a diver to make slow and steady progress toward the shore.

Strong Backwash. On a steeply sloping beach, wave backwash and surf can recreate the turbulent, sucking action of a low-head dam. Such areas make poor choices for beach dives anyway, because high surf and unsure footing can make entry and exit dangerous.

If caught in a strong backwash, a diver may be able to get out of the boiling wash by swimming away from the beach as close to the bottom as possible. Attempting to rise above the force holding you down or to gain the beach by fighting the backwash will generally be unsuccessful. Hold the mask and regulator in place. Since the water flow can be random and violent in these areas, gear easily can be lost. Divers in locations where backwashes occur frequently use surf mats or boards to stay above the turbulence when crossing the surf line and wear extra retaining straps on fins and other gear.

Beginning a dive going into the current, against the flow, will allow divers to work less hard returning to the exit point at the end of a dive.

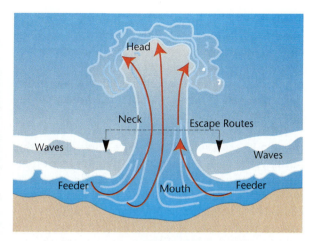

Fig. 3-9. Rip currents are usually found offshore.

Fig. 3-11. Breaking waves and a rocky shoreline are a dangerous combination for divers.

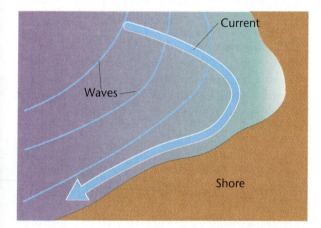

Fig. 3-10. Longshore currents can be the result of even moderate wave action. Assess conditions carefully when planning entry and exit points.

Surf. High waves and huge surf are conditions of choice for many watersports enthusiasts, but not divers! (Fig. 3-11.) Going from the shore to sea and returning in such conditions is at least a lesson in humility, and can be highly dangerous.

Successful surf entries and exits require practice, coaching, judgment, and patience. Waiting to enter until water is calmer between a series of waves is recommended. Buddy teams of beach divers often enter in pairs, with masks on and snorkel or regulator mouthpiece in place, ready to submerge beneath the incoming waves and fin their way past the breaker line at the first opportunity. Various techniques are used under different conditions. As a result, divers are advised to seek the guidance of knowledgeable local instructors who will be able to share appropriate techniques for the area. Dive shops are also good sources of this information.

When you are timing an exit in surf, it is usually best to wait until a wave set has completed and then attempt to gain the beach. If you fall, crawling on hands and knees through the foam may be best rather than attempting to stand and risk being knocked down again. Divers exiting in pairs in this manner can remove each other's fins while crawling before attempting to stand.

In surf, a scuba diver is vulnerable to gear loss and injury as a result of tumbling by a large wave. Strong backwash also is possible. Some surf areas are easier to access if kayaks, float boards, surf mats, or other flotation devices are used. Working with divers experienced in such conditions and the proper use of this equipment before attempting beach dives in surf is highly recommended. There are usually alternative sites available where more moderate conditions prevail since surf is a function of geography and weather.

Overhead Environments

Diving in overhead environments, where direct access to the surface is restricted, accounts for too many diving fatalities annually. Such environments include diving in caverns or caves, penetrating wrecks, or diving under ice. Each of these activities represents a higher-than-usual recreational dive risk that only can be deemed acceptable with extremely thorough, specialized training and suitable equipment (Fig. 3-12).

The greatest hazard in all overhead environments is inability to return to the exit point necessary to regaining the surface. Whether from disorientation, poor navigation skills, reduced visibility because of poor technique, improper equipment, gear failure or misuse, or any combination of factors, tragedy can result. NAUI recommends that divers avoid entering any overhead environments until trained to do so by qualified instructors in the specific field.

Fig. 3-12. Stay out of overhead environments unless specifically trained and appropriately equipped.

Caverns and Caves

Inadvertently finding yourself in a cave or cavern underwater usually only happens when a diver attempts to surface and unhappily finds a ceiling. Occurring at the end of a dive, when air supply is depleted, a speedy exit is crucial. Unfortunately, taking time to think calmly about your route up to that point may be difficult. Cave and cavern divers routinely deploy guidelines to enable them to find their way back to the entrance. Unless you have done so, or have followed a compass bearing into the area, accurately retracing your course to the exit is unlikely. However, waiting for rescue if you are low on air is also a poor alternative.

Observing the path of your exhalation bubbles will lead you to the highest point of the ceiling. If the roof slopes towards the entrance, following the bubbles will take you out of the obstructed environment. On a bright day, the light of the opening may be apparent. Turning off a dive light, if used, will help you identify the entrance after the eyes adjust. If visibility is suddenly lost because of carelessly disturbed silt or mud, a clear view may be found by rising above the cloud. Any of these escape possibilities is underscored by great uncertainty. Realistic consideration of the likely consequences hopefully will deter anyone without training from diving where such underwater features exist. Many of these areas have clear warnings posted.

Divers interested in learning underwater cavern and cave penetration are referred to the *National Speleological Society – Cave Diving Section* or the *National Association of Cave Divers* in the United States. Other countries have similar nationally recognized organizations.

Wreck Penetration

Shipwrecks are some of the most attractive dive sites to be found, but entering and leaving them is potentially perilous because of all the problems of other overhead environments, plus the significant risks of injury from sharp objects and entanglement from abandoned fishing gear.

NAUI strongly recommends that divers complete a Wreck Diving Specialty Course under the supervision of a qualified instructor before attempting wreck penetration diving. This course is designed to acquaint certified divers with the specialized knowledge and additional training necessary to participate in this activity without undue risk. Divers are referred to the general remarks on Overhead Environments, above, and the previous comments on dealing with Entanglement.

Diving Under Ice

Ice diving grows more popular each winter, and each season claims more unwitting victims that succumb to the potent combination of cold water and restricted overhead access without first being thoroughly trained (Fig. 3-13). Such training is readily available in all areas where ice diving is practiced. It includes the techniques, equipment, and practices experts recommend, as well as emergency and survival procedures. Venturing under ice without such training is foolish and dangerous. Readers are referred to the general remarks on Overhead Environments, above, and the previous comments on Cold Water.

Boating Traffic

Regretfully, some divers forget that their preferred recreational area is shared with others, from swimmers, sunbathers, and other watersports enthusiasts to commercial and pleasure boat operators. This last group can be especially dangerous to divers as boating accident statistics show.

Regardless of who is right, divers will invariably lose in any confrontation with a moving boat. As a result, avoiding such mishaps by following appropriate diving practices is mandatory. Central among these is to know and use the appropriate flags, floats, and signals to notify passing traffic of the presence of diving operations. These include using the internationally recognized code flag Alpha, and the traditional red-with-white-slash "Dive Flag" whenever divers are in the water, and *not* displaying these signals when they are not (Fig. 3-14).

Many states and local jurisdictions have specific rules regarding dive flags and the conduct of vessels in the vicinity of them. Some also restrict divers from certain popular boating areas, and others do likewise for boaters. Prudent vessel operators and divers know and follow these rules.

NAUI requires that its members make sure that appropriate signals and flags are used for any supervised diving activity and recommends that all divers follow suit as a means of avoiding diving accidents.

PROBLEM BREATHING PATTERNS

Involuntary and largely unconscious on land, breathing becomes a focal point upon first spending time underwater. Simple breathing interruptions, such as sneezing or coughing, assume greater importance when diving and can be sources of real difficulty in the increased pressure underwater. Choking, as when aspirating a water droplet, can be frightening, even dangerous, underwater if it leads to uncontrolled ascent or the inability to catch one's breath. So too, overexertion leading to hypoventilation when diving may be the cause of a diving mishap. Thorough training can help divers manage these problems.

Other breathing-related sources of dive accidents come from misguided attempts to extend time underwater. Practices like "skip-breathing" on scuba or excessive hyperventilation before freediving (skindiving), which can lead to "shallow water blackout," are at the root of some diving accidents. Knowledge of the detrimental effects of these practices hopefully will discourage divers from taking the risks they represent.

Choking and Coughing

The chief harms of choking and coughing underwater are that they interrupt the normal pattern of inhalation and exhalation. Good buoyancy control during these incidents will help prevent lung overexpansion injuries that can result from ascending even a few feet while regaining control.

If you are near the bottom, settling down, stopping, and finishing the episode by coughing it out or clearing the throat normally is recommended. Divers are also advised to hold their regulators in place during these moments to prevent accidental ejection.

Vomiting

Seasickness or other nausea-related illness can strike at any time, even underwater. Though disconcerting and annoying, like choking and coughing, such incidents need not result in accidents if divers maintain the presence of mind to remain at the same depth throughout and hold the regulator in place until once again feeling well. Most regulators will easily pass any regurgitated material, however,

Fig. 3-13. Diving under ice requires specialized training and equipment, rigorous preparation, and extensive support.

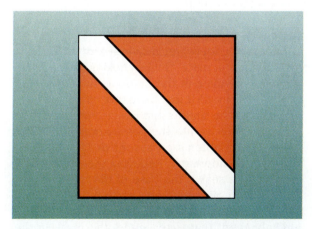

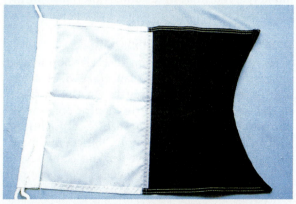

Fig. 3-14. Using authorized dive flags as routine nautical decorations aboard a vessel weakens their meaning as warning signals.

> Whenever *sneezing*, *coughing*, or *vomiting* underwater, **HOLD** the **REGULATOR** in **PLACE**, and **MAINTAIN YOUR DEPTH.**

the first inhalations afterwards should be made cautiously in case anything has been trapped. Divers should be ready to switch to an alternate second stage as they cautiously test the primary mouthpiece. If either second stage is clogged and cannot be easily cleaned by simple tapping and purging, the buddy team should ascend at the recommended rate with a precautionary stop, to deal with the clogged mouthpiece on the surface.

Most often, the regulator will continue to function without difficulty. After the situation stabilizes, divers may want to rinse the second stage clean by waving it in the water and tapping the purge valve. Divers should switch to an alternate second stage or exhale steadily while the regulator is out of their mouths.

Sneezing

Sneezing underwater requires a diver to hold the regulator in place. Unlike choking or coughing, however, the mask is also an issue since the nose is encased. In addition, sneezing causes a back pressure on the sinuses and Eustachian tubes that may drive mucus into the passageways, possibly leading to problems on ascent or injury to the areas while underwater. Relieving the pressure by breaking the seal at the base of the mask so that the expelled air can escape easily from the nose will help prevent injury from sneezing. In the unlikely event that water enters the mask in the process, it is easily cleared in the usual manner.

Overexertion and Hypoventilation

Working hard underwater, such as when finning against a strong current, can make divers feel unable to catch their breath. On the surface, breathing through an overly long or constricted snorkel can have the same effect. Although hypoventilation sounds simple, the chemical and physiological processes involved are complicated and can have serious consequences.

Hypoventilation is the term used for rapid shallow breathing that will soon result in a person's feeling breathless. Regardless of the diver's physique or fitness, hypoventilation results in insufficient gas transfer in the lungs even though a large volume of air is passing through the diver's regulator. The combination of high carbon dioxide produced from hard work and the lack of effective ventilation can lead quickly to a dangerous accumulation of carbon dioxide (hypercapnia). Avoiding overexertion underwater, and recognizing and stopping hypoventilation quickly is integral to accident prevention. If the condition persists, it will cause the diver increasing physical and mental stress until panic results from simply not being able to satisfy the need for air (air hunger).

The condition is prevented by making sure that breathing, particularly exhalation, remains effective throughout every dive. If feeling stressed or out of breath underwater, stop whatever you are doing and relax. If near the bottom, descend and hold on to something. If in mid-water, adjust buoyancy and hover. On the surface, roll over and rest on your back while buoyant.

Concentrate on complete exhalations, exaggerating their duration and depth. NAUI divers often use a problem-solving method that includes a breathing cadence: Stop–Breathe–Think–Breathe–Act that can help divers relax and regain normal breathing. Some diving leaders also recommend tapping the purge button during exhalation if you are feeling breathless. This increases the exhaust flow and may help flush out carbon dioxide more quickly by increasing the depth of a normal exhalation. Once normal respiration returns, divers can decide whether or not conditions are too strenuous to continue the dive.

Hyperventilation and "Shallow Water Blackout"

Hyperventilation is the process of exhausting too much carbon dioxide from the body by prolonged, rapid, deep breathing. Typically practiced before surface diving to increase breath-hold time, it can result in sudden unconsciousness underwater ("shallow water blackout") and lead to drowning. Excessive hyperventilation kills a significant number of people, especially young swimmers, every year.

Prolonged hyperventilation "short-circuits" the usual physiologic warning system (routine carbon dioxide increase in the circulatory system) that triggers the need to breathe, but it does not increase or "store" oxygen. The diminished level of carbon dioxide that results from hyperventilation does allow the diver to remain underwater longer but can lead to a dangerously low oxygen level before the urge to breathe is felt. During ascent, as ambient pressure on the diver decreases, so do blood gas pressures. The level of oxygen can fall below that needed for a person to remain conscious (hypoxia). When this happens, breath–

holding ends, and breathing resumes despite being underwater. Drowning results.

NAUI recommends avoiding hyperventilation entirely. Free divers who wish to increase their breath–hold ability are advised to consult a NAUI skin diving or scuba instructor to learn effective methods that entail less risk.

Skip-Breathing

Skip-breathing is an imprudent method for extending air supply by intermittently or consistently delaying exhalations, in effect, holding one's breath underwater. Besides the clear dangers of possible lung-overexpansion injuries and mild to severe hypercapnia, experience has shown that it does not work very well. It may even increase air consumption since disrupting normal breathing usually results in deeper, more labored inhalations.

The urge to breathe is governed primarily by the level of CO_2 in the circulatory system. Skip-breathing increases the amount of CO_2 and thus increases the urge to breathe. At the same time, unless the CO_2 level is diminished by normal exhalations, breathing is less satisfying. This pattern of steadily increasing CO_2 levels, although initially conserving some air, will eventually lead to greatly increased air hunger, gasping, and the inability to catch one's breath. This situation easily can progress to life-threatening panic.

The desire to remain underwater longer is, however, nearly universal among recreational divers. Fortunately, there are much better ways to do so than skip-breathing. Among the most effective and effortless are relaxing underwater, practicing Minimal Impact Diving Skills (streamlining, buoyancy control, and proper finning techniques), being warm and comfortable, and having confidence in one's ability, training, equipment, and companions. Breathing continually with a slightly slower exhalation will help relax a diver. Relaxation, accompanied by a corresponding reduction in heart rate, will naturally extend one's time underwater. In essence, follow sound practices, gain dive experience, and relax, and air consumption will surely decrease, as will the chance of underwater mishaps.

EQUALIZATION DIFFICULTIES

The inability to equalize internal pressure with the pressure of the underwater environment is a significant cause of diver stress and probably the most common cause of diving injury. Though problems can be completely prevented by exercising good judgment and using simple techniques, nearly every diver has experienced discomfort as a result of incomplete or ineffective equalization of an internal air space.

These pressure-related injuries (barotraumas) are generally divided into two types. "Squeezes" are those that occur when the air in internal spaces, such as the sinuses, middle ear, or even an artificial air space like that between the mask and face, is compressed without adding additional air to make up for the decreased volume. Tissue and fluid are then drawn into the void, sometimes with harmful and painful results.

In contrast to "squeezes," which happen on descent, "blocks" (sometimes referred to as "reverse squeezes") occur on ascent when greater-than-ambient-pressure air is somehow prevented from escaping from an enclosed space, such as when a sinus becomes clogged by mucus during a dive. Until the pressure imbalance is relieved, pain results.

Divers experiencing difficulty equalizing upon descent are advised to stop their descent immediately and breathe normally for a moment with the hands away from the face. Without trying to clear again, and with the hands remaining away from the face, ascend a few feet to relieve the discomfort and stabilize buoyancy. When ready, try to clear again. If equalization occurs, continue clearing and descending. If you are unable to equalize, aborting the dive is recommended (Fig. 3-15).

Fig. 3-15. Divers experiencing difficulty equalizing and who cannot resolve the problem should return to the surface, inflate the BC and abort the dive.

Squeezes

Difficulty equalizing pressure on descent can have a variety of causes, but it is almost always due to poor technique or delaying the process too long. For instance, though all divers know that clearing their ears throughout descent is crucial, few practice the technique at any other time. They may mistakenly wait until discomfort signals the need, increasing the difficulty of clearing because of stress. Either poor technique or delaying the clearing process can be a prescription for injury.

NAUI advises divers to ensure their ability to clear effectively when gearing up for a dive and while on the surface waiting to descend. Though there will be no actual pressure differential to equalize, loosening and exercising the involved muscles by practicing equalization maneuvers before descent will often reveal any congestion or problems that may be present. In the water, divers should begin clearing as soon as they go below the surface and throughout their descent. If making a multi-level dive, participants should continue to equalize pressure through each descent greater than about two FSW (1 MSW).

Though ear squeeze is the most common type, other air-space squeezes are possible. These spaces include the sinuses, teeth, and abdominal (gut) areas, and the air spaces created by wearing dive masks and ill-fitting wet suits. After the ears, which can be equalized through either gentle Valsalva or Frenzl Maneuvers or an individual method, and the sinuses, which, if healthy, equalize themselves, the most usual squeeze occurs when divers forget to exhale some air into their masks each time the ears are cleared or never clear water from their masks during a dive. This often happens on a second dive after a diver has been annoyed by a leaking mask on the prior dive and has overly tightened the strap so no water could enter.

Preventing less common squeezes is easy if divers are conscientious about their health and appearance. Good dentistry, a healthy diet low in gas-producing foods and carbonated drinks, and a properly fitting wetsuit will eliminate the possibilities.

Blocks

Blocks are particularly hazardous since they occur while ascending. At least as painful as squeezes, a block can make ascending difficult and uncomfortable, but because of factors like diminished air supply and nearing recommended exposure limits at the end of a dive, dealing with it quickly is essential.

Divers are advised first to stop where they are in the water column, breathe normally, and then descend a few feet to relieve the discomfort. Normal clearing efforts during the descent may help clear the block. At the slightly deeper depth, repeated efforts to clear may relieve the block. If not, the diver is advised to ascend at a greatly reduced rate, with the hands completely away from the face and making no effort to equalize, stopping when the discomfort dictates. When stopped and stabilized at depth, again try to equalize gently to clear the block. Divers can repeat the process of stopping, stabilizing, and equalizing, then ascending very slowly, to avoid or minimize discomfort, back to the surface. Carefully monitor remaining air throughout the ascent. Planning dives to surface with a good reserve supply of air is crucial to dealing with a block on ascent.

Blocks are usually caused by diving with residual congestion from a cough or cold. Strenuous efforts to equalize in spite of congestion irritates passageways, causing swelling and increased mucus that eventually stops or greatly restricts air transfer. Air introduced to equalize on descent cannot escape normally upon ascent. Blocks also can develop as a side effect of medications taken to make clearing easier! When medication wears off underwater, the condition it was meant to help, such as a clogged nasal passage or sinus, can return, possibly more severely than it was. Never diving unless completely well and equalizing gently and completely during descents, will help prevent blocks from developing. See the section on Medications in Chapter One for further information.

The problems and injuries associated with the direct effects of pressure, squeezes, and blocks are covered more fully in Chapter Seven.

DEALING WITH A BLOCK ON ASCENT

STOP!

Descend A Few Feet While Equalizing

STABILIZE!

Gently Clear the Block by Equalizing

Ascend Slowly WITHOUT Clearing

If discomfort persists, repeat the procedure

Never attempt to equalize during ascent!

JUDGMENT PROBLEMS

Given absolutely reliable technology and a carefully controlled environment, scuba diving would be perfectly safe—so long as humans did not participate! But the great diversity of human personality, motivation, abilities, and intelligence, and the unequal distribution of fundamental common sense makes the lack of good judgment a contributing factor in many, if not most, diving accidents.

As long as people continue to make bad decisions about their diving activities, including their ability to perform adequately under stressful conditions and assess conditions accurately, and their overall fitness to dive, accidents will happen. NAUI's motto, *Safety Through Education*, reflects the attitude that, basic human character aside, knowledge, thorough training, and repeated practice are fundamental to preventing diving accidents.

Making Responsible Activity Choices

Divers who thoroughly understand the risks associated with their activities, and who understand the physical requirements of successfully meeting those risks, will generally participate responsibly. For this reason, NAUI requires its members to use standardized methods, such as written waivers and detailed predive briefings, to inform divers of inherent risks in any supervised activity. By considering these risks carefully before accepting them, divers are encouraged to weigh their ability to participate enjoyably. Predive briefing information enables divers to judge whether their individual skill level, training, and diving experience are suitable for participation.

However, not all diving takes place under professional supervision or guidance. Most diving, in fact, probably does not. Individual divers and their buddies are encouraged to treat every dive they make with the same high standards NAUI sets for its leaders. Divers are urged to consider their fitness for every dive they make and to dive according to their ability and training. Leaders learn that not every dive can be made by every diver on any given day. Divers are wise to adopt the same attitude. They do well to realize that postponing a dive when conditions are marginal, or altering an activity so that it is fully within the limits of all participants' training and ability to enjoy it, is the best choice they can make.

Considering Fitness

Fitness to dive is concerned with the absence of any contraindications to participate. Diving fitness means having the physical ability to meet the demands of participating in a potentially strenuous activity. Though related, they are not interchangeable. (Both topics are covered fully in Chapter One.) They are mentioned now because inaccurate assessment of either can lead easily to a diving accident for the participant, for diving companions who are unaware of the problems, or for those who choose to support the unfit diver's participation in spite of them. The latter group is at least making an informed, albeit wrong, decision. The former group are, however, potential victims of a diver who selfishly keeps such information hidden.

No amount of desire can justify recreational activity that deliberately places others in jeopardy. NAUI urges all divers to be familiar with conditions that increase the risk of participation (see Chapter One), and to desist from diving while they are present. Furthermore, all divers must assess the wisdom of making or continuing any dive based on the conditions at the moment and their ability fully to meet the challenges they represent. Any doubt about whether participation could unduly endanger themselves or other divers is best resolved by postponing or terminating the dive.

Psychological Factors

Mental errors, poor influences or attitudes, and faulty judgment can lead to severe consequences underwater. Avoiding accidents caused by psychological factors takes concentration, maturity, self-discipline, and character.

Attitude and Judgment. Divers are unique people. Most tend to be adventurous and willing to try new things. Usually outgoing, most divers are also friendly, helpful companions, glad to lend a hand and offer advice or aid. But there are among divers, as in any group of people, those who do not fit the usual profile.

For instance, some divers may be extremely selfish, disdainful of the rights or abilities of others to participate in "their" pastime. They may deliberately leave a buddy underwater so they can enjoy "their" dive unhampered by waiting for a less capable, or simply slower, diver. Others seek extreme challenges for a variety of reasons, always striving to test the limits with a kind of "frequent survivor" behavior characterized by boasting about close calls or accidents they or their buddies have had. Still others are confrontational when presented with legitimate requests from friends, dive buddies, leaders, or others in authority. They may deliberately violate policies or rules in a wrong-headed attempt to assert their independence and superiority.

Though accidents can happen to anyone at any time, diving with obnoxious characters sets people on edge. Distracted from the tasks necessary to prepare for a successful dive, or angered by the behavior of those around them, usually-careful divers can be driven to make mistakes. Worse, competitive or combative behavior can result, threatening the peace of mind and concentration of all present. In either case, risk is increased and accidents can result. NAUI believes that diving should be a stress–reducing, pleasant recreation. Participating in that spirit of enjoyment will help make it so.

Peer Pressure. Though there are no statistics available that document how many diving accidents are due to peer pressure, it is easy to believe that many are. The desire for social approval is strong in most people. Wanting to be liked and admired by your perceived peers, and, conversely, being fearful of scorn and ridicule is part of every personality. It can be so strong in fact that it can result in bizarre or unique behavior, well outside usual conventions of society. (Consider tattooing in the Navy, for instance, or various styles of dress, appearance, or behavior among other groups, from young persons to country club members.)

History has repeatedly shown that a small group, or even a charismatic individual, can be immensely influential, leading a larger group that "ought to have known better" to ruin. In diving, when a person or group challenges an individual to act foolishly "on a dare," or join in an activity or behavior that ignores training and sound knowledge, it can lead to accidents. This includes unprepared participation in an activity that requires specialized training and equipment, such as underwater caving, or knowingly exceeding one's level of ability or training for the conditions of any dive. It also less obviously includes letting yourself be talked into making any dive about which you are for any reason unenthusiastic or uncomfortable.

Avoiding giving in to the dominion of peers requires strong self-esteem and confidence. Good training, like that provided by NAUI instructors, can help you develop the necessary internal strength to resist joining in the foolish behavior of others or being influenced by them to take unwarranted risks. Through a structured process of meeting and exceeding challenges under the guidance of a qualified instructor, such as in this course, you will grow more confident and appreciative of your own ability and judgment.

Never be afraid to say "No!" to making *any dive for any reason*.

Thrill-seeking. There are people who find danger stimulating, or for whom excessive risk-taking is necessary for bolstering their self-esteem. Whatever the reason, such behavior in divers, characterized by willfully exceeding the limits of common sense or recommended practices, will eventually cause an accident. Without debating individuals' right to harm themselves, the fact is that diving is a shared activity. Irresponsible behavior risks harm to diving companions and leaders. Most people respond unselfishly, even to the point of accepting great risk to themselves, in an effort to aid an individual in distress. Few at an accident scene will stop to consider whether the victim "had it coming," or will act differently even if so.

NAUI appeals to all divers to prevent accidents caused by this kind of behavior by carefully monitoring their own states of mind and the behavior of their diving companions. Doubts about the mental fitness of a diver or the rational basis of other divers' behavior are valid reasons at least to discuss the matter with the individual(s) or any persons in charge before entering the water.

Task Loading: "The Snowball Effect"

Diving is a complex, multidimensional activity. There are many things to consider, skills to employ, and decisions to make on every dive. Little problems, like a leaking mask, uncomfortable mouthpiece, difficulty clearing upon initial descent, greater-than-expected water current, an unfamiliar activity, or new buddy can combine to create stress. Sometimes small items are overlooked or ignored in the interest of going on with a dive in spite of them. Sometimes new or unusual activities, such as diving at night or trying out an underwater camera, may take precedence over usual preparation because there is too much to think about (Fig. 3-16). People may feel uncomfortable sharing a particular minor concern with companions, or may be reluctant to opt out of making a specific dive for fear of upsetting a buddy. In any case, any number of usually insignificant minor items can coalesce, "snowballing" into a diving accident, no matter what the diver's certification level or ability.

Preventing this type of accident takes vigilance. Anything that detracts from diver comfort or confidence or that makes a dive less enjoyable is something to correct immediately. Simply not feeling like participating for any reason is sufficient cause to sit out a dive. Constantly monitoring one's feelings, gear, and dive conditions is part of prudent diving, and resolving problems and concerns immediately will help prevent them from causing accidents.

CHAPTER 3 WHAT CAUSES DIVING ACCIDENTS?

Fig. 3-16. Too many things to think about on a dive can overload a diver's ability to cope. New underwater activities can also distract a diver from fundamental rules.

Training Considerations

Training, too, can be a source of diving accidents. The struggle to meet time and effort requirements for thorough training while making a profit can lead to short cuts in instruction. Students may get by, and operators and instructors be paid, but the learning process can suffer. Ultimately the students lose, because real ability eludes them and they are ill-prepared to dive. Poor or incomplete initial instruction, haphazard preparation, insufficient skill, or lack of practice can result in new divers going into the water less than fully ready to meet the demands of diving—pointlessly jeopardizing people's safety. Appropriate professional instruction is readily available to all divers, from NAUI or other sources.

Diving skills are learned!
Without PRACTICE and USE, they are forgotten. Keep your skills sharp by diving, and by practice.

Diving Skills

Diving skills are a complex assortment of learned responses. No one is born with them. Many of them, such as learning to equalize pressure or clear a mask, are decidedly foreign to common experience. Just breathing underwater is an unnatural event for humans. Acquiring the fundamental skill to do so, especially without a mask on, can be difficult initially because of discomfort and fear.

But patient, systematic, professional guidance will allow virtually any person to overcome normal misgivings. Given time, most people will readily acclimate to the unusual sensations and demands of the underwater environment and learn to dive.

"Passing" vs. Proficient. New divers in particular often are anxious to execute required certification skills without truly learning them. Sometimes, instructors unwittingly encourage this attitude by treating dive skills as separate tasks rather than interdependent parts of training that all contribute to proficiency (Fig. 3-17). Lack of proficiency can leave divers unable to perform effectively under the dynamic demands of actual diving, though they have been "checked off" on individual skills. Accidents can be prevented if you adopt a rigorous approach to judging quality in your own skills and those of dive companions.

NAUI training seeks to encourage proficiency in divers by the use of a simple but powerful criterion as the ultimate measure for certification. Instructors are encouraged to award certification only if they are able to answer affirmatively the

Fig. 3-17. Confidence in your buddy's ability and self-sufficiency help make your diving more pleasurable.

> Asking to see an unfamiliar buddy's logbook and sharing your own is a good way to build mutual respect and confidence. *Never dive with a buddy whose ability you doubt for any reason.*

question *Would you let a loved one dive with this person?* This self-imposed test eliminates the possibility of accepting "just passing" skills. Instead, NAUI instructors strive to foster expertise through a structured process dedicated to helping all students achieve at their highest level. Because crucial skills are taught progressively and reflexively, and lessons are built based on previous achievements and individual students' demonstrated abilities, NAUI divers meet and usually exceed all published standards and requirements.

Practice, Practice, Practice. Whether you are "getting to Carnegie Hall" or going diving, the benefit of dedicated study, experience, and practice cannot be overemphasized (Fig. 3-18). Many dive accidents can be attributed to simple forgetfulness. Persons who dive infrequently, however well trained initially, can overlook a critical part of preparation or, worse, forget how to perform some crucial task underwater. Not knowing what to do or having to spend time thinking about how to respond to a routine diving situation can progress from uncertainty to real emergency.

NAUI encourages all divers to maintain their proficiency by using their skills. After certification, frequent, thoughtful participation is the best method of refining diving skills. Practicing sharing-air methods, through mental rehearsal and discussion and practice with customary dive buddies on dry land, and in the water under controlled circumstances, will help keep your skills stay sharp and vital.

Practicing with dive gear in confined water before diving again after an extended absence, or taking a refresher course under the supervision of a qualified NAUI instructor, are also highly recommended.

Knowledge

Recreational diving is a dynamic, evolving activity, in many ways quite different today from what it was. This is a result of an ever-increasing base of knowledge and experience, the application of innovative analytical tools, and the development of new techniques and equipment. Therefore maintaining diving knowledge includes regular use and constant updating of previously learned mate-

Fig. 3-18. Practicing with your equipment under controlled conditions will help ensure your ability to deal with a real emergency.

rial. From initial certification through every level of leadership, NAUI encourages all divers to increase their readiness by expanding their knowledge of diving physics, physiology, and related fields.

Diving frequently, if you plan each dive thoroughly, is one of the best ways to maintain your diving knowledge. Careful, complete planning includes evaluating alternative times and depths (bracketing) and making air consumption calculations that include reasonable air reserves to deal with contingencies. Maintaining a logbook with this information included for each dive will provide an excellent review and reference tool.

On the other hand, depending solely on a dive computer, or the stated dive parameters of a dive guide's predive briefing, will eventually dull your planning ability and understanding and will detract from your independence and confidence. Without good understanding, experience, and practiced skills, any diver's ability to deal with changing situations is markedly reduced.

Power vs. Mastery. There are essentially two kinds of knowledge proficiency that divers can have. The first, power over information, is a person's ability to display a great deal of information on a test. While this is an impressive intellectual skill, it is less useful to a competent diver than real mastery of material. Being able to cough up information is not as important as knowing how to deal with coughing underwater. Mastering information, making it part of your repertoire of diving options so that you may call upon it to deal spontaneously with situations, is crucial to preventing accidents caused by ignorance.

> Thorough dive planning includes proposed depth and time, alternate depths and times, and making air consumption calculations that leave an appropriate reserve amount of air for contingencies.

Continuing Education. No NAUI instructor can maintain instructor status without evidence of participating in a continuing education program. Just as leaders must, NAUI advises all divers to consider their options in maintaining and building upon their base of diving knowledge. Reading this text, whether in conjunction with a *Scuba Rescue Diver* or *Advanced Scuba Rescue Diver* course or on your own, and using its information in your diving, is an example of continually pursuing diving knowledge. How you get through any diving situation will depend on how well you know what is recommended and how well you can apply or modify it to meet the demands you face.

Courses. Taking advanced and specialty diving classes is perhaps the most effective means of maintaining and improving your diving knowledge and skills. The guidance of a qualified professional instructor is invaluable for these purposes; however, most divers live in areas where participation is seasonal, so expensive travel may be necessary for the diving portions of such classes.

Many NAUI facilities offer courses devoted to strictly informational aspects of diving that will help you maintain your knowledge. Dealing with topics from equipment maintenance to dive computers, such classes are valuable preparation for diving. Not only dive shops but local schools, community organizations, libraries, colleges, and other organizations offer a choice of diving-related courses that can help focus and expand your diving knowledge. Topics range from archeology and environmental studies to marine biology, all of which can exchange with and enhance diving information. Instructors are often pleased to have an experienced diver as part of a class, because she may add valuable practical insights.

Periodicals. There are many diving publications that can expand and enhance diving knowledge. Most active divers subscribe to at least one of these. In addition to whetting your appetite for dive travel and new gear, these publications invariably feature exciting articles with vivid descriptions and photographs.

Though most people regard popular magazines as recreational reading, they can reinforce diving knowledge and be sources of new information. Imagining yourself in the story or picture is a kind of mental rehearsal for your next dive. Recalling sensations, and vicariously experiencing the situations described are useful accompaniments to actual diving.

There are scholarly and professional journals, such as *Sources*, that are excellent resources for all divers. Articles on training, medical aspects of diving, rescue, leadership, and many diving-related topics keep interested divers at all levels abreast of the latest trends and thinking in the field.

In the end, there is no simple answer to diving accidents. There are many causes, some of which are beyond divers' control. It is important, however, to recognize that in contrast to the complexity of accident causes, fundamental prevention is relatively simple: think about your diving, and dive thoughtfully at all times.

CHAPTER FOUR

Webster defines stress as "a specific response by the body to a stimlus, as fear or pain, that disturbs or interferes with the body's normal physiological equilibrium; physical, mental or emotional strain or tension." Reaction to any event, whether joy or sorrow, eagerness or fear, is accompanied by some level of stress.

Though all people live with stress as part of everyday life, its effect in diving, especially if unrelieved, can be dangerous (Fig. 4-1). Unchecked, excessive stress will quickly result in distress, a situation that requires immediate intervention. Without timely, appropriate help, strain becomes unbearable and a distressed person can no longer function. Normal reactions, however well-learned and ingrained, are suspended. Conscious thought and deliberate action are impossible, and panic, the direct cause of most diving accidents, results. The only goal of the victim is to escape from distress, regardless of the consequences.

STRESS IN DIVING

Eager, excited students on their first open water dive feel stress. Experienced wreck divers on a favorite site do, too. Mental and physical exertion, and the sheer excitement and interest of being underwater, an unusual event, can cause stress. The element of uncertainty on any dive, of not knowing completely what will happen, and being aware of what might happen, also generates some stress.

Focusing on the tasks necessary to prepare for and plan an enjoyable dive helps reduce stress. Carefully, methodically laying out dive gear before a diving excursion, going through a checklist of items, and ensuring the function of all equipment builds confidence through preparation. Making a complete dive plan, including depth and time contingencies, and planning air consumption to allow for a comfortable ascent at the recommended rate including a precautionary stop, also help relieve stress caused by uncertainty.

On the other hand, arriving to dive after rushed preparations, without taking the opportunity to thoroughly check and prepare gear, having been "too stressed" to get a good night's sleep or "too nervous" to eat a nutritious breakfast, can make a diver edgy and uncomfortable. With this poor frame of mind and stressed physical condition, small problems can become magnified and quickly grow out of control. A broken fin strap while gearing up, forgetting a mask, or a buddy's suggestion to review the dive plan can result in angry, aggressive, or otherwise inappropriate, behavior. In the water, any unusual events that would normally be dealt with routinely—a leaking mask or a dive tool that slips—can begin to trigger outsized responses because the stress level is already high. NAUI defines debilitating stress as "an imbalance between perceived demand and perceived capacity to respond to a situation."

A ship at sea is under stress.
A ship on the rocks is in distress.

Fig. 4-1. Plan to reduce stress, and act promptly to relieve it to avoid distress!

Recognizing Excessive Stress

Responses to stress include physical, mental, and emotional reactions. Recognizing stress in yourself is easy if it is not excessive. Ironically, identifying stress in others is easiest when it is excessive.

Feeling Stress

The usual mental and emotional effects of stress are similar to beginning feelings of illness—uneasiness, discomfort, and edginess. Apprehension about the dive and being able to handle it sets in. A diver may focus narrowly on the depth or some other factor like whether a piece of gear fits well or will function properly. The diver's concentration can shift from enjoying the dive to worrying about all the things that can go wrong. Although excitement is a normal part of diving, feeling physically ill, highly agitated, or a sense of dread, are not.

Being able to recognize and then act immediately to relieve excessive stress in yourself and in diving companions is fundamental to achieving NAUI's goal of eliminating dive accidents.

Stressful feelings are extremely uncomfortable. They can quickly lead to retreat, resulting in a sense of isolation. A stressed diver can begin to feel totally alone, apart from companions, as if observing them through glass or hearing them at a distance. In this state, getting ready to dive seems pointless, a task met with reluctance, or even beyond performing. A diver under such stress can start to lose focus on the here and now. Daydreaming about other activities and more pleasant places, accompanied by acute uneasiness about the surroundings or upcoming activity, are feelings associated with trying to escape from increasing stress.

Observing Stress

Increasing stress will change the way a person acts. Observing the behavior of divers around you will enable you to identify those that are feeling stressed—who might benefit from some friendly contact, or other appropriate intervention. Any one of the following signs may indicate a diver who is uncomfortably stressed about the planned dive. The signs often appear together.

At the same time, realize that knowing anything about another person's state of mind is difficult unless you have experience dealing with that person. Some people are normally better organized; others may be more experienced. What may be out of character in one diver can be usual behavior for another. Nevertheless, if a dive buddy seems nervous or agitated before a dive, going underwater without first dealing with those feelings is asking for trouble (Fig. 4-2).

Fig. 4-2. Observing dive companions closely will help you identify problem-causing stress. Deal with it tactfully before diving.

Gear Fumbling and Stalling. Divers who repeatedly make errors while setting up their gear, such as putting regulators on backward or misplacing personal equipment like their dive masks, are often reacting to excessive stress. (Even if they are just scatter-brained, disorganized, or inexperienced, such divers bear watching.) Stress also can make a diver take an unusually long time to do anything related to the dive, though it can be difficult to tell stalling from thoroughness without knowing the diver's usual behavior.

Purposeful activity is different, however, from wasting time. A methodical diver may don gear slowly but be eager to enter the water. On the other hand, an overly stressed person may remove an exposure suit two or three times to visit the bathroom, or may repeatedly ask that the regulator be checked because it seems to be hard to breathe, or complain about other items of gear or the water conditions. Any diver so stressed before the dive is likely to be a poor dive buddy underwater. Unless the stress can be resolved before the dive, usually by discussing the problem in private, this diver is best discouraged from making the dive.

Excessive Talking. There are many outgoing, talkative people in diving, but there are times when a person is clearly talking from stress. Usually accompanied by agitated behavior, this kind of speech is less concerned with topic than seeking reassurance. The talk of a stressed individual frequently is pointed at eliciting opinions from others about whether the diver will get cold, whether the current will be overpowering, or some other aspect of the dive. The person may even say, "I'm really nervous about…," sharing concern about the function of gear, inexperience, or a headache, stomachache, dive buddy, or the like. Topic is less important, however, than the behavior itself. It is usually accompanied by fidgeting, repetitive movements like tapping the foot or drumming the bench, or other signs of nervousness.

Aggressiveness or Passivity. Stress can affect a diver's normal personality, usually for the worse! A highly stressed diver often becomes aggressive and boorish. The diver may grow loud or pushy in an effort to dispel discomfort. Gear may be thrown around or become the object of anger. This same kind of inappropriate display can be directed towards other divers who encroach on the stressed person's space, touch equipment, or just try to start a friendly conversation. No buddy may be "good enough" to dive with this person.

For other stressed individuals, a sense of isolation develops, which causes them to become passive and removed (Fig. 4-3). While others are conversing normally, they may be looking down

CHAPTER 4 RECOGNIZING AND RESPONDING TO STRESS AND DISTRESS

Fig. 4-3. Isolation and passivity can be signs of stress. Sitting in the sun in a wet suit is also a bad idea. A friendly conversation can help.

listlessly at the water or staring off into space. If addressed directly, they may not respond or, if they do, answers will be indirect or uninformative nods or shrugs.

Fixation or Obsessive Behavior. Divers who spend a lot of time adjusting and readjusting things like buckles and straps and needlessly donning and taking off items usually are concerned about something other than the fit of their equipment. The same is true for divers who repeatedly ask the same question over and over.

These divers are mentally stuck in a pattern of behavior or thought induced by stress. They may spend an inordinate amount of time adjusting a single piece of gear, checking their air, hitting their purge buttons over and over, or inflating and deflating their BC "trying to get it right." Fixated on a single idea, like the depth of the dive, the current, the water temperature, the marine life, or the visibility, they repeatedly seek reassurance about it, perhaps ignoring other more appropriate concerns. It is as if dealing with this bit of equipment or dive variable is a magical key to making everything else right.

Responding to Your Own Stress

Though every diver experiences stress, recognizing and responding to it will prevent it from escalating into a problem underwater. This may be easier said than done if the stress builds unnoticed or is ignored.

Self-Awareness

Self-awareness is the fundamental tool used to avoid debilitating stress. By monitoring your state of mind, dealing openly with the issues that concern you about the dive, and gaining confidence through careful preparation, planning, training, and experience, you can effectively defuse the effect of negative stress. These same actions will help you use stress positively to heighten awareness of the dive, accepting and meeting the dynamic challenges of an underwater visit.

Developing self-awareness begins with being honest with yourself, understanding and appreciating your strengths and weaknesses. Diving beyond your ability or training is sure to cause great stress. If particular aspects of a dive worry you, making you doubt your ability to cope with them, discussing these with a more experienced diver or diving leader is a good way to start reducing stress. You will probably find that your concerns are inflated. If not, you can always opt out of the dive.

Relaxation and Visualization

Active relaxation, consciously using some method to calm yourself and clear negative thoughts and feelings, has long been recognized as an effective stress-reducing technique. Whether by meditation, rhythmic breathing, or formal exercises, such methods can be very effective. A combination of these even can be used before diving or underwater to help deal with increasing stress.

One such method is the "calming response," which combines yoga breathing (diaphragmatic or stomach breathing) with repeated phrases. Inhaling deeply, the stomach (not the chest) is pushed out, and then drawn in during a slow, deep exhalation. While inhaling, the diver thinks "I feel calm." Exhaling, the diver thinks, "I feel warm." A few repetitions can relax and focus a diver's mind. Underwater, this can be an exercise in buoyancy control, with the diver maintaining a constant depth throughout the exercise (Fig. 4-4).

Another technique that can be effective depends on the imagination. Called "visualization," it too can induce calm. By mentally seeing yourself meeting the challenges of the dive, enjoying the feelings of mastery that are generated in the process, you prepare to act properly underwater and are relaxed. This technique is often used by professional athletes, for instance, to enhance their performance under the stress of competition. In diving, it also helps to ensure that the details of the dive, from equipment preparation to exiting the water at the end, are well-instilled. Visualization is a kind of mental rehearsal of all the elements of a successful dive.

Fig. 4-4. A buoyancy control exercise that includes relaxation techniques can help calm and focus a diver experiencing excessive stress.

Helping A Buddy Deal With Stress

You can help your dive buddy deal with stress while you deal with your own. From recognition to resolution, working to reduce your buddy's stress will help reduce yours, allowing both of you to better enjoy the dive.

Observation

The key to dealing with diver stress is to be able to identify it immediately and act unhesitatingly to relieve it. As with self-awareness, monitoring the behavior of your dive companions or buddies will tell you when stress is becoming a problem.

The usual signs of stress may be present, or there may be other signals peculiar to the individual. This is especially likely when you are diving with a familiar buddy, whether a friend, spouse, or other family member. Your experience with that person, knowing what usual behavior is, will help you recognize behavior that is unusual, perhaps in reaction to stress.

Counseling

Counseling is a method of communicating that, using careful listening and encouragement, helps people identify and solve problems on their own terms. Not to be confused with psychotherapy, though it is more than just talking or giving friendly advice, counseling has elements of all three. It is particularly effective as a stress-reducing technique because it specifically helps relieve the feelings of isolation and dread that often accompany debilitating stress.

Counseling also is helpful in these circumstances because it is non-threatening and non-confrontational. The counseling approach is friendly and low key, seeking to make genuine contact with the stressed person without being judgmental or directive. By asking questions, a counselor invites persons to share their concerns, helping them explore the basis for these concerns, and explore solutions that will resolve them. In diving, the solution may be anything from limiting the dive's duration or depth or making some other modification in the plan, to agreeing to sit one out.

Paying attention to your buddy, making eye contact, sitting close by, and being open and available will help the diver feel comfortable about discussing any issues about the dive with you. If not, taking the initiative and expressing your own feelings about the dive *can*, if done in a matter-of-fact way, help get the process started. Your intention is not to talk this person out of having feelings, or "to tell another person how to feel," but to help the diver put personal feelings in perspective by examining them in the open. Frequently, just getting the thoughts out alleviates any distress they may be causing (Fig. 4-5).

Very often, discussing ways to prevent or deal with possible problems can help make problems less threatening and alleviate stress. Going over the recommended emergency procedures for situations like separation underwater, rehearsing out-of-air procedures calmly on the surface beforehand, and thoroughly planning the dive and checking each other's gear will help build confidence and relieve concern.

Do not wait to "see" if stress will grow.

Act to **RELIEVE STRESS IMMEDIATELY** before it does!

CHAPTER 4   RECOGNIZING AND RESPONDING TO STRESS AND DISTRESS

Fig. 4-5. Discussing concerns about a dive with a buddy or diving leader will reduce stress.

You also may make some suggestions that will help the person deal with a particular problem. If the dive's depth is a concern, for instance, you may volunteer to serve as the buddy team's depth indicator, agreeing with your buddy that you will be the person who descends first, and that you may remain in that lower position, close by, throughout the dive. Other problems will have other solutions.

Note however, that you are there to enjoy a dive, not to deal extensively with the problems of a buddy. If a casual but direct approach on your part is rebuffed, or if the problem seems greater than one you can resolve easily, it is probably best to discuss the matter with someone in charge. If no one else is available, the feasibility of making the dive with this person must be examined responsibly. Diving with a buddy about whose fitness you are unsure is an insupportable risk.

DISTRESS

Distress is defined as a condition of acute anxiety caused by excessive stress. An individual in distress must be relieved of the stress, either by removal from the source of stress or some other active measure, or panic will result. Distress, and especially panic, easily can lead to injury of the diver and very possibly to anyone trying to help.

A person in distress is usually beyond asking for help (Fig. 4-6). Fortunately, distress is generally quite easy to recognize. However, anyone requesting aid, like signaling for pick-up at the end of a dive after surfacing far from the exit, is wisely attempting to deal with stress *before* it becomes distress. If the diver is not helped immediately, a dangerous situation can result. Any diver can go quickly from stress to distress and, once in distress, will need immediate assistance.

Signs of In-Water Distress

Careful, consistent, and wide observation is the chief tool divers have to use against distress. Detecting and relieving stress *before* a diver enters the water is the easiest way to prevent a diving accident. Some of the signs of stress and distress will be quite obvious, particularly those that occur on the surface. Underwater, recognizing problems often will require keen awareness to subtle differences in diver behavior or in easy-to-overlook but obvious cues like the amount of bubbles a diver may be exhaling.

At The Surface

Agitated behavior of any sort, generally accompanied by splashing or flailing about, is easy to recognize as distress. This is often caused, or accompanied, by difficulty staying afloat or in one place. The uncontrollable movements of the diver's arms and legs make remaining stationary impossible. A person struggling on the surface or, worse, sinking inappropriately regardless of struggling, is a clear signal for immediate response (Fig. 4-7).

Fig. 4-6. A person in distress is unable to ask for help.

Before a diver is obviously distressed, however, some other signs usually point to a deteriorating state of mind and ability. Breathing patterns, especially erratic gasping for air often signal growing distress, as does unusual behavior involving breathing equipment. Taking out a regulator or snorkel and gasping for breath, or tearing off the mask is almost always a sign of anxiety and distress. Seeing a diver clutching the second stage tightly, possibly with both hands, breathing heavily for no apparent reason or depressing the purge button continuously is cause to respond immediately and attempt to restore calm.

Eyes almost always mirror an individual's state of mind. Diving instructors routinely monitor students' eyes and facial expressions for signs of difficulty. It is an indicator any diver can use. A distressed person almost always will be wide-eyed, either blinking rapidly or staring wildly. This may be accompanied by other signs. Agitated expression is often the first and only warning you will receive that the person is in distress and requires immediate investigation and response.

Finally, any diver alone on the surface, whether agitated or not, is a sign that something is wrong. If the diver is not joined shortly by a buddy, or the diver fails to respond to an OK signal, action is necessary.

Underwater

Signs of distress underwater center around breathing and movement (Fig. 4-8). A stream of excessive bubbles, such as from continuous purging or gasping breaths, or few or no bubbles, are signs that require immediate attention. Even if the diver is not in distress at the moment, such behavior can lead quickly to a problem. Either rapid, shallow breathing (hypoventilation) or skip-breathing will ultimately result in a dangerously high level of carbon dioxide, making it hard for the diver to satisfy the need for air. This easily can trigger panicked flight. Excessively deep breaths accompanied by poor buoyancy control can result in lung-overexpansion injuries.

Buoyancy Problems. Divers who have difficulty controlling their buoyancy throughout a dive are often the victims of injury. They may suffer a lung-overexpansion injury or can run out of air through excessive use of the BCs low-pressure inflator mechanism coupled with stress from working harder throughout the dive to maintain appropriate buoyancy. They may be overweighted and consequently labor strenuously throughout the dive. These factors together are a potent combination of skill- and gear-related problems that can be recognized by a pattern called "elevator diving."

Fig. 4-7 A, Any distress signal from a diver in the water requires an immediate response.

Elevator diving takes place when a person is constantly going up and down through a dive, never achieving stable buoyancy. With the focus on just staying underwater or not rapidly sinking, a diver can ignore or inadvertently violate depth and time limitations and may not monitor remaining air carefully. Any of these, or the constant changes in depth themselves, especially if the diver is not conscientious about maintaining normal breathing, can result in a serious accident (Fig. 4-9).

A diver who appears to be relaxed but continues sinking also may need help. This is especially true if the dive is taking place where maximum recommended depths are easy to exceed, like when diving the top of a deep reef or when wall-diving.

These problems related to overweighting are best handled before the diver enters the water, and definitely on the surface before submerging. It is wise to question any diver, especially your buddy, about the amount of weight worn. A diver who looks this up in a logbook entry for a previous dive is most likely to be more appropriately weighted than one who just guesses.

CHAPTER 4 Recognizing and Responding to Stress and Distress

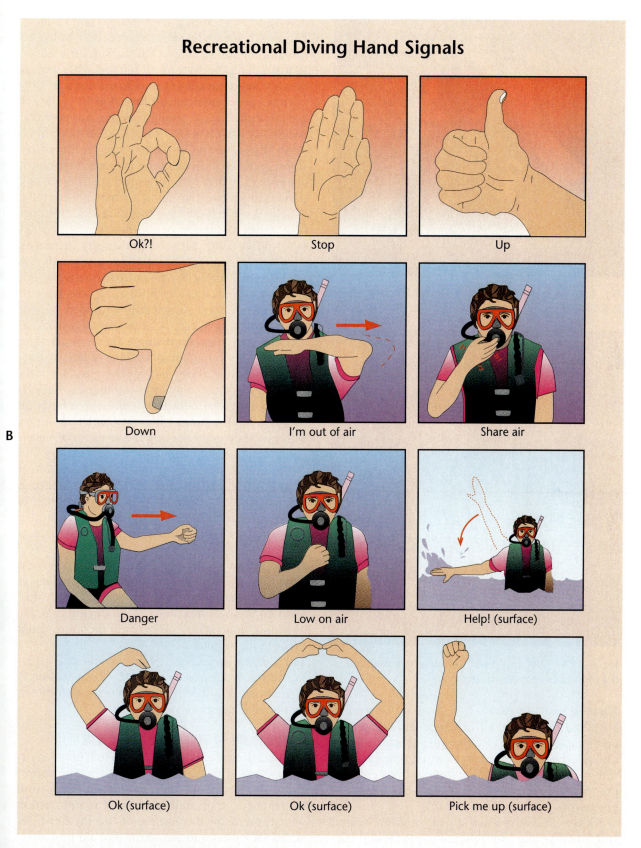

Fig. 4-7 cont'd. B, Recreational diving hand signals.

Fig. 4-8. Distress is often caused by sudden breathing difficulty that occurs close to the surface.

Fig. 4-9. An "elevator diver" is highly stressed and risks lung over-expansion injury.

Movement and Trim Problems. Diving should be a relaxing, almost effortless activity once you are geared up and underwater. Hovering weightless or gliding through the water in a natural swimming position with slow, controlled, and graceful movement is at the core of good technique. A diver behaving otherwise may be in trouble.

A diver in distress can appear literally "scared stiff," unable to move from fear. This person may appear rigid, muscles tense, perhaps not even breathing, terrified by some aspect of being underwater. If not completely immobile, any movements will be stiff and jerky and they will usually occur suddenly, as in intermittent struggle. There will be little or no connection between kicks, or furious kicking or flailing with little effect, as if stabbing the water with the fins. This person needs immediate aid to return to the surface.

Other problems can be revealed by a diver's being vertical while trying to move horizontally. Swimming underwater is easiest when horizontal. Apart from ascents, descents, and precautionary stops, most of a diver's time is spent face-down, observing. A vertically oriented diver is poorly trimmed to move through the water horizontally. Usually accompanied by a bicycling kick, this posture is often a result of too much weight or an over-inflated BC. Either significantly increases drag and the difficulty of moving through the water, contributing to stress from overwork and possible carbon dioxide build-up. It also is more difficult for a diver to maintain neutral buoyancy when swimming in this position, which is likely to contribute to "elevator diving." These are all signs of divers who through poor training or lack of practice are diving under harmful stress. A poorly trimmed diver also may be breathing very deeply, creating excessive buoyancy in the upper body by overinflating the lungs with each breath. Coupled with poor buoyancy control, this is especially dangerous and can result in life-threatening injury.

Under any of these circumstances, especially if the diver is your buddy, signaling to return directly to the surface at the appropriate rate is recommended. At the surface, once you are buoyant and if surface conditions are comfortable, discuss your observations with the diver. Readjusting the placement and amount of weight worn will often relieve the problem. If the diver is "falling backward" underwater, moving weight forward on the belt may help. If the person is small, switching to a smaller air cylinder on future dives can also be helpful.

Gear Rejection. Rejecting any gear underwater, tearing off the face mask or removing the regulator, is a definite sign of a diver in distress who needs immediate, aggressive assistance.

Responding To Stress and Distress

Identifying diving stress in yourself, or recognizing a diver in distress, requires a speedy, appropriate response to prevent the situation from worsening to the point of injury. The right action will depend on the nature of the incident, its potential for harm to the victim and aid providers, and the location. Who is available to render assistance and their qualifications to do so, including preparation and training, will also govern what can be done to help the diver.

At the Surface

Most diving incidents occur at or near the surface. The nagging problems or minor annoyances on the shore or deck that seemed insignificant crop up again or may snowball upon entering the water. Other problems, like difficulty clearing, an equipment failure, or being overweighted, may only become apparent in the water.

Self-Rescue. You are your own best first resource for dealing with increasing stress, whatever its cause. Being vigilant about what you are feeling and how it will affect your diving performance will help you know active response is necessary. NAUI recommends that all divers who feel they may need help ACT IMMEDIATELY by relaxing and taking whatever measures may be necessary to relieve the difficulty.

Establish Buoyancy. Simultaneously with relaxation, establishing buoyancy at the surface will help prevent stress from rapidly becoming distress. It also ensures that you will stay on the surface, not take a problem or deteriorating situation underwater.

Becoming buoyant is best and most rapidly accomplished by discarding the weight belt or jettisoning ballast carried in a BC. Lead is cheap. Weight belts are disposable, easily replaced items. No dive operation is without sufficient spares, and a dropped belt often is easily recovered at the site. There should be no hesitation or doubt on any diver's part immediately to discard weight if feeling overly stressed on the surface. This maneuver should be practiced regularly on land. Once free of the belt, inflating the BC adds additional lift and comfort.

Relaxation. Thoughtful, problem-solving activity, the basis of self-rescue, is best accomplished in a calm frame of mind. Relaxing, through practicing the "calming response" or by any other means you may find effective, is the first step to take when confronted with difficulty diving. By relaxing and breathing normally with an extended exhalation time, you are best able to reason, preventing stress from taking over and short-circuiting the chance for rational action.

Surface Resting in Cold Water. Even with a wet suit, an extended stay on the surface in cold water can lead to hypothermia. (Without an exposure suit, the chance of survival in colder water diminishes rapidly.) Immersing your face repeatedly in colder water is not recommended because it quickly will draw vital warmth from your body. Inflate the BC to a comfortable level, and draw the legs up towards the torso as if sitting in the water. (It may be possible to maintain this position without a BC if the exposure suit is buoyant enough.) If

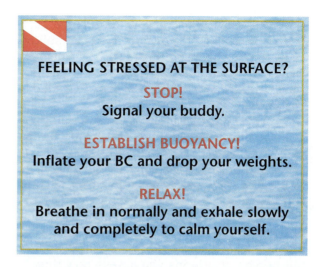

FEELING STRESSED AT THE SURFACE?

STOP!
Signal your buddy.

ESTABLISH BUOYANCY!
Inflate your BC and drop your weights.

RELAX!
Breathe in normally and exhale slowly and completely to calm yourself.

you are with other divers, link arms to make a tight circle facing inward, to help everyone better monitor each other's condition and to lessen exposure to wind. Keep arms close to the body and the head out of the water.

Assisting Another Diver. As with helping yourself deal with stress at the surface, the two main requirements to helping your buddy or another diver in distress are to establish buoyancy and to stabilize breathing. These acts alone may be sufficient to allow the diver to regain control and even go on with the dive after resting for a time.

Establishing Buoyancy on the Surface. Dropping a fellow diver's weight belt if that person apparently is in distress is a positive, helpful action that will have no negative consequences. But, it is better to get the diver to do it instead of doing it yourself. If possible, check beneath the diver first to make sure no one will be hit by the falling weight, then call the diver by name, or simply tell the person to drop the belt and to inflate the BC. A strong, authoritative order will often result in correct action. The advantage of this is that the diver is in charge, focused on dealing with the situation. The ability to respond also indicates that the stress level has not reached the point where rational behavior is impossible.

If the diver is unable to perform either maneuver, however, removing the belt and inflating the BC for the person is necessary. If you are dealing with a buddy, you already will have grown familiar with the release mechanism's operation and placement during the predive equipment checks. Most weight-retaining devices, such as a quick-release buckle, or hook and loop-fastened pockets, or a rip-cord release in an integrated weight BC, are easily operated with one hand under normal circumstances. But finding and then dealing with them under the stress of an emergency is not always simple. The release may have become inaccessible by shifting position during the entry or dive. Doing it for the diver is further complicated by the fact that the diver may be difficult, even dangerous, to approach. More complete information on dealing with panicked divers is included in Chapter Six.

Stabilizing Breathing. Helping a stressed diver stabilize breathing, once buoyant, can be accomplished as simply as by holding the diver's arm firmly, and calmly and repeatedly telling the diver to breathe. Any encouraging gestures, such as nodding, looking into the person's eyes sympathetically, and smiling will also help. By expressing such concern, you are helping to relieve the isolation and fear the diver is experiencing. Touching the person also helps you assess how deeply affected the diver is. Signs of excessive stress, such as trembling or rigid, tense muscles, usually mean that continuing the dive is unwise. The diver is best helped to exit from the water.

Rescue

NAUI defines *to rescue* as "to act to release from imminent danger by prompt action." Divers need to be rescued when they can no longer effectively help themselves and harm will result without immediate intervention from someone who recognizes the problem and has the knowledge and skill necessary to deal effectively with it.

The main purpose of a diving rescue is to prevent death by drowning. In diving, drowning results from a combination of loss of control, unconsciousness, and not having air to breathe. Secondarily, diving-related or other illnesses or injuries may incapacitate a person to the point that drowning may result. Successful rescues remove the danger of drowning first by ensuring buoyancy and breathing, then aim to sustain life by dealing with any injuries by the most effective means available.

Assessment

The time spent thinking about what needs to be done and deciding how best to do it is in many ways the most crucial part of the rescue. Just as in dive planning, assessing the variables and preparing to meet them usually will result in success. Acting without thinking likely will lead to more than the original victim's needing help. At the same time, unduly delaying intervention defeats the purpose and risks failure.

Personal Risk. Would-be rescuers must first assess the risk to themselves. No matter what the rescuers' levels of certification or experience, they too can drown, or suffer injury or a diving illness.

> Thorough **TRAINING** that includes stress-producing, realistic scenarios is **CRUCIAL** to being able to react quickly and surely in a diving emergency.
>
> Take a NAUI *Scuba Rescue Diver* or *Advanced Scuba Rescue Diver* course.

Dealing with a panicked individual is dangerous at any time, and especially so in the water. The dive that the person needing rescue made is the same dive that the rescuer will make to render aid. Success is not guaranteed under the best of circumstances, and failure carries its own personal risks, from severe emotional trauma to the possibility of protracted lawsuits.

Confidence in one's rescue skills, such as those acquired in this course and through continued practice, is the first step to reducing your risk. Having the right equipment on hand and having a clear plan of action to deal with an emergency situation will also help.

Emergency Plan of Action. Deciding that attempting to rescue is an acceptable risk can take just seconds. Similarly, figuring out what to do can also be done swiftly if the initial planning and preparation is done well in advance, appropriate gear is on hand, and the rescuer is ready to act (Fig. 4-10).

In commonly prepared-for emergencies, like the need to share air with a buddy, response can be almost instantaneous. A buddy team or diver missing after other group members have returned to the exit point, however, is a situation in which planning a coordinated response effort that includes outside resources like the Coast Guard or local rescue agencies can take more time. Knowing about these resources in advance, and being prepared to contact and work with them, is part of preparing for the dive. So, too, is identifying anyone present that may be able to help because of their rescue training, experience, or professional expertise. Even as an underwater search effort is begun, if appropriate, such outside help can be activated. (See Chapter Eight for a more complete discussion of emergency planning.)

Act

How to accomplish any dive rescue depends on the circumstances, but the actions are all directed first at removing the threat of drowning. If the victim is underwater, the person must be brought to the surface. On the surface, buoyancy must be established. Once buoyant, removal from the water is necessary. At all points in the process, maintaining or restoring breathing is a paramount concern.

Evaluate

As soon as practical, usually upon reaching the surface but certainly upon removal from the water, appropriate first aid is begun. What this entails will be determined by the qualifications of the rescuer, equipment on hand, and the needs of the victim, but further professional evaluation and follow-up care also are necessary.

NAUI recommends activating local Emergency Medical Services (EMS) for any rescue, but particularly in any instance where breathing was interrupted even momentarily, or where other injury or illness is present or suspected. Professional medical evaluation is mandatory under these circumstances to ensure proper care.

In cases where an individual in distress was rescued without apparent injury, never lost consciousness, nor had to have breathing restored, such as a person who may have panicked on the surface, follow-up care is still needed. Rescues generate emotional trauma for all concerned. After an appropriate interval, counseling—quiet, directed conversation about the incident and the participants' feelings—will help alleviate lingering negative emotions that can affect adversely any future dives. Such conversation also will help foster understanding of the events with the goal being to avoid similar problems in the future.

Evacuate

In rescues where injury results, evacuation and emergency medical evaluation and care are necessary. Again, planning for these events in advance will make sure that appropriate care is provided swiftly. Evacuation can be as simple as driving an injured person to the closest emergency medical center or having an ambulance dispatched to the accident scene. It also can be as complex as having injured persons removed from a vessel offshore by helicopter, or taken into care by a mobile intensive care unit. In any case, knowing how to contact the appropriate resource for the help you need, and having complete information available for responding aid-providers, will help ensure a successful outcome.

Accident management procedures are discussed more fully in Chapter Eight.

Fig. 4-10. Personal risks are only increased if the rescuer in untrained and poorly equiped to effect a rescue as seen here.

CHAPTER FIVE

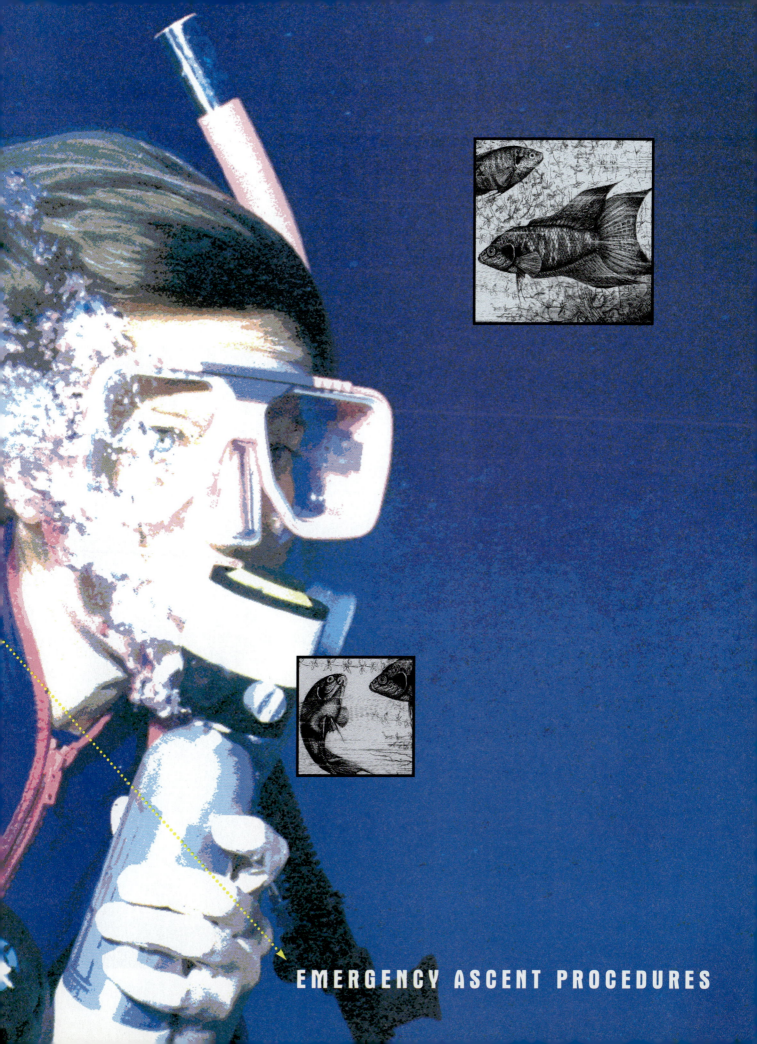

EMERGENCY ASCENT PROCEDURES

The need to make an emergency ascent can arise from any of the common causes of diving accidents but it is most frequently the result of an out-of-air or other breathing-related incident. Following recommended procedures can help prevent injury or will help ensure accident victims' chances of survival and recovery.

OUT-OF-AIR EMERGENCIES

Careful attention to dive planning and preparation, and diligently monitoring a functioning submersible pressure gauge (SPG) will almost invariably prevent running out of air underwater (Fig. 5-1). Even so, the possibility exists on every dive. As a result, training in techniques of sharing air and self-rescue are included in every NAUI scuba diver certification class. NAUI also recommends that all divers be appropriately equipped with an alternate air source, like a redundant scuba back-up system, and regularly review and practice procedures for its use. These measures will help decrease the chance of injury if a diver actually does run out of air or has another air supply problem.

THINK before you ACT!

Is it safe for me to help?

A dangerous out-of-air emergency may also result, however, when a diver for some reason feels unable to breathe underwater, or is compelled to believe that immediate escape to the surface is the only response possible to overwhelming stress. Panic can occur virtually without warning because of excessive carbon dioxide levels, nitrogen narcosis, physical and mental stress, a breathing difficulty, fear, or some combination of these and other factors.

Dealing With Panicked Flight

Also known as "bolting," fear-driven retreat from a dive is a life-threatening emergency to the victim and potentially to any rescuers. A panicked diver is unconcerned with anything except getting to the surface as quickly as possible. Rescuers, and even dive equipment, are obstacles to that goal. As a result, the diver and rescuer face significant risks of decompression illnesses from an uncontrolled, rapid ascent from depth and as possible consequences of struggling underwater and at the surface. Rescuers must consider these factors when making the decision about how best to aid a bolting diver—whether to attempt to control the person underwater, or monitor the ascent and deal with the problem on the surface. Most of the time, being ready to aid the distressed diver on the surface is the far wiser choice.

Fig. 5-1. Careful dive planning and monitoring a functioning SPG make running out of air nearly impossible.

Controlling The Diver

It is unlikely that you will be close enough to prevent bolting under normal diving circumstances, but if you are, it is probably better for you to let the diver go than to seek to hamper the ascent. Attaching yourself to a diver in extreme distress is dangerous, and even the most fit diver can be overcome easily. Incidental tension and the strain of exertion can cause you to forget to breathe, resulting in lung overexpansion injury. Struggling with a fear-maddened, probably air-hungry diver also can result in other serious injuries, including life-threatening overexertion or loss of your own air supply underwater.

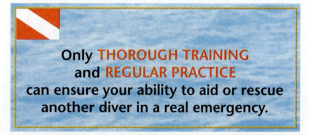

Only **THOROUGH TRAINING** and **REGULAR PRACTICE** can ensure your ability to aid or rescue another diver in a real emergency.

> Except in rare instances, it is best for a rescuer to ascend at the recommended rate, breathing continually, and attempt to keep visual contact with the distressed diver.
>
> In control or in trouble, a rapidly ascending diver is experiencing a potentially life-threatening emergency. Losing consciousness from hypoxia (inadequate oxygen level in the brain) or decompression illness before reaching the surface is a clear danger.
>
> By remaining in control and being close enough and prepared to help near or on the surface, a rescuer can save a life.

Monitoring the Ascent

Seeing a diver ascend rapidly is frightening. The urge to intervene is strong, but care should be taken not to confuse a diver making an emergency swimming, or buoyant, ascent with one who is out of control. If the diver is exhaling a steady stream of bubbles, arching backwards, venting the BC, and preparing to drop the weight belt, attempting to intervene is unwise.

On the other hand, a diver ascending rapidly, with stiff, jerky movements, clawing and climbing towards the surface with few if any exhalation bubbles, may benefit from aid if it is possible to give. A rescuer who happens to be close enough to get attention may be able to signal the diver to exhale, but approaching a panicked, fleeing diver, let alone attempting to exert control and share air, is highly dangerous. Even getting close easily could result in harm to either or both divers. (Methods for dealing with these contingencies are discussed more fully in Chapter Six.) Under no circumstances should a rescuer attempt to force another diver to exhale by striking their abdomen or squeezing their chest or diaphragm, even if a would-be rescuer is close enough to do so. Injury is almost certain to result.

Maintaining the Airway. A diver overcome in mid-water as a result of a rapid ascent needs immediate aid to the surface. The recommended procedures are discussed in this chapter under the topic Surfacing an Unconscious, Unresponsive Victim.

INDEPENDENT RESCUE PROCEDURES

Whatever the problem, the well-trained, skilled diver who acts deliberately and remains in control will most probably be able to solve it. Independent rescue is the term used to describe the personal problem-solving activity characterized by thoughtful, decisive action based on training, practice, and experience.

Stop-Breathe-Think-Breathe-Act

Practicing the "calming response," or just stopping all activity and breathing calmly for a moment, either relaxing on the bottom or hovering in mid-water, is the first step in deciding what to do for most diving problems. Exaggerating exhalation and breathing slowly will help you plan an effective response. Even if slow, relaxed breathing is impossible, such as when faced with an out-of-air emergency, thinking before acting will help ensure proper action.

INDEPENDENT EMERGENCY ASCENTS

Though diving is a shared activity, all divers are first responsible for themselves. If buddies are not within touching distance or are not within each other's field of view when an out-of-air emergency occurs, a diver must choose between attempting to reach the buddy or making an independent emergency ascent. From depths shallower than 33 feet if the buddy is not close by, an independent ascent can be a wiser choice, when a diver is well practiced in the procedures and completely prepared to take immediate action (Fig. 5-2).

Fig. 5-2. Frequently monitoring your own and your buddy's remaining air supply will almost eliminate the chance of running out of air.

Redundant Scuba Ascent

If divers are equipped with an appropriately sized pony bottle, a redundant scuba ascent will resemble a normal ascent in every way, even including a recommended precautionary stop. This is the great advantage of such equipment.

On the other hand, having one of the highly marketed small-volume, mouthpiece-equipped cylinders usually will not allow the luxury of a relaxed ascent, except from shallow depths. In either case, NAUI urges divers to regard redundant scuba systems as emergency ascent equipment, not as means of extending time underwater, and to terminate immediately any dive in which these devices must be employed.

Divers are strongly discouraged from depending on these systems to make precautionary stops. It is a foolish diver who deliberately depletes the main air supply and then uses an auxiliary emergency supply to complete the dive or as a means of equalizing buddies' uneven air consumption rates. Such practices violate common sense principles of dive planning and air management and needlessly increase the likelihood of a diving accident.

Emergency Swimming Ascent

In an out-of-air situation at depths shallower than about 33 FSW (10 m), if making a shared-air or redundant scuba ascent is not immediately possible, an emergency swimming ascent can be the most efficient and dependable means of returning to the surface. The ability to perform this technique, as it is taught in all NAUI scuba diver certification classes, relies on fitness and control. It is impossible to maintain this ability without regular practice under controlled conditions, preferably supervised by a qualified instructor.

In an emergency swimming ascent an out-of-air diver swims directly to the surface with the regulator in place, exhaling continuously, and, should the need develop, attempts to breathe (Fig. 5-3).

EMERGENCY SWIMMING ASCENT

❶ LOOK UP!

❷ REACH UP with the Low Pressure Inflator to CONTROL YOUR BUOYANCY.

❸ SWIM UP with the eyes on the surface while EXHALING.

Fig. 5-3. Keep the regulator in place, exhale constantly, and swim directly to the surface at the recommended ascent rate.

The left hand is used to control buoyancy by venting the BC, if necessary, and the right hand is poised at the weight belt or other ballast release, ready to establish buoyancy at the surface. The ascent speed approximates the normally recommended rate.

If you are feeling the need to breathe, it may be possible to draw air from a seemingly empty cylinder as the ambient pressure is reduced. The act of attempting to breathe will not seriously disrupt ventilating the lungs and may even help relieve air hunger.

If reaching the surface conscious is in doubt, using the techniques of the emergency buoyant ascent is recommended. These will help make sure that you will be positively buoyant and face-up on the surface, even if unconscious.

Emergency Buoyant Ascent

NAUI recommends using an emergency buoyant ascent only if you are in doubt about your ability to return to the surface in full control, such as when feeling faint or otherwise threatened with loss of consciousness underwater, and there is no other aid available. By becoming positively buoyant in these situations, you make certain that you will at least reach the surface where you will be able to receive appropriate aid. Emergency buoyant ascents are not recommended if you are diving in overhead environments.

The chief risk in an emergency buoyant ascent if you are unconscious is that the rapid rise will result in decompression sickness. This possibility is preferable to the near certainty of drowning if you become unconscious underwater. Since breath-holding is a voluntary action, lung overexpansion injury is not an issue during a buoyant ascent if the diver is not conscious. (This is why an emergency swimming ascent at the recommended rate is preferred until your ability to reach the surface is in doubt.)

An emergency buoyant ascent is initiated by jettisoning the weight belt or other ballast. Raising or lowering one arm, if you are in the usual horizontal, face-down swimming position, generally forces you if you become unconscious, to turn over and arrive at the surface face-up. If you are vertical, arching backward while still conscious, flaring arms and legs will usually have the same result and it also will slow your ascent (Fig. 5-4).

Fig. 5-4. An emergency buoyant ascent.

An **EMERGENCY BUOYANT ASCENT** is a diver's last resort before losing consciousness underwater.

SHARED-AIR ASCENTS

Running out of air is prevented through careful air consumption planning and monitoring and good equipment maintenance procedures; however, it can happen. If it does, your buddy is the most likely source of ready aid. As a result, NAUI recommends that all divers consistently review their preferred method for dealing with an out-of-air emergency with buddies as part of pre-dive preparation, and regularly practice preferred techniques under controlled conditions. Routine practice and commitment to good buddy diving procedures, like maintaining close proximity and frequent visual contact throughout all dives, will help prevent an out-of-air emergency leading to an injury.

By any available method, sharing air under the stress of a real emergency is a rigorous test of training and competence. It can entail greatly increased risk to both divers, especially if unrehearsed. There may be insufficient air available to support two divers back to the surface if both are using the same cylinder at the end of a dive. Shared equipment can be overworked to breakdown. Poor, uncoordinated technique caused by buddies' unfamiliarity with each other's methods can cause overwhelming stress, even panic, and injury easily can result. Traditional buddy breathing, in which a single mouthpiece is shared, may entail the possibility of disease transmission, though this is extremely unlikely because of the cleansing effect of passing the shared second stage through water.

NAUI recommends that all divers who make shared ascents be carefully monitored at the surface for any ill effects and refrain from further diving until they are examined by a diving physician, regardless of lack of symptoms.

Your buddy is your first source of aid. How long will it take for you to reach each other in an emergency?

Redundant Scuba Systems

Whether by an appropriately sized pony bottle (Fig. 5-5), or multiple cylinders with separate regulators, a redundant scuba back-up system is probably the most effective means of making sure that divers who must share air reach the surface unharmed. The problem of running out of air again, ever present when two divers must share an already-depleted cylinder, is eliminated under normal recreational diving conditions. So too is the possibility of overbreathing a single first stage, or the remote risk of infection in sharing a single mouthpiece. With enough air available, the ascent rate, including a precautionary stop, can be as recommended.

When two divers employ redundant scuba for an ascent, the donor has three options depending on the equipment:
1. Use the primary cylinder, sharing air by giving the pony or other cylinder's second stage to the donee.
2. Use the pony or other cylinder's second stage, sharing air by giving the main cylinder's second stage, or alternate second stage, if available.
3. Hand over the pony bottle and its dedicated regulator.

Though all of these methods work well, the third has the advantage of separating the divers completely, allowing each to independently monitor the other's ascent without having to remain attached throughout. It also requires that divers be equipped with a quick-release pony harness, or a BC that has a built-in quick-release pocket for the extra cylinder.

Divers who employ redundant scuba back-up systems also have numerous mounting options (Fig. 5-6). NAUI encourages all divers to keep alternate second stages intended to share air visible and easily accessible in the triangle area, described earlier as the area between the mid-chest and navel (see Fig. 2-11), and to include familiarizing your buddy with its placement and function as part of routine predive preparations.

Small Volume Redundant Scuba System Ascent

The same sharing options apply to divers equipped with a small-volume, integrated-mouthpiece scuba system as with larger-sized pony bottles or multiple cylinders; however, available capacity and lack of SPG are important limiting factors. Another hazard can be that of dropping a small, possibly slippery cylinder from a gloved hand. As with any emergency procedure, repeated practice in handling the equipment will lessen the chances of making errors in the field.

At depth and under stress, a diver may need significantly more air to ascend at the recommended rate than such systems provide. With no submersible pressure gauge, a diver using this equipment is unable to monitor consumption and appropriately modify ascent rate to ensure reaching the surface with air. As a result, a precautionary stop is probably out of the question. Though some air is better than no air, misplaced confidence in inadequate equipment contributes to accidents.

NAUI recommends that divers give due consideration to the use of such equipment, including noted limitations. Although useful under some circumstances, depending on these systems as primary back-up for an out-of-air emergency is probably unwise.

Fig. 5-5. A pony bottle with its own regulator is an excellent back-up system.

Fig. 5-6. A redundant back-up system with twin air cylinders, two first stages, and a transfer manifold.

> More AIR gives a diver more OPTIONS, especially in an emergency.
>
> *Is your redundant scuba back-up system sufficient for the diving you do?*

Alternate Second Stage ("Octopus") Ascent

Like a redundant scuba system, using an alternate second stage ("octopus" regulator) to share air makes sure that both divers will have equal, uninterrupted access to air on demand through independent mouthpieces. However, unlike a redundant back-up, both divers will have to rely on the remaining air in the same cylinder and breathe through the same first stage. Despite these drawbacks, given conservative air planning and management and well-tuned equipment, an alternate second stage can save lives (Fig. 5-7).

NAUI recommends that all divers whose primary method of sharing air depends on a single air source, like divers equipped with alternate second stages, *plan their air consumption to include sufficient air at the end of the dive to support a two-person buddy team to the surface at the recommended ascent rate.* Such planning best includes basing air calculations on the divers' actual usage rates, and considers depth, the demands of the dive, probable stress level, and a conservative margin to arrive at the surface with approximately 15% to 20% of original cylinder pressure on every dive (Fig. 5-8).

Alternate second stage ascents may be made with either the primary or alternate second stage given to, or taken by, the donee. After two or three stabilizing breaths, the donor signals the donee to begin the ascent, paying careful attention to the donee's expression and eyes for signs of distress or flight. Each diver should use the right hand to hold onto the BC, backpack strap, or forearm of the other diver, and the left hand to vent air from the BC, controlling buoyancy throughout the ascent.

Each diver, as much as possible, monitors the ascent rate and continual breathing of the other diver. To avoid the possibility of decompression sickness, if air supply permits, maintain an ascent rate as close to normally recommended as possible. Divers with sufficient air, and confident of each others' control, *may* elect to include a precautionary stop.

Buddy-Breathing Ascent

Many lives have been saved by buddy-breathing. Before the widespread availability of alternate second stage systems, it was in fact the only air-sharing technique divers had. Even today, divers in many parts of the world depend on buddy-breathing rather than other methods for dealing with out-of-air emergencies. Citing its traditional universal acceptance, lack of extra gear requirements, and dependency on thorough training and control, vocal advocates abound.

Despite these seemingly compelling arguments, many training agencies, NAUI among them,

Fig. 5-7. Practicing air sharing techniques with your customary buddy will ensure your ability to deal with an emergency.

Fig. 5-8. With an alternate second stage, both divers have air as long as the remaining air lasts. Plan air consumption to ensure a sufficient reserve for yourself and your buddy.

are moving away from teaching buddy-breathing as the primary air-sharing method. (See the NAUI Standards and Procedures Update in this book's Appendix.) Other methods, notably using alternate second stage ("octopus") and redundant scuba systems, are far simpler to learn. More important, these less complex methods are much easier to use in the stress of a real emergency.

Simply put, the chief drawback of buddy-breathing is doing it. Two divers under stress must maintain sufficient control to alternately breathe from one mouthpiece, regulating their breathing rhythm and air demands to each others' while ascending. Uneven diver air demands, fumbling, poorly remembered technique, the need to repeatedly clear the regulator and breathe cautiously, and the possibility of inadvertent breath-holding, increase buddy-breathing's difficulty and risk. Second, some divers are reluctant to share a mouthpiece with anyone else because of the remote possibility of contracting illness. (See Blood-Borne Pathogens in this book's Appendix B.) Realistic or not, any hesitation to aid someone in an out-of-air emergency adds danger. It is easy to see why buddy-breathing is being supplanted by other means, however equipment-oriented.

Even so, two practiced divers comfortable with the technique can use buddy-breathing effectively to deal with an out-of-air emergency. Signaled by the needy diver, the donor inhales a breath, handing over the mouthpiece while retaining control of the hose to ensure that the purge button is accessible (Fig. 5-9). While the needy diver is taking an initial shallow (clearing) breath and another deep inhalation, the donor exhales slowly, reserving some breath, if possible, to clear the mouthpiece when it is returned.

Clearing water from the second stage also can be accomplished without breath, and without wasting air by using the purge button, by making use of the water itself. By expelling water into the mouthpiece, drawn from the mouthpiece or the surrounding water, the regulator will clear. The first breath should be drawn carefully to make sure that no water is inhaled from a partially cleared regulator.

After the second inhalation, the needy diver relinquishes the mouthpiece to the donor, exhaling slowly while the donor breathes. Once returned, the donor signals to ascend, and the divers swim directly to the surface, continuing to pass the regulator between them. It is recommended that the donor retain control of the mouthpiece at all times and that the donee hold onto the donor's arm throughout the ascent (Fig. 5-10).

Fig. 5-9. Signaling for aid is easy when buddies stay close underwater.

Fig. 5-10. Maintain physical and eye contact with your buddy during a shared air ascent.

Successful buddy-breathing ascents depend on the proficiency of both divers. Without practice, skill is impossible to retain. Divers who team with individuals who declare buddy-breathing is their preferred sharing-air method are justified in questioning the diver's expertise and experience with the technique. Practicing together under controlled conditions is highly recommended but may be impractical under the circumstances of the dive. If unsatisfied with the response *for any reason*, choosing a more reliable buddy is recommended.

UNDERWATER RESCUE

Dealing with out-of-control individuals underwater places any rescuer in great jeopardy. Though there is less immediate risk with an unconscious diver, the emotional trauma that accompanies what may very well be an unsuccessful attempt to save or restore life can be extremely distressing. If you are not dealing with your own buddy, there may be another diver in distress, the victim's dive partner, who also needs aid; or two divers may be in difficulty at one time. Even the most well-prepared, competent diving leader likely can only help one diver at a time. Considering these issues, it is easy to understand why accident prevention, "Safety Through Education," is NAUI's fundamental training goal.

Risk Assessment

Every dive rescue begins with three questions whose answers depend upon each other:

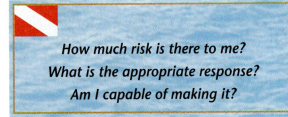

How much risk is there to me?
What is the appropriate response?
Am I capable of making it?

How the answers translate into action will be unique for each diving situation, depending on environmental conditions, the nature of the distress, available support, and personnel.

Personal Risk

All divers accept an amount of risk on every dive. This is a normal part of diving. But deciding to attempt to rescue a diver in distress is simultaneously a decision to assume an extraordinary risk. This risk comes from attempting to deal with an unpredictable set of circumstances, not the least of which are highly increased physical and mental stress and personal danger and the aftermath of even a successful rescue. Without some duty to respond, such as exists for professional diving leaders under some circumstances, whether to act is a question that must be carefully examined.

Most people respond unselfishly to another's distress. Reports of heroic rescues and attempts filled with courage and self-sacrifice inspire admiration. Yet such reports often include the names of lost rescuers, some who joined the victims they tried to save, others who were taken instead. *The possibility of grave harm to the salvor attends every underwater rescue* and NAUI urges divers to carefully weigh that risk against their willingness to intervene (Fig. 5-11).

Fig. 5-11. Evaluate personal risk before a rescue.

Appropriate Response

An appropriate response is one that quickly resolves the difficulty with the least amount of risk and fanfare. It is a reasoned, considered reaction with the goal of removing everyone involved as swiftly as possible from the chance of (further) harm. Most often, rescue is unobtrusive, such as when subtly supporting and reassuring a coughing diver with buoyancy problems until control is regained. At other times it can be exciting and dramatic, even to the point of restoring life to an unresponsive victim brought up from the bottom. At either extreme, the rescuer remains dedicated to solving the problem without calling undue attention to the difficulty or the distressed individual, or highlighting the efforts made on the diver's behalf.

Ability

A rescuer's ability to intervene is a function of motivation—willingness to accept the risk and determination to obtain training and knowledge to meet the challenge that the rescue represents. There are no easy answers for motivation, but training and knowledge are at the heart of this course, and they are NAUI's approach.

By learning and practicing the skills in this class, and by increasing your knowledge of recommended practices and procedures, you are building on the foundation of your previous dive training. Continuing to practice and refine your skills and capacity, increasing your fitness, and maintaining your fitness to dive will help give you the confidence necessary to respond to another diver's distress, and it will make you a better diver.

However the events of any emergency unfold, the rescuer's best answer remains,

> *I will do as much to aid as I am able, consistent with my training, ability and qualifications, with the least amount of risk to all concerned.*

Dealing With A Responsive Diver In Distress

A responsive diver in distress may be aware of the predicament, and may even be attempting to resolve it. This can include a number of things, from dealing with an equipment problem like a second stage freeflow or lost mask, to entanglement. Minimal intervention often will bring such incidents to a successful close. A responsive diver may also, however, be deep in the throes of nitrogen narcosis, suffering some breathing difficulty like choking or coughing, or on the verge of losing control or consciousness. It is dangerous to assume that any diver in apparent distress will be okay without aid, or "should" be able to help you effect a rescue.

Assessing the Problem

Careful observation is the starting point of assessing a diving problem. Knowing how to respond depends on knowing what's wrong. If questioned with an OK signal, a responsive diver may be able to signal the source of the distress, which may be anything from pain in the ears caused by difficulty clearing, to breathing difficulty or a problem with some specific piece of gear.

Bubbles. For a distressed diver underwater, breathing difficulty is the primary concern. A lack or excess of bubbles is an instant clue to a potentially life-threatening emergency. Approach such a diver extremely carefully, prepared to share air while at the same time protecting your own mouthpiece.

If not exhaling, signal the diver to do so by placing a hand on your own chest or tapping your own mouthpiece while exhaling forcefully. Whatever problem may be present may have made the diver forget to exhale, even if this is not the primary source of distress. If exhalation begins, immediately check the diver's air supply. Breath-holding may have resulted from difficulty drawing the last breath. If there is air, and normal breathing is apparently restored, stay in contact with the diver, holding on to her arm or other gear, prepared to share air or otherwise help, until the diver responds affirmatively to an "OK" signal or indicates some other source of distress.

On a deeper dive, apparent confusion, including forgetting to exhale or agitation, may be caused by nitrogen narcosis. Even if not, no harm is done by helping this diver to the surface where discussion of any breathing difficulty is possible. It is advisable to monitor carefully any divers who have experienced underwater breathing problems, regardless of how minor they may seem or how quickly they were resolved.

Gear. After observing for exhalation bubbles, a quick check of usual equipment, starting from the head down, will generally reveal a gear problem that may be contributing to, or may be the major cause of, observed distress. Gear that is out of place, or the object of attention or fumbling, will be obvious. A trapped or twisted hose, overly tight weight belt or BC strap, torn mouthpiece or purge diaphragm, or folded mask skirt will not be easy to spot unless you are looking carefully for attendant signs like struggling or breathing and buoyancy problems.

Most gear problems, particularly those arising from over- or under-weighting, are best dealt with before the dive or on the surface. It is unwise to remove a diver's weight belt for adjustment underwater. Doing so could easily result in an uncontrolled buoyant ascent. On the other hand, misplaced or ill-fitting equipment, or problems like a loose air cylinder or weight belt, often can be resolved underwater (Fig. 5-12). If the person calms sufficiently, the dive may be successfully completed.

If the diver is relatively calm, make eye contact with the person, and signal that you see the problem and will attempt to fix it. Before beginning, give an "OK" signal and wait for a response. If the diver does not respond, preferably by hand signal, though a simple nod will do, signal the diver to return to the surface, and assist the diver during

Fig. 5-12. Correcting problems before the person enters the water will help avoid having to rescue the diver later.

a direct, controlled ascent at the recommended rate, following the procedures detailed below. If the diver responds appropriately to your offer of aid, fix the problem. Again, give the diver an "OK" signal, and wait for an appropriate response. Maintain eye, and possibly physical, contact, or at least remain close by and monitor the diver's condition for a few moments before signaling to continue the dive. Make sure the diver signals and appears "OK" before moving on.

Buoyancy. Buoyancy difficulties often are the cause and sign of underwater distress. "Elevator diving," rapidly cycling short ascents and descents, places divers under a great deal of stress from the repeated necessity of equalizing to the fear that arises from being out of control, unable to prevent sinking, or finding a comfortable level. These are more a problem for infrequent or inexperienced divers, who also are least practiced in effective buoyancy-control techniques.

Help the diver by grasping the forearm, upper arm, or shoulder, in order to provide stability. Touching the diver coincidentally enables the rescuer to assess more accurately the person's stress level, but should be done carefully so as to avoid frightening or offending the diver. Once under control, the person may be able to continue the dive. If the diver is still agitated, escort the person to the surface, maintaining close proximity or contact to keep within the recommended ascent rate.

Buoyancy problems also may be indicative of gear-related problems, from overweighting to BC bladder failure or low-pressure inflator malfunction. They also can be the result of unfamiliar gear, a change to a new BC or exposure suit, especially a dry suit, or a result of diving in uncustomary water temperature or type.

A distressed diver's buoyancy problem also may be the result of struggling underwater with a more serious issue, like a breathing difficulty caused by some restricting gear, or an overload of stress from trying to cope with too many tasks at once.

Trim. A diver's physical orientation underwater can sometimes indicate distress, and it may even point to its cause. Most divers who stop swimming

---

Never assume a diver is now "OK" because you have fixed the apparent problem.

Make sure by
WAITING and WATCHING!

BUOYANCY AND TRIM PROBLEMS CAN BE A TIP-OFF THAT SOMETHING EVEN MORE SERIOUS IS WRONG. LOOK AT AN "ELEVATOR" OR OUT-OF-TRIM DIVER CAREFULLY:

1. Are the diver's eyes focused?
2. Is the diver under- or over-weighted?
3. Is the BC properly fitted, too full or leaking air, or the cylinder loose or out of position?
4. Do the bubbles indicate that the diver is breathing normally?
5. Is the diver kicking properly?
6. Does the diver "feel" stressed to the touch?
7. Does this problem need to be handled on the surface or out of the water?

underwater, are about to head for the surface, or are distracted will assume an upright position. Further, trying to swim horizontally while in a vertical position is almost always a self-defeating, stress-producing activity that usually indicates poor training or an overweighted, inexperienced or infrequent diver.

Trim also can indicate a diver trying to deal with an increasingly difficult situation caused by any number of things from exhaustion to ear pain, or a hard-breathing regulator. Seeing a diver lying on the bottom, holding on to some part of the terrain, finning upright against a current, or in any unusual position, from upside-down to hunched over, can indicate exhaustion or pain.

Surfacing a Responsive Diver

Signal the diver to stop, and maintain position in the water column. If the diver appears unable to do so, slowly grasp the diver under the upper arm to help the person relax, judge their level of stress, and establish control. If the diver is rigid or trembling, or apparently losing control as evidenced by eye movement or facial expression, immediately take charge and assist the diver in making a direct, controlled ascent at the recommended rate.

The rescuer must be in position and able to control the rate of ascent and, as much as possible, ensure adequate breathing for both divers. Though responsive, the distressed diver should not be depended upon to aid in the rescue, and may even inadvertently or purposefully hamper a rescuer's efforts.

Establishing firm control takes strength. The rescuer has the option of holding on to the diver or the diver's equipment, but in either case a strong grip is required. It is usually preferred for the rescuer to be facing the diver, making constant eye contact possible. Observing the eyes and expression will help the rescuer monitor the diver's state of mind throughout the ascent. Hand signals also are recommended to help calm the diver. Even just using an "OK" signal and getting a feeble response can be reassuring to both participants, though the diver is clearly not "OK"!

After signaling the diver that the ascent is beginning, the rescuer begins swimming upward, observing the diver for breathing, especially exhalation. The ascent should approximate the recommended rate, given sufficient air supply. Under the best circumstances, responsive divers will be able to fin upward while controlling their own buoyancy. If not, the diver should be signaled to vent the BC of any air, or the rescuer may do it to avoid excessive buoyancy, which will cause a rapid ascent as they near the surface.

Under most circumstances, a rescuer's BC provides the best source of adequate lift for both divers because it is most easily controlled. Both divers' weights should be kept in place unless the rescuer's inflated BC and effort are unable to raise both divers. This may occur when there is a great weight or size disparity between diver and rescuer, or when aiding a severely over-weighted diver. Ditching the weight belt should be done only if you are confident that you will not release the diver before surfacing, and if you are also of the opinion that losing the ballast will not adversely affect the ascent rate of both divers. For instance, if the distressed diver is in a buoyant dry suit, dropping the diver's weight belt may be unwise.

At the surface, establish positive buoyancy for both of you by ensuring that both BCs are inflated, and by dropping both weight belts or other ballast, if they are still in place. If other help is available, call or signal for aid. While waiting for help, monitor the rescued diver by maintaining eye contact and conversation. Both will help you assess the diver's mental state. Remain in contact with the diver while awaiting pick-up, or, if no other aid is available, commence towing, assisting, or escorting the diver to the exit point.

If at any time breathing may have been interrupted, there was any period of out-of-control buoyant ascent, possible or certain unconsciousness for any duration, or air was shared, speedy follow-up medical examination is mandatory. A brief neurological examination of both divers is wise in any case.

Surfacing an Unconscious, Unresponsive Victim

An unconscious, unresponsive diver underwater will surely die unless immediately brought to the surface. Breathing or not, this person has a chance to survive. That chance is increased by knowledgeable assistance.

Making sure the diver can ventilate on the way to the surface is paramount to survival. Lung overexpansion injury is a dangerous possibility regard-

> A conscious diver who is too stressed or confused underwater to respond properly to an "OK" signal should be assisted immediately to the surface.

less of any scuba dive's depth or duration. After determining that the diver is unconscious and unresponsive, usually by touching and shaking an arm, the rescuer must act immediately.

Grasp the diver from behind, holding the regulator in place firmly, but gently, if still in place. If the regulator is out of the diver's mouth, do not attempt to replace it. Lift the person to the upright position and check the mask. If the mask is clear, leave it alone. If the mask is filled with water, remove it, sealing off the nose without dislodging the regulator. The diver is now upright against your chest, all other gear in place, and ready for the ascent.

The diver's buoyancy will affect your actions. If the diver is close to neutral buoyancy, it will be relatively easy to move upward. Check for air in the BC by venting a small amount.* Be prepared to control the diver's buoyancy throughout the ascent by venting the BC if there is air. Drop the diver's weight belt or other ballast. Using one hand to hold the regulator in place and seal off the nose, begin the ascent. Air will flow from the diver no matter what position the head is in so long as the diver is unconscious. You can control buoyancy for the diver and yourself with your left hand as usual, or your left hand may be needed to maintain the regulator in place (Fig. 5-13). Swim directly to the surface breathing continually. Establish buoyancy for the diver and yourself immediately upon surfacing by dropping your own weight belt or other ballast and inflating both BCs. (Techniques for dropping weight belts for yourself and another diver are demonstrated in NAUI's *Safety Through Education* Video Series.)

If the victim is apparently not breathing or the regulator is out of the mouth, the diver is likely to be heavy and difficult to raise. It will probably be necessary to partially inflate the victim's BC to move from the bottom.

*If the victim is in a dry suit, make sure it is also vented throughout the ascent.

Fig. 5-13. An unconscious victim's airway will be open throughout the ascent. If the regulator is in place, hold it there while ascending.

SURFACING AN UNCONSCIOUS DIVER

1. Check for responsiveness.

2. Check the mask. If full of water, remove it. If empty, leave it on. Check the mouthpiece. If out, leave it out. If in, hold it in throughout the ascent.

3. Tap the BC low-pressure inflator to determine if there is air in the BC. If so, be prepared to control it throughout the ascent.

4. Drop the victim's weight belt or other integrated ballast. Don't worry about ankle weights.

5. Raise the diver to the surface as quickly as you can without risking DCI. If necessary, inflate the victim's BC and follow at an appropriate ascent rate.

Time is of the essence in this case, so the ascent rate should be as fast as the rescuer finds acceptable. From any but the shallowest depths, especially if at the end of a dive near or at the recommended maximum no-decompression time limit, rescuers must consider how the ascent rate will affect their own risk of decompression sickness.

Under circumstances in which a rapid ascent would be especially dangerous for the rescuer, making the victim fully buoyant by inflating the BC and removing the weight belt or other ballast, and sending the victim to the surface alone may be a necessity (Fig. 5-14). The rescuer is advised to follow at an appropriate rate, monitoring the ascent. Surface conditions that will make quickly finding and aiding the victim on the surface especially difficult or impossible, such as when diving in overhead environments, night diving, or diving in high waves, make this technique inadvisable unless there is no other choice. Though the victim will make a rapid buoyant ascent, the need for abundant air and immediate surface care outweighs the victim's risk of decompression sickness. With or without the regulator in place, the airway is unlikely to be obstructed in an unconscious, nonbreathing diver made buoyant and sent to the surface.

Fig. 5-14. Make sure that the weight belt or other ballast is completely clear of the diver before ascending.

CHAPTER SIX

TOWING, ASSISTING, AND SURFACE RESCUE

No dive rescue can be considered successful until everyone—rescuers and aided divers alike—is out of the water and receiving appropriate care (Fig. 6-1). This would be impossible without the skills and ability to transport incapacitated divers on the surface, and then get them out of the water. Most diving-related injuries and accidents, including decompression illnesses which can be signaled by life-threatening sudden incapacitation or unconsciousness, occur at or near the surface. Whether the dive's exit point is on the shore or aboard a boat, timely surface aid, often including in-water life support and evacuation by emergency medical services, dramatically increases injured divers' chances of recovery.

CHAPTER 6 TOWING, ASSISTING, AND SURFACE RESCUE

Surface assisting skills, from the ability to calm an agitated diver in the water before a dive, to helping make sure an exhausted diver returns unharmed, are also crucial to achieving the goal of accident-free diving. Your diving experiences will undoubtedly include many more opportunities for preventing accidents through unassuming, appropriate intervention than it will provide chances to perform underwater rescues or deal with major injuries or emergencies.

RISK AT THE SURFACE

Surface rescue is no less risky than underwater rescue. For instance, struggling with a panicked diver on the surface has many of the same perils as it does underwater, including loss of air supply. Further, unlike most underwater rescue, which, although stressful, often make few strenuous physical demands on a rescuer, surface rescues and towing require physical strength, stamina, and technique. Wind, waves, current, and surface air temperature add hazards that can greatly increase the difficulty of any surface rescue. Drowning is an ever-present danger for an exhausted person in the water, regardless of the diver's role or certification level. Strenuous postdive activity also increases a rescuer's risk of decompression sickness.

As with all rescue and all diving, risks can be minimized with training, knowledge, and conscientious application of conservative judgment. But as in all rescues and all dives, risks cannot be totally eliminated. Your decision to aid another diver on the surface is best based on your honest assessment of your ability, including physical capacity, to do so successfully with the least amount of additional risk.

This includes being prepared to seek and direct appropriate aid from other divers and outside resources and also having on hand additional specialized equipment. Though independent action and self-sufficiency are hallmarks of leadership and diving competence, successful surface rescues, after initial intervention, are usually the result of planned, cooperative efforts, as detailed in Chapter Eight.

Panic At the Surface

Panic is unreasoning fear most usually characterized by the overwhelming need to escape. In diving, it can occur from an overload of stress resulting from a group of (individually) minor problems that go unresolved, a single seemingly minor problem like losing one's mask unexpectedly, or a major difficulty like an out-of-air emergency.

Panic also is the end result of carbon dioxide excess (hypercapnia). This condition can result from poor ventilation caused by deliberately using improper breathing patterns underwater like "skip-breathing," from breathing restrictions due to wearing ill-fitting or poorly adjusted diving dress, or even from diving with a regulator that has hard breathing action. Any of these alone or together, along with anxiety or excessive physical effort, can lead to panic. As carbon dioxide levels rise and stress is allowed to build, the need to breathe increases until no amount of air can satisfy it. The feeling or fact of impending suffocation can lead anyone to panic. Though panic and its distress can be prevented by careful diving practices, as detailed in Chapter Four, it still occurs. Once panicked, any diver's ability to cope is overcome.

Panic is life-threatening for its victims and anyone who would aid them, no matter why or where it occurs (Fig. 6-2). Whether divers have survived an uncontrolled flight from depth or are yet to descend, panic can lead individuals to do anything believed necessary to survive. This includes severely injuring, or even drowning, those attempting to save them, which is sure to cost their own lives. Approaching any panicked individual requires extreme caution and a clear plan of action that considers methods of escape.

Fig. 6-1. Rescue continues until all divers involved have exited the water and are receiving appropriate care.

Fig. 6-2. Panic is life-threatening for its victims and anyone who gets close to them.

Fig. 6-3. Approach a struggling or panicked diver extremely carefully and only if necessary to keep the diver from sinking.

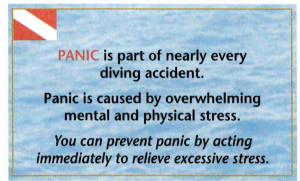

PANIC is part of nearly every diving accident.

Panic is caused by overwhelming mental and physical stress.

You can prevent panic by acting immediately to relieve excessive stress.

Approaching A Panicked Diver

A rescuer seeing a person in violent struggle on the surface is advised to respond immediately, but you should nevertheless avoid getting within touching distance until you are able to assess the situation (Fig. 6-3). Whether aboard a boat or on shore, bring a buoyant device, preferably one with an attached line, that can be floated to the diver. If you are wearing scuba gear, inflate your BC to be consistent with the level of mobility you will need to maneuver freely and remain buoyant. The weight belt or other ballast is initially best left in place in case the panicked diver sinks and underwater rescue becomes necessary.

Making sure the panicked diver stays afloat is the first thing to do after ensuring your own buoyancy. A panicked diver on the surface is trying to get free of the water and anything else that is perceived as dragging the diver down. This often includes the person's mask and regulator but, ironically, rarely includes the weight belt or other ballast.

From a safe distance, shout at the person to drop the weight belt and inflate the BC. Repeat this, attempting to get the diver's attention and direct it towards the float that you are cautiously extending. Seeing you or hearing your voice may make the panicked diver act as directed. More likely the diver will lunge toward you or the float. If the distressed diver grabs the float, deploy the line to maintain separation and begin to back up toward the exit point, pulling or swimming ahead of the victim while observing the diver constantly. Without the float, be prepared to back up. Getting such a person to chase you back to the exit point or additional help is a fine way to rescue the diver without undue risk to anyone, but it will not work if you cannot reliably out-swim the distressed person. Unfortunately, it is easy to underestimate the speed and ability of a person driven by panic.

If the diver does not give chase and appears in no danger of sinking (for instance if the person is floating high because the BC is inflated or because of furious kicking and arm movement) maintain position beyond the victim's reach. Attempting to calm the diver through reassuring words is another risk-free rescue option. Victims are likely to tire quickly and may soon regain control sufficiently to listen, or even to help themselves back to the exit.

On the other hand, if the struggling is causing the diver to drop beneath the surface intermittently, the diver is choking, and the BC appears empty or ineffective, intervention is necessary to prevent the victim's drowning. Approaching quickly from behind or below the surface and releasing the weight belt or ballast is recommended. No matter how quick or strong you are, being attacked and dragged under by a panicked diver is likely if you venture within arm's reach. Being kicked, scratched, strangled, or punched, and having your regulator, mask, or snorkel dislodged are almost guaranteed. Getting free and clear of this onslaught takes swift action, whatever method may be employed.

Defense and Escape

Rescuers must understand that panic is aggressive and unreasoning, and act accordingly whenever approaching a victim in this distress. It is far preferable to avoid getting close enough to be trapped than to depend on the chance that you will be able to fight free. It is certainly far easier to aid someone else when you are thinking of actions and in control than it is when you are struggling to escape.

In every case, a rescuer who is caught by a panicked diver is in trouble. Escape from a panicked diver is mandatory to ensuring survival for the rescuer and eventual rescue for the victim. Planning carefully and using conservative judgment in approaching an out-of-control diver will help avoid having to fight your way free. Like all diving techniques, blocks and escapes can only be mastered through training and practice and will only be useful in a real emergency if they are consistently reviewed under controlled conditions.

The Defensive Position.
Though your arm strength may be excellent, it is unlikely to surpass the power of your legs. It is recommended that these be a rescuer's primary defensive tools. By reclining backwards away from a lunging victim, the rescuer helps make certain that the legs and fins will be ready to block any attack made with the victim's arms. Keep your legs extended toward the victim, and keep moving horizontally, ready to react. Maintaining this position will generally prevent the victim from grabbing your life support equipment or your vulnerable face, head, and neck area (Fig. 6-4).

Escaping From A Panicked Diver.
It is easy to be surprised by the speed, reach, or guile of a panicked victim. Such attacks also may come without warning from a diver in mild distress who just seconds before, appeared in control. Watch any panicked victim carefully for signs of attack, even as you try to calm the person through reassuring talk.

Escapes.
Most dangerous surface attacks will concentrate on the neck and head. Besides the chance of injury to delicate areas like the eyes or nose, strangling and suffocation may result. The chance of the rescuer swallowing water, becoming breathless, or even losing control makes determined efforts to escape essential. These possibilities also make preventing being caught far preferable to having to escape.

DON'T *REACT*!
Stop-*Breathe*-Think-*Breathe*-Act

Fig. 6-4. Legs are longer and stronger than arms. If there is no float or other device available or you must get close to distract a panicked person so that another rescuer can render aid from behind, use this technique.

Most surface escapes are variations on the theme of quickly dropping out of a panicked embrace (Fig. 6-5). Since the water is the object of the panicked diver's fear, it can be a trapped rescuer's refuge. Preceded by breathing to ensure control and, if snorkeling, breath-holding ability, the rescuer submerges. With forceful, surprise action against the holding victim, the rescuer either will be freed immediately or will (hopefully) be able to outlast the panicked diver's ability to stay underwater.

In any case, getting free in any way possible and inflating your BC and dropping your weight belt or other ballast will keep you on the surface (Fig. 6-6). If possible, do the same for the victim. Once free, regroup and plan how best to aid the diver. A rescuer's training, practice, and efforts to maintain fitness and ability will directly affect the probability of success in any escape maneuver. (Obviously, dropping underwater attached to a panicky diver is a poor choice after losing the regulator to the victim.)

Dealing With A Responsive Diver

A responsive diver is probably less liable to hamper a rescuer's efforts, but a victim's awareness and consciousness neither guarantees the ability to aid in the rescue nor ensures that the diver's condition will not deteriorate dramatically before leaving the water. Even if a victim is apparently uninjured or only complaining of fatigue, careful monitoring is required. Debilitating fatigue can be an early sign of decompression illness. Rescuers are advised to never take any in-water or underwater rescue or assist lightly. The same high level of vigilance and caution with which they would approach any extraordinarily hazardous in-water situation is required until the rescue is concluded.

Approaching A Responsive Diver

A responsive diver is breathing, although possibly with some difficulty, and may be able to tell a rescuer why help is needed. Ensuring buoyancy is, as always, the first goal of surface rescue. If the victim's BC is not inflated, direct the diver to inflate it and to drop the weight belt or other ballast if still worn. Speak in a firm, calm, reassuring tone. The victim can be directed to nod or signal in response to questions, keeping the mouthpiece in place. If the diver can speak comfortably, the rescuer should ask what happened.

If the diver is slow to react, fumbling, or responding in a confused manner, drop the weight for the diver, informing the person as you do it. This will help ease any anxiety the diver may have about sinking, and reduces the possibility of frightening the diver into an aggressive response.

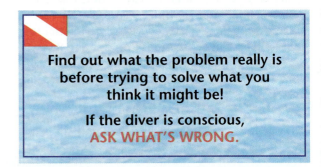

Find out what the problem really is before trying to solve what you think it might be!

If the diver is conscious, ASK WHAT'S WRONG.

Fig. 6-5. Aggressive, deliberate action can get you free.

Fig. 6-6. Get free and make yourself and the victim buoyant.

> **OBSERVE CAREFULLY FOR CLUES!**
>
> 1. Is the diver buoyant?
> 2. Is there an obvious injury like bleeding or any breathing difficulty?
> 3. Is the diver conscious? Coherent?
> 4. Is the BC over-inflated and hissing air?
> 5. Is there a regulator freeflow or broken hose?
> 6. Are the skin and lips blue?
> 7. Where is the diver's buddy?

If the diver has removed the mouthpiece or mask, ask why. Locate the diver's mouthpiece in case it will ease breathing during transport, such as in rough surface conditions. This is most easily done by tracing the hose from the first stage. Whatever the diver's response, check remaining air supply, particularly if you are planning to replace the mouthpiece. An empty cylinder often denotes having made a fast ascent driven by an out-of-air incident.

Any breathing difficulty, gasping, wheezing, whistling, blood in the mask or on the face or mouth, difficulty hearing, or other signs of disorientation or confusion, with or without apparent injury or pain, especially in the chest and neck area, are reasons to suspect decompression illness, barotrauma, or possible cardiac problems. This also may be the case if the diver's BC is fully inflated when the rescuer arrives, perhaps even hissing air from its relief valve, such as might happen if it was not vented during a rapid ascent or was overinflated on the surface. If the BC is fully inflated, it is likely to be constricting the diver's breathing. Tell the diver you are adjusting buoyancy, and release some air from the victim's BC to make the diver float more comfortably.

Observe and evaluate details like the BCs inflation, cylinder pressure, and any physical signs carefully. They alert a rescuer that the responsive victim may soon lose consciousness, breathing, or both. At the same time, lack of physical signs and symptoms is no proof against these possibilities. In any case, this victim must be aided or towed to the exit, monitored throughout the process, and evaluated out of the water.

Dealing With An Unconscious Diver

Unconsciousness on the surface is as life-threatening as it is underwater, although mitigated somewhat if the victim is face-up and buoyant. After establishing buoyancy, check for breathing by looking, listening and feeling as described and begin in-water resuscitation, if required. As soon as possible after unconsciousness is verified, rescuers are advised to notify emergency medical systems of the need for immediate evacuation. Regardless of the reason, all unconscious divers, even if rapidly revived, require professional emergency medical care.

Approaching an Unconscious Face-Down Diver

An unresponsive diver on the surface may be found in a face-down, prone position. Immediately turn the diver face-up. When approaching head-on you can do this easily by grasping the victim's right wrist with your right hand, pulling towards you and down in a counter-clockwise rotation. This will cause the victim to turn face-up, beside you. Follow the procedures given for an Unconscious Face-Up Diver.

Approaching an Unconscious Face-Up Diver

Call out to the diver as you approach. Tap the collar bone area of the chest to verify unconsciousness. This may wake the victim, so be prepared to respond to disorientation, agitation, or panic. If the victim does not immediately respond, notify divers or other support personnel to activate emergency services. Next check for breathing by careful observation of the chest, by placing your face close to the victim's nose and mouth, or by holding the exterior glass of the victim's mask close to the nose and observing for fogging. In rough sea conditions this will be difficult to verify precisely.

Air is a priority. If the victim is apparently not breathing, commence rescue breathing as described in the following section, checking the victim's weight belt or other ballast, and dropping it if it is still in place. If more buoyancy is needed, further inflate the victim's BC from the cylinder or by oral inflation between breaths, if necessary (Fig. 6-7). Observe the victim's face for signs of injury, particularly bleeding from the mouth, nose, and, if no dive hood is worn, ears. Blood here can indicate a life-threatening, pressure-related injury requiring immediate evacuation for emergency medical treatment. Observe skin color and lips for cyanosis (blue color), a sign of possible suffocation. If present, make certain that the victim's dive cylinder is recovered if possible, and do not allow the victim or anyone else to use the cylinder for breathing.

Fig. 6-7. Even though the victim is at the surface, make sure she is buoyant. Drop the weight belt and check the BC.

RESCUE BREATHING

How best to perform effective in-water rescue breathing is a controversial topic in diving. Though all agree on its necessity for a nonbreathing victim at the surface, favored techniques vary with expert practitioners. Despite the absence of universal consensus, the fact remains that a nonbreathing victim will certainly die without immediate breathing aid.

Effective in-water rescue breathing, especially while the rescuer is towing, is extremely strenuous. Any choice of method must take into account the rescuer's actual ability to continue with the technique over time under the highly stressful and difficult environmental conditions likely to accompany a real incident. Once begun, like other techniques aimed at restoring or maintaining life, it is best continued as long and as regularly as the rescuer is able without incurring undue risk or compromising efforts to move rescuer and victim to the dive's exit, or until the rescuer is relieved by another qualified person or medical personnel.

NAUI recommends that any combination of the methods suggested below be adopted and practiced until rescuers are completely proficient and confident of their ability to perform them for an extended period in the water, at least to the published standards of their certification level.

Mouth-to-Mouth Rescue Breathing

The rescuer must stabilize the victim's head and make sure that the airway is open by gently tilting the diver's head backward before beginning (Fig. 6-8). With the victim on your left, hook your left arm under the diver's left. Using your left hand to support the back of the victim's head or neck, remove the mask and pinch the victim's nose closed with your right hand. Care must be taken not to overextend the neck or sink the victim by leaning down with the right hand. Make sure that the head is supported and the airway open. The victim's head will lie in the crook of the rescuer's left arm or on the forearm.

Roll the victim towards you, and give two full, deliberate breaths, observing the victim's chest for evidence of effective respiration. This will be difficult to see in some conditions and impossible to tell in some types of exposure suits. By giving two breaths initially with a good seal and open airway, a rescuer can be confident that the diver is getting some air (Fig. 6-9). In any case, once towing commences, there may be little sign of breathing effect unless the victim revives or regurgitates.

In rough water, the rescuer may attempt to time the breathing cycle so that the breaths are given when water is passing over the rescuer's and victim's heads. This has the advantage of preventing water from entering either the rescuer or victim's mouths, which will be protected by the seal.

During towing, preferably in the "do-si-do" position described under Towing and Assisting, *a respiration cycle of two full, deliberate breaths every 10 seconds or one full, deliberate breath every 5 seconds* will allow a single rescuer to maintain an acceptable rate of progress through the water without rapid exhaustion. If more than one rescuer is aiding the victim, rescue breathing can be administered more easily.

Fig. 6-8. Ensure that air gets into the victim by gently tilting the head back to open the airway.

Fig. 6-9. Full, deliberate breaths help ensure that air will enter the lungs instead of the stomach.

Fig. 6-10. Using a Rescucci-snorkel® has the advantage of avoiding mouth-to-mouth contact with a victim.

Mouth-to-Snorkel Rescue Breathing

This is sometimes an effective alternative to mouth-to-mouth, especially in rough water where relatively full BCs may be needed to float participants high enough to give breaths. Under those circumstances, the rescuer will have to rise higher out of the water to get close enough to perform mouth-to-mouth, and as a result will likely tire sooner. Mouth-to-snorkel breathing also minimizes any concerns about the possibility of disease transmission (Fig. 6-10).

Despite these advantages, mouth-to-snorkel rescue breathing is much more difficult to master than mouth-to-mouth. This is primarily because making an effective seal, crucial to preventing the victim from filling with water and to giving breaths, is much harder when using a snorkel than with mouth-to-mouth rescue breathing. Unless the seal is carefully maintained, water can be blown into the victim, leading to drowning. Because of this possibility, rescuers are advised that under most circumstances, unless you are completely proficient as a result of long practice with the technique, mouth-to-mouth rescue breathing is preferred because it will be more effective.

Positioning for mouth-to-snorkel breathing is different from mouth-to-mouth. Instead of having the left arm under the victim's left arm with the hand supporting the head or neck, the victim's head is cradled against the rescuer's chest by the right arm, though the left may be used if the rescuer is on the victim's right. The chin is held by the encircling hand and used to raise the facial area above the water and keep the airway open. Both divers are on their backs, heads toward shore or boat and preferably the wind and waves, with the rescuer behind the victim.

The hard part of mouth-to-snorkel breathing is making an effective lip seal. Getting the mouthpiece into an unconscious diver's mouth, if possible, is time-consuming and uncertain. If the mask is in the way, discard it.

After clearing the snorkel by either draining it or blowing the water out, place its mouthpiece down between the fingers of the cradling arm. This hand will be used to hold the mouthpiece in position and help make the seal. Insert the mouthpiece into the victim's mouth, using the hand holding the snorkel to seal the flange tightly all around. The bite tabs will be inside the victim's mouth, against the teeth. With the seal made, pinch off the victim's nose, or seal it with the same hand that is holding the snorkel by pressing the mask's skirt against the victim's nostrils. Again give two full, deliberate initial breaths, observing the chest for evidence of

PRACTICE with your preferred method and equipment.

The goal is to be able to give a nonbreathing victim as consistent an air supply as possible until he is out of the water and receiving professional care.

inhalation, and feeling for exhalation with the cheek at the end of the snorkel. To prevent CO_2 build-up in themselves, rescuers are advised to make sure that they do not inhale the victim's expired air.

If it is difficult to effect a seal, the rescuer can give the initial breaths by mouth-to-mouth and then attempt to place the snorkel for subsequent breaths. Rescue breathing should be maintained by mouth-to-mouth until the snorkel is in place. Once the snorkel is in the victim's mouth, a seal can be easily and reliably maintained.

In mouth-to-snorkel breathing, respirations should be slightly longer and deeper than normal mouth-to-mouth to overcome the dead-air space of the breathing tube. When you are towing from behind, cradling the head will allow you to maintain the necessary position to administer breaths through the snorkel. There also will be less necessity to roll the victim or rise up to make a seal with this method, however detecting an airway obstruction will be more difficult than with mouth-to-mouth. It is important to prevent water from entering the tube, usually by pinching the snorkel between the fingers to close the tube and raise it up. A hard plastic snorkel must be kept up out of the water.

Flexible tube snorkels are more difficult to work with than simple J-bend types. Should mouth-to-snorkel rescue breathing become your preferred technique after practice, experiment to find a good tool and to familiarize yourself with the characteristics of generally-available snorkels in case you need to use someone else's in an emergency. A snorkel with a purge valve, for instance, may be employed but will require practice in learning to close off the purge so that breaths will get through. Also practice using the snorkel while it is still attached to a mask. This can save time trying to free it before use.

As discussed previously, use either one full, deliberate breath every 5 seconds or two breaths every 10 seconds, and maintain rescue breathing as long as necessary or possible until the victim is out of the water and receiving additional care.

Using a Pocket Mask™

Some divers have begun to carry "Pocket Masks™" (Laerdal Med. Corp) in their BCs on all dives, to use for rescue breathing. Standard emergency gear on land, and usually found in all dive first-aid kits, these soft plastic or rubber devices are just as effective in the water. Having one available to use in an in-water emergency can make rescue breathing more effective in some cases (Fig. 6-11).

Pocket Masks™ have two specific features that make them excellent for use in the water:

1. The flexible skirt makes an easy seal over virtually any victim's mouth and nose simultaneously, ensuring effective ventilation.
2. The one-way valve prevents any material from entering the snorkel or mouth of the rescuer. There is no direct contact.

Using a Pocket Mask™ in the water requires the same diligent practice as other methods if proficiency is to be achieved and maintained. As with mouth-to-mouth breathing, rescuers will need to be relatively close to administer breaths, but the mask may extend this to a more comfortable distance. Some masks also may be equipped with an extended flexible tube and mouthpiece to facilitate their use in the water. Like mouth-to-snorkel breathing, rescuers also may prefer having a barrier between themselves and the victim and may possibly respond more willingly to strangers in distress. The victim's dive mask will always be discarded if a Pocket Mask™ is used.

The technique will vary with the type of mask employed, but most divers will find some variation of the chin-lift from behind most effective. By using only one arm and hand to cradle the head as in mouth-to-snorkel breathing, and holding the mask in place, the rescuer has a free hand to aid in transport or gear removal while towing. Easier swimming position also increases towing speed. On the other hand, extensive practice will be required for you to become proficient at deploying and maintaining the mask in place, especially if you are diving in colder water where gloves or mittens may be worn.

Fig. 6-11. With extensive practice, a pocket mask can be effective for in-water rescue breathing.

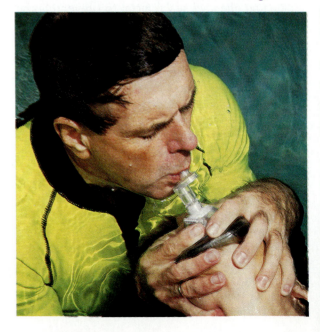

TOWING AND ASSISTING

Unless a victim is washed ashore or deposited on deck by a lucky wave, towing is most often the only way to get an unconscious diver back to the exit point quickly. Similarly, an incapacitated diver, whether injured, fatigued, or cramped, will have to be assisted.

Towing and assisting over even relatively short distances can take great effort (Fig. 6-12). The environment, wind, waves, and current almost always will multiply difficulty for the rescuer. Though usually fit to dive, a rescuer must evaluate the added demands of moving another diver any distance in challenging conditions, especially at the end of an already strenuous dive. Minimum fitness is not enough.

To some extent, additional risks can be reduced with careful dive planning and execution. Having appropriate rescue equipment and trained personnel available is prudent whenever possible. Many recreational dive operations use rescue swimmers/divers who enter the water only if required and carry extensive additional equipment. Groups may divide themselves into teams that dive alternately, ensuring that someone is on the surface on watch and ready to render aid, if needed. NAUI advises that all divers carefully assess environmental conditions, especially water current and visibility, and use underwater navigation skills on every dive to help ensure surfacing near the exit point. If aid becomes necessary, being close to where it is readily available is invaluable.

Fig. 6-12. Towing a diver is hard work. Get help whenever possible.

Before Beginning

After considering one's ability to tow a victim, the following decisions still need to be made:

1. *Where is the best place to tow this person?*

   This may not be the dive's planned exit, particularly if you are far down-current from an anchored vessel. The shore may be an easier choice and may have the advantage of quicker access to appropriate emergency aid.

2. *What about gear?*

   Breathing and buoyancy are priorities. An empty cylinder and jacket BC may be unnecessary drags for a diver and rescuer in buoyant exposure suits. Inflated BCs discarded before towing almost always will be returned. Masks, so long as they are free of water, are best left in place to prevent water from entering the nose. Taking a few moments to prepare will pay off later in a faster, less taxing swim.

3. *Can anyone else help?*

   Unless diving solely with a buddy who needs your help, there often are other divers available and willing to help if they are told how. Use them to help avoid fatigue. They may provide the towing power while you ventilate the victim, or, if they are trained, they can alternate roles with you. Other help may be found on the boat or shore, if it can be obtained by signaling or dispatching a fast swimmer for help while the tow commences. Passing boats also may be helpful, as transport and to communicate with emergency service providers.

Spinal Injury Considerations

In cases where spinal injury may be present, such as when a diver is injured in a collision with another diver or with an air cylinder, or has fallen from or been hit by a platform, boarding ladder, or boat, it is crucial to attempt to maintain the head and neck in stable alignment. Under most circumstances, rescuers are advised to seek professional aid immediately to transport and remove the victim from the water. However necessary to immobilize the victim's spine, it is probably impossible during in-water transport without several professional rescuers' best efforts, and without the use of a rigid backboard and cervical collar. Nevertheless, rescuers can be faced with conditions that may make moving the victim necessary. These conditions include diving in remote locations far from timely help, being on the surface in rough water where violent movement is unavoidable, or the need to deal immediately with a major wound or provide CPR to a victim with no pulse or heartbeat.

> Let professional rescuers handle all spinal- or neck-injury victims whenever possible. Monitor and reassure the victim until they arrive.

Towing and Assisting Methods

Mastering several towing and assisting techniques will make you a more versatile rescuer. Not all divers are equipped the same way, and most diving situations are unique. Conditions can favor one method over another or, as with rescue breathing, they can make combining techniques most effective. Resourcefulness and good judgment are important to successful rescues.

The "do-si-do" Tow

Probably the most popular method, especially if mouth-to-mouth rescue breathing is used, all rescuers are advised to practice and perfect the "do-si-do" tow technique. The rescuer approaches a face-up victim from the side, placing the rescuer's own near arm inside the near arm of the victim, then reaching up to hold the victim's head, neck, or gear. Similar to the intertwining arms of square-dancing, this grip gives the tow its name (Fig. 6-13). Comfortably attached, the rescuer begins the tow, using the free hand for swimming, or to turn the victim to administer breaths, if necessary.

With a conscious diver, the rescuer can maintain frequent eye contact in this position, helping to reassure the victim, as well as effectively monitor the aided diver's condition.

Fig. 6-13. If air is available, the rescuer can use the mouthpiece throughout the tow. This is much easier than having to use a snorkel. Plan air consumption for contingencies on all dives.

Gear Tows

A buoyant, tired diver may be towed by any convenient handhold that allows comfortable and efficient movement for the rescuer. This can include grasping the strap of a back pack, or holding on to a wet suit collar or dry suit shoulder, or the cylinder valve and first stage (Fig. 6-14).

Most gear tows are easiest with the rescuer still on scuba or snorkeling. This spares the rescuer from having to strain out of the water to breathe. The rescuer reaches back, grabbing the gear palm-up with the hand nearest the victim. Gear tows are especially useful if the diver is conscious and can help the rescuer's efforts by kicking, even if only for short periods of time.

Gear tows are unsuitable for unconscious victims for whom constant monitoring and rescue breathing are required unless there are two rescuers. In that case, one rescuer can provide extra propulsion while the other continues to aid the victim. When fatigue occurs, the rescuers can switch positions.

> Handle all victims GENTLY!
>
> Rough treatment increases the chance of worsening an injury and shock.
>
> WAIT FOR HELP if it is available and delay will not endanger the victim or you!

Fig. 6-14. The cylinder valve makes a good handle for a gear tow.

Underarm Assisting

This is a simple but effective technique for reassuring a fatigued or agitated diver and helping the diver move toward the exit point (Fig. 6-15). It is often used by leadership-level divers charged with escorting students underwater or at the surface. Divers are cautioned that any physical contact with a conscious diver, especially at the surface, should be preceded by requesting and receiving permission.

The aiding diver grasps the diver under the arm, holding on to the biceps area with the hand lodged in the armpit. The divers both may swim face-down on snorkel or scuba, or the stressed diver can be resting face-up, finning as much as possible. The assisting diver can use the contact to help judge how the aided diver is faring, noting shivering and tension. This technique also can be used underwater to help a diver regain the surface and while performing a precautionary stop (Fig. 6-16).

"Wheelbarrow" Assist

Useful for helping a conscious, fatigued, or cramped diver, the rescuer acts as the "engine" in a composite unit in which the aided diver is floating face-up. Grasping the disabled diver's ankles, heels, or fins like the handles of a wheelbarrow, the rescuer, breathing from either snorkel or scuba, pushes the diver to the exit point. In another variation, the aided diver rests both feet on the shoulders of the pushing diver. In either case, the rescuer must maintain some visual reference, or follow a compass bearing to the exit point to ensure kicking in a straight line. In addition, the rescuer must make certain that the victim is buoyant enough so that the upper body does not submerge while being pushed in this manner, and that the victim's snorkel tube, if being used for breathing, does not submerge.

Additional Towing and Assisting Considerations

Any tow or assist goes more smoothly if abundant fresh air is available. In rough water, a regulator is the best source, particularly when you are helping a conscious diver. Leave the mouthpiece in place if the cylinder has air, to ensure that passing waves do not hamper breathing, and if the gear's weight and drag will not compromise the rescuer's ability to complete the tow. If the cylinder is empty, orally inflating the BC and discarding the gear, if this is not excessively time-consuming, may be desirable.

Navigation while towing, especially during rescue breathing, is difficult but necessary. Extending

Fig. 6-15. Most rescues are as simple as providing contact and support to a fatigued or agitated diver at the surface and assisting him to the exit.

Fig. 6-16. An underarm assist is probably the most frequently used rescue skill.

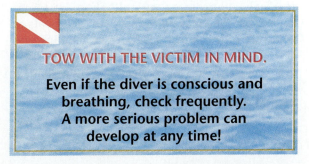

TOW WITH THE VICTIM IN MIND.

Even if the diver is conscious and breathing, check frequently. A more serious problem can develop at any time!

the length of a tow needlessly increases risk to all concerned. Treatment is delayed, and the rescuer ultimately works harder. Taking the time frequently to check one's bearings, allowing for the effects of surface current and wind, is wise.

Providing aid to another diver on the surface heightens your responsibility to the extent that you are expected to do all that is prudent to prevent additional harm. Rescuers are advised to check victims at frequent intervals, even if they are only professing fatigue or cramps. The possibility of loss of breathing or unconsciousness always exists. Some degree of shock, a life-threatening reduction in circulation, attends all injuries, and any victim's condition may be worsened by fear and thermal stress.

Masks and snorkels left in place should be monitored as well. A snorkel well may become a source of water instead of air. If the end of the tube dips beneath the surface, a diver can suffocate, aspirate water, choke, or drown. The mask also may slip, admitting water. In any event, vigilance to such details will prevent them from becoming problems.

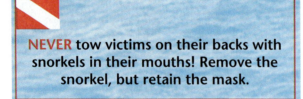

NEVER tow victims on their backs with snorkels in their mouths! Remove the snorkel, but retain the mask.

AUXILIARY RESCUE EQUIPMENT

There is no substitute for having the right tool at hand when performing any task (Fig. 6-17). Appropriate, functional equipment is as important to successful rescue as it is to enjoyable diving. How much gear divers accumulate "just in case" will depend on the amount and type of diving they do and their diving role. Working leadership divers will have different requirements from vacationers, but all divers can benefit from knowing how best to use available equipment.

Some rescue gear can fit easily into any diver's gear bag. Other items are unlikely to be transported, but they may be available aboard boats or at popular dive sites. Careful dive planning and preparation will help identify what gear is most desirable for the diving in which you participate.

Rescue Craft

A variety of small boats make excellent rescue craft, helping effect rapid and efficient transport of injured divers. Larger, motorized inflatables often

Fig. 6-17. Having great equipment is no substitute for thorough training and practice using it.

serve as dive boats themselves. Smaller rowing craft frequently function as auxiliary vessels on larger boats or may be additional recreational items found on boats or beaches. Water jet-driven personal watercraft are becoming extremely popular, and many diving clubs and professional rescue services are adding them to their equipment inventory for their versatility in an emergency.

Whatever the choice a diver makes, boating is another activity entirely. Many public organizations and private agencies provide free or low-cost boating education that will make using these craft, even if only as adjuncts to diving, much less hazardous to the operators, other boaters, swimmers, and divers. At the same time, learning to use boats properly will make them much more useful tools in any diving emergency. NAUI recommends that all divers who use boats make certain that they are qualified to do so by seeking additional information and training from recognized sources.

Small Power Boats

Small power boats can make most rescues much easier. Used as ferries for injured divers or to deliver rescue personnel to an accident site to provide in-water care before transport, speed is their chief asset. If large enough, they are also

> Using boats for any reason without specific training and practice is dangerous and irresponsible.
>
> Take a **SAFE-BOATING COURSE** from a recognized agency like the U.S. Coast Guard Auxiliary. Never use boats unless qualified and confident of your ability.

excellent interim-care platforms, providing rescuers with a flat, stable surface on which to begin administering first aid or life support to a victim.

Hard Motor Boats

Many dive boats use small motor boats for rescue purposes. Larger commercial craft are often mandated by regulations to carry them and must have qualified operators as part of their crew. Authorities recognize that using a motor boat around people in the water is an activity that requires training. Attempting to do so without information and mastery of many skills will likely lead to grief. The risks of extensive injuries from collision or being hit by a propeller always are present, especially with an inexperienced operator. Swamping and sinking are possible unless boats are equipped with additional buoyancy. Hard, steep sides can make entry and return difficult for even sound divers and complicate an unprepared rescuer's tasks.

However, well-equipped and in competent hands, a small motor boat is an excellent rescue craft. It has the speed and maneuverability to retrieve injured or fatigued divers before their condition deteriorates and to deliver timely aid. It is an advantage if any boat used for rescue can be rowed or paddled, especially when in close proximity to divers.

Inflatable Motor Boats

Speedy inflatable motor boats are probably the most popular type of rescue craft (Fig. 6-18). Many are able to run fast in rough water by virtue of their inherent buoyancy and special keel configurations. This is particularly true in hybrid types that combine a hard hull with an inflatable collar. Such craft are virtually unsinkable and can be very seaworthy, although sacrificing some of their easy portability.

Inflatables are relatively cheap and easy to acquire and maintain, great advantages for any additional dive gear, though they carry the same

Fig. 6-18. Many professional water rescue services use inflatable craft.

legal equipment and registration requirements as any other motor vessel of comparable size. If purely inflatable, some types, such as those with inflatable keels, may be difficult to control at low speeds. Like other small boats, they are weight-sensitive. Loading them with divers and equipment will seriously compromise their handling and performance and severely limit working space.

Personal Water Craft

Ridden more than driven, such craft can be used to deliver a rescuer quickly to the site of an accident, but without extensive modifications they may be useless in transporting an injured, unconscious diver. Newer models, however, combine greater passenger capacity with additional stowage. Such vessels blur the distinction between "water bikes" and small boats.

In any case, the chief advantage of personal water craft, apart from speed, is that they use a water jet for propulsion, eliminating the danger of a spinning propeller when operating around people. Coupled with very shallow draft, this makes them useful in situations where launching and returning to shore is necessary. As with all boats, additional training and familiarity with their unique handling characteristics and legally required equipment and registration is required.

Paddle Craft

Oar or paddle-powered boats are slower than motorboats, but have the advantage of being less dangerous, and are subject to much less legal regulation. Nearly anyone can paddle a boat, and most people can learn to row effectively. Some paddle craft, like kayaks, can be used even in rough water. Others may endanger operators in anything but calm conditions. Knowing how and when to use the tools you have available will make the difference in whether you need, or make, the rescue.

Kayaks and Canoes

These small craft are becoming more popular with divers as a means of extending their diving range and supplementing the outdoor experience in an environmentally sound, fitness-oriented way. In the right hands, they make good rescue craft for delivering aid and additional flotation to tired divers, even towing conscious divers back to a boat or shore. They also may be useful for covering larger distances more effectively than a snorkeler or diver could, especially when searching for a missing diver.

Because they are generally light and narrow, their stability may leave something to be desired. Recovering a diver into a kayak or canoe, especially if the victim is unconscious or disabled may be impossible without additional help, and without swamping the boat. Techniques for dewatering and righting such craft are central to all recognized training.

Rowboats

The humble wooden rowboat, heavy and stolid, can be a life-saving rescue craft if an injured or tired diver can be boarded from the water. This generally will require forethought and additional equipment, such as a ladder or straps, as described in this chapter. Useful close to shore, or as an auxiliary craft for a larger vessel, a rowboat or dinghy usually has the load-carrying capacity and stability to recover more than one diver besides the oarsperson. Oars can also extend the operator's reach and eliminate propeller danger and problems associated with carrying volatile fuels. Many dive operations in high-visibility water areas, from the tropics to inland springs, utilize rescue personnel in row boats to monitor divers from the surface.

Floats

Floats are decidedly low-tech and far less glamorous than boats or personal water craft, but they have undoubtedly saved more lives in the water than any other rescue device (Fig 6-19). Whether worn like a BC, personal flotation device (PFD), or rescue tube, or held onto like a buoy, paddleboard, or surfmat, they help a tired or injured person stay afloat, the first requirement of survival.

Fig. 6-19. Auxiliary rescue tools.

"Lifejackets"

Required aboard all vessels, most PFDs are designed to support a conscious or unconscious person face-up in the water for at least a day, generally far longer than necessary to locate and retrieve the individual. Though not specifically for diving rescue, PFDs, because of their high visibility and buoyancy, can be very useful during an emergency. Their chief asset is that they are readily available on all boats.

Several PFDs together can be used to construct a kind of piecemeal raft under a diver, which can make transport easier. Such a makeshift arrangement also will help support rescuers. However, attempting to put PFDs on an unconscious diver in the water in the traditional manner can be frustrating and time-consuming.

Soft Rescue Tube

A rescue tube is a life-saving device that has a high visibility, closed-cell buoyant foam tube attached to a floating line and strap (see Fig. 6-19). It can be used in a variety of ways to more easily transport a conscious or unresponsive breathing diver than traditional tows. The tube can also provide additional buoyancy to a non-breathing victim, but a single rescuer generally would be better off towing by some other method because of the need to maintain proximity for rescue breathing. Rescue tubes with enough line attached are especially useful for dealing with panicked divers at the surface, where they can be floated to the person in distress without the need to get within touching distance.

The tube can be held by the assisted diver or it may be fastened in position around the upper body. The rescuer can hold the tube's strap at the closure or use the attached line to extend the distance between the divers. When towing, the rescuer should not wear the shoulder strap. Rather, the line should be held to extend the rescuer's reach making it possible to swim using one arm and both legs to pull the victim (Fig. 6-20). With a long line attached, a rescuer may swim the tube out to the diver from the exit point. Aides on shore or a boat can then pull both divers back using the line (Fig. 6-21).

Rescue Can

Similar to a rescue tube, a rescue can is a buoyant device, generally constructed of a hard plastic enclosing flotation, which has handles and provision for attaching a line at one end (see Fig. 6-19). Shaped like a flattened torpedo, or rounded surfmat, it can be used easily to tow a conscious diver able to hold on, such as one with leg cramps. Like a rescue tube, if brought out to a diver in distress with a long line attached, it can be used to tow both divers back, or floated to a panicked diver for towing at a reasonable distance.

When used for tandem towing, the injured diver may be between the rescuer and the float, ensuring that the victim remains in contact with the float back to the exit (see Fig. 6-21).

Paddle Boards, Surfmats, etc.

Generally rectangular-shaped with a rounded end, if equipped to have a line attached, these can be used to provide additional buoyancy to an injured diver. Many shore divers use them to transit the surf area on the surface, avoiding strong backwash and water turbulence, and later as staging points for groups before and after dives. So-called "boogie boards" and "body boards" used for wave-riding purposes, especially if equipped with retaining lanyards, also can be used to help tow tired divers, providing them with comforting addi-

Fig. 6-20. Monitor the victim throughout the tow.

Fig. 6-21. Outside aid and additional tools can help get a victim to medical treatment more quickly.

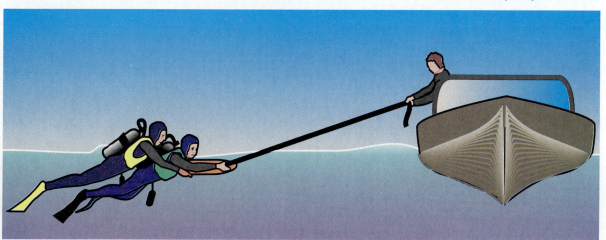

tional buoyancy. All such devices are best used with conscious victims only or to help transport rescue personnel to an injured diver.

Some paddle boards are large enough to be used by divers as primary transport to an offshore dive site. Paddling these with the arms, a rescuer can often transit waves, the surf zone, and even kelp easily and swiftly. The ability to reach a victim quickly, especially a non-breathing one, makes such gear extremely useful.

Inflatable Buoys, Beach Toys, Boat Fenders and Cushions

When necessary, buoyant material of any type is preferable to none. Boat fenders and many, but not all, upholstered cushions aboard boats will float for long periods of time. Boat fenders also are equipped to carry a line at either or both ends, increasing their utility for rescue purposes. Even inflatable lift bags or blow-up toys can have their place in a dive rescue if nothing else is available. Under some circumstances, these devices can help a rescuer provide a convenient resting point for tired divers, or they can aid in dealing with a panicked diver without getting close.

Heaving Lines and Throw Bags

These devices can greatly extend a rescuer's reach from shore or a boat, or from boat to boat. Heaving lines have a weighted end that helps guide the line where it is thrown. Accurate in practiced hands, they should be used cautiously in dive rescue since the weighted end can injure a surprised receiver. Though often found aboard boats, they are best used to send a line to another boat or ashore to aid in docking. If available in an auxiliary boat, they can be used to get a line out to the main vessel quickly, and they may be useful for that purpose in rescues conducted from rowing craft.

On the other hand, throw bags (Fig. 6-22) overcome many of the drawbacks of traditional heaving or messenger lines. Usually consisting of a nylon or other light-weight material bag within which a light, braided floating line is stuffed, these devices allow almost anyone to deliver a line accurately to a person in the water at a considerable distance. With practice, a distance of 75 feet (23 m) or more is possible—much farther than most experienced sailors can throw a carefully coiled line. Since the bag arrives virtually empty, injury from being hit by the weight is not an issue. The floating line does not absorb water, and it may be grabbed by the diver if it lands close enough. If the line misses its mark widely, it can be retrieved quickly and thrown again—the wet bag providing soft weight, and the line deploying as before. Restuffing a throw bag can be done quickly with practice.

While no amount of extra gear can replace a committed, trained rescuer, such items will frequently make the job easier. Having appropriate equipment ready and knowing how to use it properly is a necessary part of a rescuer's preparation. At the very least, throwable buoyant devices can sometimes make it unnecessary for a rescuer to enter the water, by extending the effective reach of aid, and thereby giving fatigued divers a chance to relax and collect themselves. Having available at least a throw bag, rescue tube, or buoyant float is a highly recommended leadership practice that all divers can follow.

A float in particular is extremely useful for purposes besides rescue. In conjunction with a dive flag, it is used to warn passing boats of the pres-

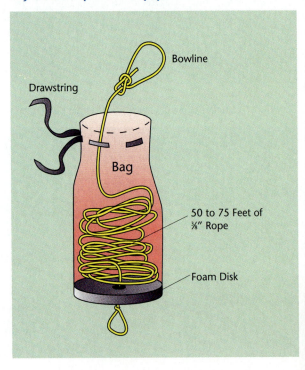

Fig. 6-22. A throw bag is an excellent addition to any rescuer's personal equipment.

> Rescuers need to be resourceful. Use whatever you have on hand that will meet your goal of moving the victim quickly and efficiently to professional care without further harming the victim or endangering yourself.

ence of divers and can reduce the incidence of boat and diver accidents. In many places such flags are required by law for all dives, even as they are for all boats engaged in underwater operations. NAUI recommends that floats and flags be used whether or not legally required whenever divers are in the water. Used with a shot line, or attached by a line to the surface from the crown of a boat anchor, they can help reduce accidents by giving divers on the surface a convenient visual reference, providing easy guidance to a dive site, and making good surface resting points before and after dives.

REMOVING A RESCUED DIVER FROM THE WATER

Arrival at a dive's exit point with a diver in tow presents a rescuer with a new set of problems. Getting an injured or unconscious person out of the water without worsening the victim's condition takes a combination of appropriate equipment, technique, ingenuity, and raw strength. The first three factors can lessen the need for the last, but careful handling of even a small person will take a fair amount of brawn.

Backboards and Spinal Injury Management

Whenever a spinal injury is suspected, it is better to act as if it is present than to hope it is not and possibly aggravate a serious problem through mishandling. Divers who become unconscious upon water entry, or who are involved in collisions with other divers or objects, or who complain of numbness or lack of muscular control before diving after a slip or fall in which they hit their heads or necks may well have suffered a spinal injury. After a dive, even if decompression illness of some type is suspected, evidence of some injury to the head or neck from any cause is sufficient reason to handle a victim as if spinal injury were present. Such extra care can do no harm and may make a significant difference in the chance for recovery if a spinal injury is indeed part of the problem (Fig. 6-23).

Backboards are specially constructed, lightweight rigid structures with retaining straps to immobilize a victim's head and neck. Using them in the water is fairly easy since the victim is buoyant, but extra help will make the job easier, particularly if gear removal is involved.

In any case, one rescuer should be assigned to hold the head aligned in place throughout the process. If available, a cervical collar may be fastened around the victim's neck as soon as possible. This will make the rescuer's job much easier

Fig. 6-23. Professionals use great care whenever dealing with possible spinal or neck injury. Let them handle these problems whenever possible.

ONLY MOVE A SUSPECTED SPINAL INJURY VICTIM:

1. When the water is rough and stability of the victim is impossible to maintain.
2. When CPR is necessary.

Professional handling is always preferred for spinal injury victims.

Wait for their help whenever possible.

and is more reliable for holding the head in position than relying solely on a person's steady hands, particularly in the water.

If you are alongside a boat, the approach will most likely have been made to the stern of the vessel. If this area is rough, or if a stern anchor has been set, moving into the sheltered (lee) side of the boat is recommended. On a shore dive, a backboard may be brought out beyond the surf line, or the victim may be towed into the shallows using an appropriate tow, then placed on the board.

After gear has been removed, the board is slid underneath the victim and the closures are fas-

> **IF CIRCUMSTANCES MAKE YOU SUSPECT A SPINAL INJURY:**
>
> 1. Summon help immediately.
> 2. Approach the victim gently; avoid making excessive waves.
> 3. Stabilize the head and neck in the position in which they were found.
> 4. Turn a person found floating face down in the water according to the recommendations of the National Safety Council.
> 5. Check for breathing, and, if none, have a second rescuer begin administering breathing after opening the airway via a jaw thrust.
> 6. Keep the head and neck stable until emergency medical professionals arrive.

> Cutting is quick and efficient and disturbs the victim least. Remove only enough garment to treat the injury or provide care. Keep the victim warm and comfortable.

tened snugly enough to ensure support, but not so tightly as to hamper circulation. The head and chin straps are particularly important, and when used in conjunction with a flexible or rigid cervical collar, if available, they will help ensure complete immobility.

In-water Gear Removal

Starting at the top, the rescuer should work down the victim's body opening all fastenings retaining the diver in the equipment. If the victim is in a jacket BC, front closure straps and any waistband should be opened. If there are fast releases on the shoulder straps and they are simply opened and the BC submerged, the victim is freed. If the jacket does not release at the shoulder, or only on one shoulder, the victim's arm should be bent naturally at the elbow and pushed gently through the BC armhole, freeing it. Repeat the procedure for the other arm, if necessary. Sometimes rolling the victim slightly away from the armhole will make BC removal smoother. Other means may be necessary in cases where there is a shoulder or arm injury; under some circumstances, this may include cutting the BC at the shoulder. Paramedic shears, which combine tough, sharp edges with blunt tips and a transverse spade on the end of the bottom blade, make excellent dive tools for rescuers for this reason.

It may be necessary to deflate the BC partially to handle it easily and, especially, to sink it below the victim for removal. If so, it may be necessary to reinflate it so that it may be recovered later.

With older-style "horse collar" BCs, removing gear without at least two rescuers is difficult, especially if it is necessary to stabilize the head because of possible neck injury or if rescue breathing is needed.

Removal on a Backboard

On a boat with a spacious, water-level swim platform, or up a gently sloping shore, handling an immobilized victim is easy. In either case, the board acts like a rigid stretcher, making moving the victim relatively easy, albeit strenuous, depending on the victim's size. On a suitably configured boat, timing the rise and fall of the boat, and coordinating the lift with persons on board, the victim is first raised to the platform, and held there. Rescuers then reach down and either lift the victim over the vessel's transom, or through the boarding door from the platform to cockpit. On a boat equipped only with boarding ladders or minimal platforms, other methods will have to be tested and perfected before an emergency.

Removal on a rocky shore, ironically where spinal injury from a slip and fall accident while wearing dive gear may be likely, even before entering the water, can be a difficult problem requiring outside aid. The variety of shoreside terrain makes specific advice too general to be of great value, but rock-climbing in scuba gear is not unusual for some intrepid divers. Such dive sites require great caution and good plans for emergency management that include the ability to call upon outside professionals if the need arises.

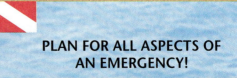

> **PLAN FOR ALL ASPECTS OF AN EMERGENCY!**

Getting A Victim Aboard

The difficulty in getting a diver aboard a boat will be inversely proportional to the amount of thought and preparation spent working out an effective system in advance. The type of vessel, boarding system, swim platform (if any), and the ability of the crew all will be factors to consider in determining a specific method. The following suggestions will undoubtedly need modification, trial, and repeated practice in the conditions you customarily face before you will be able to use them reliably in a real emergency.

Parbuckling

A medieval system for moving large casks of wine, parbuckling is easily adaptable to the rescuer's needs for an efficient means of raising even a large victim from the water relatively easily. Parbuckling by net or webbed straps also can be employed for a victim with a spinal injury if used carefully in conjunction with a backboard and cervical collar (Fig. 6-24).

The method is simple. Using a net or three (but preferably four) webbed straps at least 1½ inches (3.8 cm) wide, attach one end to the boat. The length of the net or straps should be at least two and a half times the distance from the boat's lowest accessible freeboard (distance from the lowest point on the gunwale, or upper hull deck joint, to the waterline).

The other ends are dropped in the water to the rescuer(s) aiding the victim. Each strap is then passed under the victim, and the end of that strap is then given back to the assistants on the boat. Following the in-water person's directions, the rescuers on the boat or dock begin recovering the net or straps, making sure to coordinate the speed so that the victim is raised parallel to the water. It is important that each handler recover strap or net at the same speed, keeping the victim from shifting from a position parallel to the water, or being hung by one section. Lines should also remain parallel to each other for the same reason. Uneven tension will injure the victim, who also may slip free and fall back into the water.

Since the victim will roll as the net or straps are tightened, gear removal prior to lifting is mandatory. The victim's arms should be stabilized alongside the torso or resting on the abdomen, possibly by a loosely tied line or buckled, empty weight belt if unconscious, to prevent them from becoming trapped or injured in the net during lifting. Once at the gunwale, a conventional stretcher, the attached backboard, or available hands can be used to lower the victim to the deck inside the boat. Care must be taken not to drop the victim to the ground or back into the water when lifting the diver onto boat or dock.

Fig. 6-24. A net makes parbuckling easier and supports the victim more evenly.

Line Roll-Up

This is a variation on parbuckling that uses knotted lines to achieve the same purpose. It can be improvised at a site, and long lines need not be cut. If the lines are long enough, they can be doubled, and thus provide more support.

The lines are knotted at the dock- or boat-side end of the rope, and rescuers may stand on, or preferably in front of, the knots to secure them. This makes deployment quicker than searching for appropriate attachment points, if not arranged in advance. As with the above technique, the free ends, or the closed loops if doubled, are passed under the victim in the water and then returned to the people on the boat or dock. Again under the direction of the in-water rescuer, the lines are recovered evenly and slowly, rolling and raising the victim to the level of the boat or dock for further handling without injuring or dropping the victim (Fig. 6-25). Like parbuckling, a stretcher, attached backboard, or willing hands can take the victim from there (Fig. 6-26).

Surfboards and Paddle Boards

A rigid paddle board or surfboard can be used to help raise an injured diver to the level of a swim platform or small boat. The victim is first

Fig. 6-25. Lines can be used effectively, but extra care must be taken not to injure the victim. Raise slowly and steadily with one person in charge.

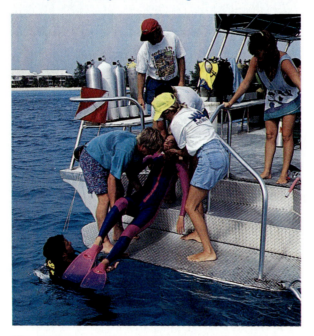

Fig. 6-26. No matter what equipment is on hand, careful, extra help is necessary to move a victim.

placed on the board, usually by sinking the board beneath the person and allowing it to rise under the diver. With very buoyant devices, this may take the weight of two rescuers to accomplish.

Once the victim is on the board, the rescuers raise one end of the board onto the vessel's swim platform, or, if there is a line attached, hand it up to others who will drag the board and diver on. With minimal outside help, two rescuers likely can maneuver the end of the board onto the step, allowing one to get on the boat while the in-water rescuer maintains the board in position. This can be difficult in rough water.

The in-water rescuer stabilizes the victim on the board, while the one on the boat slides the board and victim as far into the boat as possible. Once certain that the victim and board will stay on the boat, the in-water rescuer comes aboard the boat, and the two complete the job. In cases of a small victim, it may be possible for one person to do this alone in calm water.

Carries and Lifts

Getting a victim away from danger and to appropriate aid rapidly is the goal of any rescue. Despite the usefulness of many rescue aids, they may not be at hand, or they can be too time-consuming to rig during an emergency. Additional help also may be unavailable. If waiting is not possible, transporting a victim from the water alone is often the quickest, most direct method.

Carrying a heavy load is hard work, but the need for great delicacy for an injured person increases the work significantly. There is no substitute for coordinated effort—the strength of many hands—when transporting a victim; unfortunately, this may not be available. NAUI advises that all divers consider the physical demands on the rescuers of any carry or lift. Serious back injury and other muscular problems easily can result from improper methods or overzealous effort.

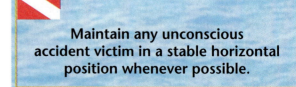

Maintain any unconscious accident victim in a stable horizontal position whenever possible.

CHAPTER 6   TOWING, ASSISTING, AND SURFACE RESCUE

The average person weighs 150 lbs. How much can you lift and carry alone?

GET HELP!

Fireman's Carry

A fireman's carry takes strength, though not as much as you might think. A single rescuer can carry an injured diver of about equal physical size from the water using this technique. When begun in the water, the lift is simplified by buoyancy (Fig. 6-27).

The tricky part is lifting the victim up onto your shoulders in one swift motion. Float the victim to shallow water. When the water is at the height of your sternum, remove your fins. The victim's gear already will have been discarded. The diver will be floating face-up. Grasp the victim's arm and place the victim's abdomen on your shoulder. The other hand is used to hold the injured diver's leg, and the weight is borne by your upper back and legs, with the diver draped over your shoulders. If lifting the injured diver clear to that height is not possible, the pack strap carry described in this section can be used.

A fireman's carry generally is not suitable for victims with breathing distress, abdominal pains, shock, possible DCI, or spinal injury unless there is no other choice.

Ladder Carry

Getting a victim up a ladder from the water to a boat or dock definitely will require strength, but like other carries, technique can help offset the amount of strength needed (Fig. 6-28). It will be difficult to control an unconscious victim's head when doing a ladder carry since a single rescuer will have both hands occupied. By draping the diver's arms over your shoulders, you can cradle the diver's head against your chest. Move slowly and steadily upwards. The fatigue of holding on will diminish your arm and wrist strength more rapidly than climbing.

BC Carry

It is possible to use a version of this carry to get a victim up a ladder or onto shore, if the victim has on a jacket-style BC. In order to use two hands to support yourself and the diver on the ladder, you and the victim wear the BC together (Fig. 6-29).

The cylinder and regulator(s) are removed from the diver's BC, and the BC is deflated. (This tech-

Fig. 6-27. By using the large muscles of the legs, buoyancy and timing, most rescuers can lift a victim of about equal size.

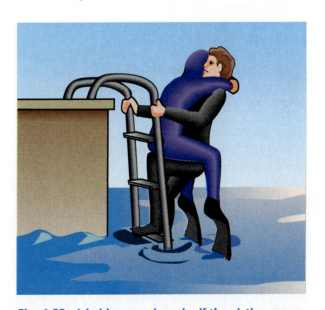

Fig. 6-28. A ladder carry is easier if the victim can hold on.

nique is only for a victim with a buoyant exposure suit or if the rescuer is certain that the victim can be maintained at the surface.) Shoulder straps, if any, should be opened to permit your arms to enter, and the chest straps undone. (If it is a fixed-armhole type, there usually will be enough space for two arms.) Put the BC on with the diver in it. The BC will keep the diver on your back as the ladder is climbed.

Fig. 6-29. A BC carry can help a rescuer move an injured diver up a ladder if no other aid is available.

Fig. 6-30. Since there is less handling of the victim, a pack strap carry is sometimes better than a fireman's carry.

Pack Strap Carry

A pack strap carry can be used when the rescuer is unable to lift the victim up onto the shoulder as in a fireman's carry (Fig. 6-30).

Reach across the diver from either side, grasping an arm with your same-side hand, left or right. Lift the arm over your shoulder, sliding your body beneath it and rolling the diver. Grab the other arm, and duck low to allow the water to lift the diver onto your back. Both arms are draped over your shoulders, with one or both your hands holding the arms down. Be sure not to submerge the victim during the roll-over.

As the water level recedes, the full weight of the diver will be borne on your shoulders. If the victim is taller than you are, the feet will drag on the bottom as land is approached, making movement more difficult. It is not necessary to get to completely dry shore before carefully placing the diver down, so long as there is no longer a chance of drowning. Do so at the earliest opportunity.

"Bounce" Lift

If a boat has suitable dive platform, and the rescuer is alone, it may be possible to use the victim's buoyancy to get the person on the platform and subsequently aboard. Upon reaching the boat the rescuer secures the floating victim face-up and climbs aboard. The victim is freed and turned to face the platform, or side of the boat if the lowest freeboard. (This is often the case with an inflatable boat, or rigid dinghy.)

The rescuer tips the boat, lowering the entry point as much as possible. Timing the boat's movement with the lift, the rescuer pushes the diver low in the water, about chin level, then raises the victim sharply. This will often bring the diver's torso over the edge of the boat or onto the platform. The next wave or surge and the rescuer's strenuous dragging will often get the person aboard. Abrasions are likely, even if the victim is wearing an exposure suit, but the injured diver will be out of the water (Fig. 6-31).

Removal to Shore

Any of the above techniques, except "bouncing," can be used to help a victim ashore. However, shorelines, surf, and current add additional problems. Rocks, debris, and uneven terrain increase the chance of falling resulting in serious injury to rescuers and victims alike. Current and steep or slippery river banks or lakefronts can require climbing and additional help. Surge, surf, and geographic currents also can complicate beach landings with an incapacitated diver.

NAUI recommends that the unique nature of diving areas be considered as part of dive and emergency planning. Such plans best include procedures to transport injured divers to treatment should the need arise.

Current

A rescuer is advised to consider how current will affect the difficulty and duration of any tow or

CHAPTER 6 TOWING, ASSISTING, AND SURFACE RESCUE

Fig. 6-31. Dragging a victim over the side of a boat can cause injury to rescuers or victim. Having the victim facing the boat is generally preferred. Move carefully and slowly.

Environmental conditions usually make rescue more difficult. Working in and around water is always hazardous.

Rescue is *not* recreational diving.

Surf

Surf is especially hazardous during a rescue. Surf can overwhelm any diver, especially one with another in tow. The chance of losing the victim increases in turbulent water. Falling in surf while carrying a victim from the water not only risks the victim, but it can injure the rescuer as well.

Conservative judgment is mandatory under such circumstances. It may be better to wait for shore-based aid, small boats, or additional personnel beyond the surf line than to attempt to land a victim through it. The likelihood of aid can be increased if rescuers are able to signal people ashore of the need for help with a small, waterproof personal strobe, a signaling mirror, a good whistle, or even submersible pyrotechnic flares.

If outside help is not an option, the greatest caution is recommended. Pause to watch the pattern of the breakers, and time the attempt in order to take advantage of any lulls you observe. Assessing the beach zone may reveal a less violent landing area. Once in breaking surf, you must take care to protect an unconscious victim's airway by sealing the nose and mouth with one hand during transport.

Multiple Person Shore Carries

Carrying a victim to shore is frequently a group effort since onlookers often are available to help. However, even with people present, assistance is not always assured. Bystanders sometimes remain so, engrossed in the struggles they are witnessing, unless the rescuer is able to enlist their support and direct them effectively.

Two-Person Carry

A two-person carry can be done two ways. If the victim is responsive and can stand, the two carriers grip each other's wrists, forming a seat for the injured person. The victim sits down on the carriers' forearms, and the rescuers' other arms encircle the victim's back. The victim's arms are draped over the shoulders of both rescuers (Fig. 6-32).

If the victim is unresponsive, and no spinal injury is suspected, one rescuer may take the diver under the arms, with the other lifting the

assist. It also may be possible to use the current to advantage. If the vessel lies offshore, for instance, a favorable current leading to shore may be the quickest means of reaching additional aid.

Dive boats routinely deploy current lines, long lines with attached floats at the end that trail with the current, to enable divers to pull themselves back to the boat or rest on the surface before and after diving. These lines often can be extended greatly if enough rope is available, and they can be used to help a rescuer tow a victim back to the boat. A swimmer also may be able to bring the end of a long line ashore, so that additional help can be gathered to haul in a rescuer and diver at the float's end.

Rescuers departing from shore may be able to bring a rescue sling attached to a large reel of line on shore, such as those found at some popular beaches. By extending the reach of fresh, land-based assistance, quicker response to overcome currents and other difficulties can be assured. The help of professional lifeguards is always beneficial to gaining swift, appropriate treatment of any water casualty.

The effects of current can also be minimized by planning dives to take advantage of published slack-water times. Diving in areas with geographic currents, such as rips and longshore currents, if it must be done at all, requires special planning and extra precautions.

legs. If an injury may be present, the rescuer at the head can use the forearms to help stabilize the head and neck, or may be close enough to rest the victim's head against the rescuer's body. Rescuers are cautioned to initiate the lift with the large muscles of the legs, straightening carefully to avoid injury to themselves.

Three-Person Carry

A three-person carry is useful in cases of an unresponsive victim, where there may be a spinal injury or when rescue breathing is being administered. One rescuer is responsible for immobilizing the head and neck and giving breaths. Another rescuer must direct the carry and watch out for obstructions.

The primary rescuer assumes position adjacent to the victim's shoulder, and the second rescuer is positioned on the same side just below the victim's hip. The third person is on the opposite side roughly midway between the other two. A cervical collar, if available and necessary, should be put on the victim before lifting. The rescuers kneel, sliding their arms gently beneath the victim, with each rescuer grasping one of each of the other rescuer's wrists. The interlocking arms form a cradle under the victim's mid-back and lower buttock/hip area, and the rescuer at the head uses the forearm to help stabilize the spine. At the lead rescuer's direction, the three lift in tandem, raising the victim in a horizontal position, and start walking.

Four-Person Carry

Similar to the three-person carry above, the fourth person adds support and strength to the effort. The chief benefit of the fourth person is the substantial reduction in the weight the three other helpers must bear, and also the increased control that results from additional strength. As with all group rescue efforts, one person must take charge and direct the activity or confusion results. Carrying a victim with more than four people can be counterproductive to effective handling.

Drags

When no help is available, a rescuer may have to resort to dragging a victim along a shoreline. This can be accomplished even with a possible spinal injury if no backboard is available and waiting is not an option. If a victim is conscious and

> **Wait for help unless doing so will endanger the victim or yourself.**

Fig. 6-32. Watch your footing when carrying another diver in shallow water. Uneven terrain and extra weight make balance difficult. A fall will injure everyone.

breathing without difficulty and the resting place is secure, leaving the diver momentarily to get help or activate emergency services is often the wiser choice. Never leave a severely injured diver alone unless there is no other option. However, if the tide is rising or the exit point is otherwise precarious, dragging the victim up a bank or shoreline may be necessary.

If it is, care must be taken to ensure that any additional harm is minimized. Booties or other foot covering can be left in place to prevent cuts and abrasion. The victim should be dragged slowly, with the rescuer supporting as much of the torso weight as feasible. Grasp the diver beneath the armpits from behind, as best as possible stabilizing the head and neck with your forearms while dragging the victim backwards. Choose the route carefully to avoid obstructions that will injure the victim or make movement more difficult. This sometimes means traveling farther to get to a suitable area more quickly.

Bank Drag. A steep, possibly slippery bank makes transporting a victim even harder, particularly for a single rescuer. A variation of dragging may help overcome the combination of incline and poor footing. This technique also can be used if the rescuer is unable to make progress in dragging a large victim or because of fatigue. Before attempting it, however, a rescuer is advised to assess carefully whether or not it is necessary, or if getting additional help would be better.

The rescuer kneels or stands behind the prone victim, reaching under the arms and encircling the chest. Lifting with the legs, the rescuer raises the victim as high as possible and sits back into the bank, digging in the heels to maintain position. The victim winds up on top of the rescuer, and some progress upwards will have been made. Similar to an inch worm's movement, having a victim repeatedly fall on top of the rescuer on rough ground is bound to become painful and can cause injury.

Additional Shore Transport Equipment

Some items can make transporting a victim on shore much easier. These may be gear designed to transport victims, like traditional stretchers or cloth rescue mats, or found items such as beach or other blankets, chairs, ladders, removable table tops or discarded doors. Any flat, portable surface of sufficient size and strength may be used, if enough hands are available to lift and carry it, while making sure that the victim stays on it.

Carry Mats and Stretchers

Stretchers and especially carry mats are good additions to a shore dive first-aid kit. Cloth carry mats are extremely easy to carry folded into a compact bundle. Usually constructed of some rugged canvas-like synthetic material, and reinforced around the edges where handhold straps are attached, they often have diagrams printed on them detailing their use. They also are easy to construct. The rescuers place the mat under a diver, then lift the mat, carrying the victim in either a supine or sitting position depending on the mat and condition of the diver.

Stretchers are less easy to stow, but they may be more useful for some kinds of injuries, particularly when there is an unconscious victim, or when an injured person must be passed or transported from one level to another. Rigid poles make this easier.

Blankets

Unlike other multiple-person carries during which using more than four rescuers is difficult, the ability to spread the load of a victim along the edges of a blanket to more rescuers makes even a long shore transport possible. Maintaining stability of the head and neck also is facilitated by extra hands in this case. Roll the edges of the blanket under and towards the victim's sides for better stability and to give carriers a more secure grip.

Ladders, Doors, Etc.

Any of these found items can make good rescue gear. If possible, the surface can be padded with a blanket or mat. This is particularly true of ladders, in which the rungs may be uncomfortable to the victim, or if splinters or any sharp protrusions exist.

Two-Person Chair Carry

If a sturdy light-weight chair is available, even without legs, it can easily be used as a transport device. The (preferably responsive) victim is placed in the chair and may be secured by a band, belt, or line, if available, across the chest. The rescuers lift the chair, just as in a two-person carry, keeping the victim inclined slightly backward to ensure that the person remains in the chair throughout the carry.

Removing Exposure Suits

Deciding to remove a victim's exposure suit requires considering more than technique. Such actions should only be performed without the victim's explicit permission when justified by the need to initiate CPR to a non-breathing diver with no pulse, when dealing with an unconscious diver in acute thermal distress, or by some obvious injury that requires clear access to the wound and surrounding site. In some cases, removing the exposure suit may hasten or worsen the onset of shock or hypothermia.

The following techniques may be used if preserving the suit is necessary. But swift access to a life-threatening major injury, or the need to commence CPR, may make such efforts an insupportable waste of time. If so, paramedic shears are fast and efficient tools.

Wet Suits

Most wet suits can be removed normally, if laboriously, by undoing zippers and hook-and-loop fasteners, then by removing the garment. Hoods should be rolled up over the ears and eyes, then removed. Jackets are best taken off over the head, up the back by the beaver tail, if any, with the arms winding up inside out. Farmer John-style pants are rolled down the body, also winding up inside out. If the victim is in a one-piece jumpsuit with a central zipper in front or behind, more handling and victim movement will be necessary to remove the suit, but complete removal may be unnecessary. When cervical (neck) or head injuries are suspected, but suit removal is necessary, always cut the wet suit; never pull the wet suit because more severe injury can result. Wait for professional help whenever possible.

Dry Suits

Techniques of removal will depend on the design of the suit. Rear-entry suits may be easier to take off an unconscious victim, but most dry suits will be somewhat less difficult for the rescuer than a wet suit. Underwear will add problems and may best be removed by cutting, if necessary.

CHAPTER SEVEN

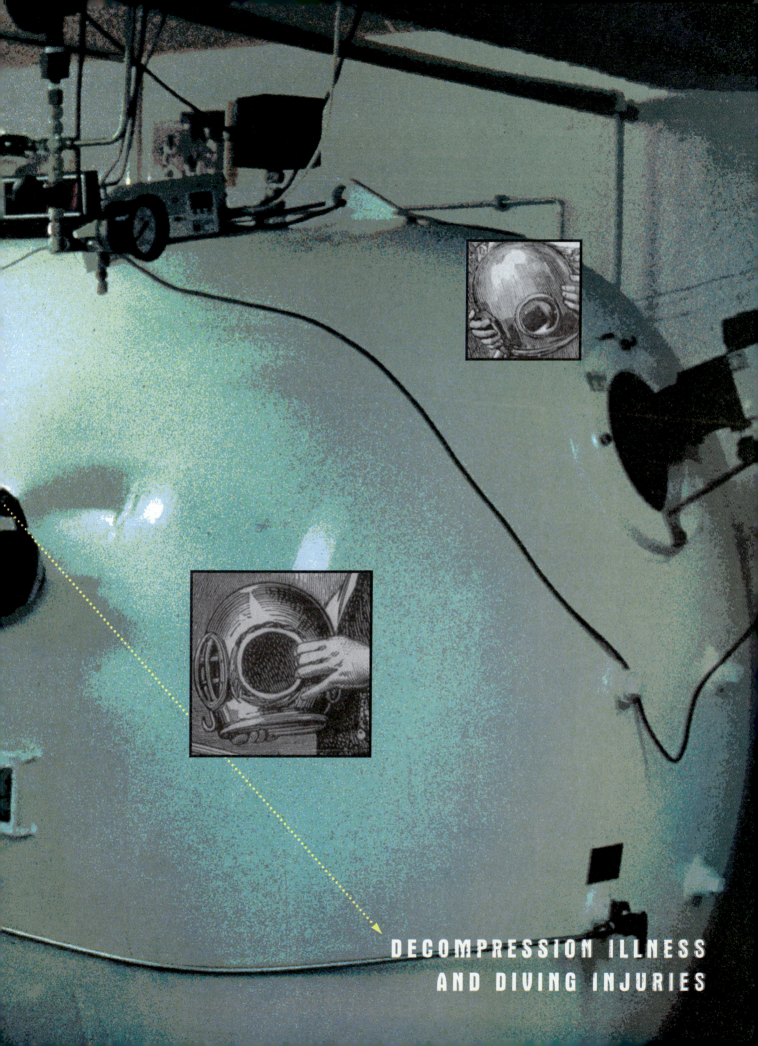

DECOMPRESSION ILLNESS
AND DIVING INJURIES

Every dive carries risk of injury from factors unique to the aquatic environment and from strenuous exercise. Most of these risks can be reduced greatly through thoughtful planning, preparation and judgment (Fig. 7-1). Careful practices and attention to your own and your companions' fitness to dive—and dedication to maintaining diving fitness—can reduce the chance of harm. Yet entirely eliminating the possibility of diving mishaps may well be impossible considering the nature of diving, and especially the uncertain nature of decompression illness (DCI).

Every year a few divers are afflicted with decompression sickness (DCS) or serious pressure-related injury (barotrauma), despite scrupulous adherence to published exposure limits, ascent rates, and recommended diving practices. More frequently, others suffer because they may ignore the presence of some temporary contraindication or continue a dive in spite of discomfort or pain. And there are certainly other divers whose diving methods or choices make DCI, in hindsight, entirely predictable. Balancing these incidents, there are probably many more divers who voluntarily or inadvertently surpass limits and disregard accepted practices and advice without apparent ill effects.

Deserved or not, completely known or misunderstood, DCI happens—just as other common diving-related injuries can happen regardless of diligent efforts to prevent them. Early recognition that a problem exists and appropriate first aid, including immediate administration of oxygen and rapid medical evaluation for virtually all types of DCI, will definitely help limit their effects on victims.

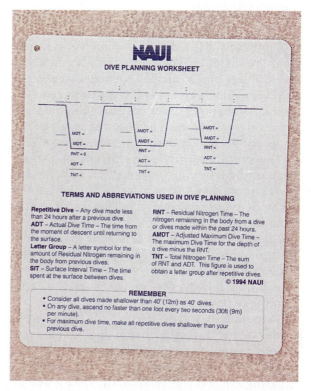

Fig. 7-1. Thorough dive planning can greatly reduce the chance of decompression illness.

SIGNS AND SYMPTOMS

Signs of a problem can be observed externally, and evaluated without cooperation from the victim. They include tangible signs of trouble such as external tissue damage, bleeding, unconsciousness after diving, or excessive coughing. Obvious changes in behavior or usual function such as suddenly confused speech or difficulty standing or walking also can signal trouble.

Symptoms of an injury or illness are experienced internally by the victim. They may be *physical*, such as pain or dizziness, or *emotional*, such as acute anxiety, nervousness, or depression. For a rescuer, discerning symptoms even by astute, sensitive questioning often is hindered by a victim's denial or rationalization. This frequently results in delaying treatment until more serious problems develop.

All signs and symptoms need to be taken in the context of events so a rescuer can determine an appropriate response. For instance, vomiting (a sign) and nausea (a symptom) on a boat ride *before* diving most likely are attributed to seasickness—debilitating but not generally life-threatening, despite the victim's assertions. The same signs and symptoms after surfacing from a dive may be indicative of serious DCI.

In addition, some DCI signs are very similar and others can be very subtle. Differentiating one problem from another is virtually impossible in the field, no matter how knowledgeable or vigilant the rescuer. Immediately recognizing there is a problem and beginning aggressive treatment that usually includes oxygen administration, life support, if necessary, and evacuation for professional medical care that may include recompression therapy is more important than detailed evaluation.

BAROTRAUMA

Barotrauma is the term for any injury that results from the direct effects of pressure. It is used to describe any of the common squeezes on descent or reverse blocks on ascent. Lung overexpansion injuries (sometimes called reverse squeezes), the most serious barotraumas, are discussed below under the heading of decompression illness (DCI).

The great majority of barotraumas can be avoided by following universally recommended diving procedures. These include ensuring the ability to equalize pressure before diving, equalizing pressure gently throughout descent, never holding your breath while scuba diving, and refraining from diving unless completely fit. Procedures are reviewed here as a means of helping prevent the injuries themselves, as well as accidents they can cause.

Pain causes great stress. Excessive stress underwater can lead to dangerous actions and severe injuries. Sudden pain underwater can lead to uncontrolled, unthinking reaction. Difficulty clearing can be the final factor that moves a stressed, anxious diver into panic and flight. Any pain can add a layer of difficulty to a growing "snowball" of problems.

Squeezes

Squeezes are barotraumas that occur on descent. They are caused by incomplete or ineffective efforts to equalize pressure between natural, internal, or artificially created external airspaces and the ambient environment. Air within these spaces acts according to Boyle's Law, compressing on descent as ambient (water) pressure increases.

If more air is not introduced to the space, usually by active equalization efforts, the tissue surrounding the area is drawn into the space in an attempt to fill it to its original volume. This results in discomfort and, if unrelieved by clearing, pain and injury.

Ear Squeezes

Ear squeezes are the most common, and most easily avoided, barotraumas. They usually occur in the middle ear but can affect the external and inner ear under some circumstances.

Middle Ear Squeeze. Middle ear squeeze takes place when the space between the tympanic membrane (ear drum) and inner ear is not equalized by admitting extra air into the space through the eustachian tube (Fig. 7-2). This can happen because of poor equalization technique or because of an internal blockage or external pressure on the tube.

Fig. 7-2. The structure of the ear.

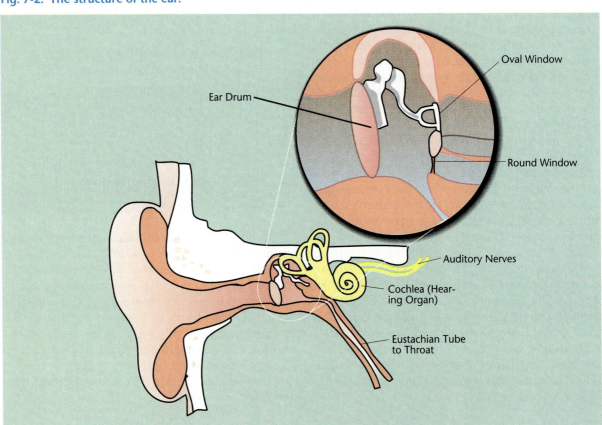

Equalization is easy for most divers, and a choice of several methods is available. Most divers use the Valsalva maneuver, in which the nostrils are pinched and the diver gently exhales against them. This creates slight back pressure that encourages air to enter the middle ear through the eustachian tube. Others use a Frenzl maneuver, combining jaw and facial movements similar to attempting to wiggle the ears and swallow at the same time, to open the eustachian tube and admit air to the middle ear. Many divers develop their own unique methods of equalizing pressure, from facial gyrations to specific head, neck, jaw, or swallowing movements.

While a diver is descending at the recommended rate or is stationary in the water column, all such momentary, minimal back pressure is virtually harmless and usually effective. However, if the back pressure applied is excessive, such as from too forceful or too long an exhalation, or through repeated attempts to force the ears to clear, damage to delicate tissue membranes can result. The same problems can stem from delayed or partial clearing, from attempting to clear while ascending, or any combination of these factors.

Too forceful or extended an exhalation can result in injury to delicate tissue in the middle and inner ear. The ear drum (tympanic membrane) can tear, allowing water to enter the middle ear through the external ear canal, causing pain and vertigo, sudden debilitating dizziness, and spatial disorientation. Literally not knowing which way is up is obviously a dangerous and frightening experience, even more so underwater. Complete or partial hearing loss can result if other membranes of the inner ear are similarly ruptured by excessively forceful clearing efforts (see Fig. 7-2). Bacteria admitted when an ear drum ruptures can easily cause a middle ear infection—a serious illness marked by high fevers, dizziness, nausea, and vomiting for an extended period.

Back pressure on the lung tissue brought on by continuing attempts to clear while inadvertently or deliberately rising through the water column, or a mistaken effort to clear a reverse block while continuing ascent, can result in tearing that will release air into the body or circulatory system. The effects of such errors or inattentiveness can be disastrous.

Delayed clearing, which can occur when a diver is already experiencing discomfort or pain on descent, can contribute to problems. In this case, the diver is already under stress, physically tense from the difficulty, and anxious to resolve it and get on with the dive. The muscular tension in the neck and throat area, from the pain and the urgency of dealing with it, can pinch the eustachian tube, defeating any efforts to equalize. This can lead to excessively forceful efforts and associated problems.

Equalization cannot be forced. Efforts to do so almost invariably will result in injury. NAUI recommends that all divers ensure their ability to clear before any dive, begin to clear on the surface, and continue throughout all descents well in advance of feeling the need to do so.

Divers who cannot equalize pressure or who experience discomfort or pain on descent are advised to stop trying to clear immediately, remove their hands from their faces, signal their buddies of the problem, and breathe continually while ascending at the normal rate until all discomfort is gone, even if this means surfacing. Never attempt to equalize while ascending. If at a shallower depth where there is no pain, appropriate efforts to clear are unsuccessful or pain again develops, postpone the dive until effective clearing is possible.

Outer Ear Squeeze. Outer ear squeeze is not usually a problem for healthy or knowledgeable divers, but it can occur, even in shallow descents, if the external ear canal is blocked. Wearing earplugs or a wet suit hood that covers the external ear too tightly, so that water is not allowed to enter before descent can create an artificial, temporary airspace between the ear drum and the external barrier. Since this space cannot be equalized except externally, a squeeze results.

Divers are advised never to descend below the surface with the ears blocked or plugged and to admit water to wet suit hoods before descending. Skin divers in particular are cautioned against the use of ear plugs, which will cause problems upon executing even a shallow surface dive. Besides outer ear squeeze, plugs may be driven deep into the ear canal by water pressure and the ear drum can be damaged by the partial vacuum created.

Difficulty Clearing on Descent?

STOP!

Take hands away from the face and breathe normally.

Ascend until all pain is gone.

Stabilize at the shallower depth, then GENTLY try again!

Sinus Squeeze

Sinuses are hollows in the skull bones, lined with mucous membrane (tissues) and most are connected to narrow airways that end in the nasal cavities (Fig. 7-3). They become literally squeezed when the air normally within them compresses upon descent and the slight vacuum created pulls the surrounding tissue into the space.

Healthy sinuses are equalized as a by-product of efforts to equalize the middle ear. If blocked by an active cold or infection, the residual effects of such illnesses, allergy, growths, or other damage, pain results. Although ignoring severe pain is unlikely, people have different tolerances. Others may believe that the pain will stop if they just put up with it for a while. In either case, continuing a descent will result in injury.

Sinus squeezes are usually signaled *after* the fact by blood in a dive mask beneath the nostrils or actual nosebleed after diving. Residual symptoms similar to severe headaches or facial pains like toothaches are common.

Ill effects are avoided easily by normal clearing methods and making sure of your fitness to participate before every dive. Some divers mistakenly hope to avoid sinus squeeze through the routine use of decongestants and nasal spray whenever diving. NAUI strongly condemns this practice because it can have dangerous side effects and may in fact lead to worse problems underwater. If the drug wears off while diving, severe increased swelling of the sinuses is likely to result. This will prevent normal air movement from the space on ascent (reverse sinus block), and return to the surface will be extremely painful.

Lung Squeeze

More a problem of skin divers than scuba divers, lung squeeze can result from deep surface dives or from breath-holding during a scuba descent. Air within the lungs compresses normally during any breath-holding descents. If the descent is very deep or prolonged, as is possible for experienced and talented skin divers, the normal elasticity of the chest cavity may be exceeded. Tissues and fluid can be drawn into the air sacs (alveoli) and into the lung passageways. Fluid may build up in the lungs, causing severe breathing difficulties. These same effects can result when a scuba diver forcibly exhales, emptying the lungs, and then descends without breathing, U*sing forceful inhalations or exhalations for buoyancy control while diving is a poor choice*.

Lung squeeze, also known as "thoracic (chest) squeeze," is avoided easily by common sense skin- and scuba-diving practices and by confining your diving to reasonably recommended limits.

Tooth Squeeze (Barodontalgia)

Though extremely unusual, poor dentistry or a hidden cavity beneath the gum line that creates a gas pocket in the tooth can lead to a tooth squeeze. Accompanied by excruciating pain, and possibly the loss of dental fillings, there is virtually no chance of continuing a dive comfortably with tooth squeeze.

NAUI recommends that all divers discuss their diving activities with their medical professionals, including dentists. Discussions usually will reveal any noteworthy medical concerns.

Gear Squeezes

Some dive equipment, notably dive masks and dry suits, is designed to create airspaces that must be equalized on descent. At other times, ill-fitting gear, most often wet suits, may create unwanted airspaces that can result in squeeze.

Mask Squeeze. The result of a mask squeeze, caused by failure to equalize pressure in the mask during descents, is dramatic and easy to spot. The diver's eyes will be red and blood-filled from the damage to capillaries around the surface of the eye, and the clear imprint of a dive mask will be etched into the face. There may be no pain except from the uncomfortable constriction of the mask, or the victim may feel soreness around the eyes caused by their having been literally pulled on by the vacuum that developed in the mask.

Fig. 7-3. The sinuses.

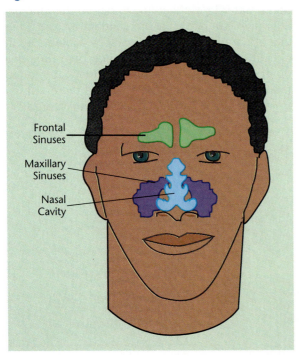

This problem can be avoided by simply remembering to exhale slightly through the nose into the mask after clearing the ears while descending (Fig. 7-4). It often appears on a second dive, in which a diver had a leaking mask through the first and overtightened the strap to avoid having to spend so much time clearing the mask on the next dive. With the mask on tight, the skirt up against the nostrils restricts usual slight exhalation, and the lack of any leakage removes the necessity to clear water from the mask during the dive. The victim believes the discomfort is from the tight mask and ignores it, providing amusement for companions upon surfacing. Fortunately, this is more a cosmetic issue than a serious injury. Cool compresses can relieve some discomfort and can control swelling.

Dry Suit Squeeze. Dry suits create an artificial airspace around the entire body, using the insulating properties of air to provide divers with increased comfort in colder water. As with other airspaces, this one requires equalization throughout a dive. Dry suit squeeze is unlikely to result in barotrauma, but it may have an effect on tissue gas transfer rates and retention that could invalidate normally recommended dive exposure limits. As a result, NAUI urges all dry suit users to become practiced in their proper use, including methods of avoiding squeezes, controlling buoyancy and trim, and unique emergency procedures, by seeking professional training from a qualified instructor.

Hood Squeeze. Hood squeeze can result in external ear squeeze, the mechanism and prevention of which have been described.

Ascent Squeezes

Barotrauma on ascent can occur if compressed air introduced to equalize pressure in natural or artificial airspaces on descent is not vented normally. It can happen also if gases produced naturally as a by-product of digestion become trapped in the body rather than exiting through the usual channels.

Reverse Blocks

The most common reverse block occurs when the middle ear is unable to release air upon ascent because of excessive tension or mucus in the eustachian tube. It also can occur when sinuses become swollen or inflamed during a dive, usually from excessive clearing efforts or misguided use of medications.

Reverse blocks have symptoms similar to their respective descent squeezes, ranging from mild to excruciating pain. Unlike descent squeezes, however, which can be relieved by returning to the surface, reverse blocks interfere with ascent. This generally happens at the end of a dive when the diver

Fig. 7-4. Normal mask clearing or slight exhalation into the mask while descending completely prevents mask squeeze.

has reached the planned minimum air for ascent or has neared the planned exposure limits. *Anything that prevents a diver from returning to the surface at the end of a dive, is serious and best dealt with by prevention.*

Divers who develop a reverse block in either ears or sinuses are advised to stop the ascent, descend slightly, and stabilize buoyancy. Immediately check air supply, depth, and time to determine whether running out of air soon is possible. Signal your buddy of the difficulty, and to make similar checks. Try to clear the block by "yawning-type" jaw movements, pinching the nose and gently swallowing, moving the head from side to side, or any individual maneuvers you may prefer. If there

Ascent Problem?
STOP!
Descend Slightly
Stabilize Buoyancy
Check Remaining Air and Time
Signal Your Buddy
Relax
RESPOND

is sufficient air, ascending extremely slowly, pausing at frequent intervals to attempt gentle efforts to clear and reduce pain before rising again, will likely be effective in clearing the block or relieving its worst effects. Remaining air and time should be carefully monitored throughout such an ascent.

If low on air with a reverse block, divers must judge whether there will be enough air available to make a shared-air ascent. If you are forced to make an emergency ascent with a reverse block, serious injury will be the likely result. This underscores the desirability of effective prevention.

Reverse blocks are prevented by making certain of your fitness to dive, including the ability to clear, not using medications to "aid" diving, and the complete absence of any temporary contraindications to diving that may affect equalization.

Gut Squeeze

A gut squeeze can develop if a diver has eaten or drunk excessive amounts of gas-producing liquids or foods before diving. Digestion and digestive gas production will continue throughout the dive. These gases, like any other, will expand on ascent. If trapped internally, their expansion will result in severe abdominal pain, particularly in the lower intestinal area. Sometimes assuming a horizontal position momentarily, or rotating while horizontal, will help relieve such pains by causing the gas to exit normally. If not, the pain usually can be relieved by slowing the ascent rate to allow the gas to dissipate through the intestine. Again, this is possible only with sufficient remaining air and time, and highlights the need for conservative dive planning, including air consumption calculations for every dive. Obviously, avoiding foods and beverages that produce gas when diving is the easiest method of preventing gut squeeze.

DECOMPRESSION ILLNESS

NAUI uses the term decompression illness (DCI) to cover the various ascent-related lung overexpansion injuries (pulmonary barotrauma), or to describe syndromes associated with the excessive or uncontrolled release of formerly dissolved inert gases—commonly called decompression sickness (DCS). Either can occur at any time during any ascent while you are breathing compressed air (or other mixtures) underwater, or as a result of even gradual reductions in ambient pressure, such as when surfacing at the end of a dive.

The likelihood of DCI when following prudent diving practices within published exposure limits is extremely small. Nevertheless, until the actual mechanisms of gas transfer in humans under increased pressure are better understood and documented by the scientific community, the risk of DCI exists on every dive. As a result, learning as much as possible to reduce or prevent factors that increase the possibility of DCI, and learning to recognize and deal with the injuries it may cause, are essential for any rescuer.

Lung Overexpansion Injuries

Whenever the internal pressure of the lungs is greater than the ambient pressure, lung tissue—extremely fine and normally pliant—expands. This happens every time a person breathes. However, if the difference between the internal (lung) and external (ambient) pressures continues to increase, such as when expanding air underwater is trapped, by some previous damage to the lung or by voluntary or accidental breath-holding upon ascent, lung tissue will rupture. When it does, the air or other breathing gas it contained will escape. Depending upon the amount of air or gas that escapes and where it goes, a variety of injuries, some of which can be fatal, can result.

Avoiding the problems associated with lung overexpansion, which can occur at any depth, is easy for healthy divers. Simply maintaining continual breathing throughout all scuba dives will virtually eliminate the possibility, but there are times when breath-holding may unwittingly occur. A diver coughing or choking underwater is interrupting normal breathing. The same is true for sneezing or vomiting. E*qualizing*, part of every dive, is a momentary interruption of normal breathing, and is accompanied by deliberately increased back pressure on

---

Even momentary breath-holding on scuba can lead to injury!

NEVER HOLD YOUR BREATH

Whether coughing, sneezing, or experiencing other breathing difficulty:

STOP!!

Stabilize at depth until completely under control and again breathing normally!

Continue your dive, or ascend, at your option.

the lungs and other delicate tissues. Some divers use momentary breath-holding or unusually large inhalations as tools to help stabilize buoyancy. Whatever the cause, deliberate or not, breath-holding on scuba can lead to overexpansion injuries in ascents as small as 3 to 5 feet (1 to 1.5 m) of sea water (FSW).

Any lung disease, such as asthma, emphysema, or advanced stages of tuberculosis (TB), is an absolute contraindication to participating in scuba because of the unacceptably increased risk of overexpansion injuries, as detailed in Chapter One. Smokers are advised to be cautious for the same reasons: reduced lung function and other physical damage associated with long-term use of tobacco.

Mediastinal and Subcutaneous Emphysema

Emphysema, besides being a chronic lung disease, describes any condition in which air, or another gas, expands in part of the body or an internal organ, swelling it. The mediastinum is the mid-chest area around the heart, one of the first places that air leaking from the lungs will go. Enough air in this space can actually shift the heart and attached blood vessels. From there, air can rise through the chest cavity, along the outside of the trachea, and accumulate in the neck and shoulders. This air causes subcutaneous (literally, "under the skin") emphysema (Fig. 7-5).

Though neither condition may in itself be life-threatening, any evidence of air leaking from ruptured lung tissue is extremely serious. The presence of mediastinal or subcutaneous emphysema is best considered a warning to rescuers that the victim's problems may be just beginning.

Signs and Symptoms. Mediastinal emphysema may have no external signs, or there can be pronounced breathing difficulty and shortness of breath. This can be accompanied by circulatory distress caused by air pressure around the heart and major blood vessels. Erratic pulse may be detected, as well as the usual signs of shock, if there is a major air leak.

Symptoms will include difficulty breathing and pain directly under the breastbone, as well as those of shock if enough air has leaked and expanded to displace the heart or other organs.

Subcutaneous emphysema also may be difficult to detect unless sufficient air has accumulated to "bubble up" under the skin in the neck and shoulder areas. This skin will crackle if touched as air migrates between layers of tissue. The voice may change, depending on whether the trachea is displaced or there is pressure on the voice box.

There may be no symptoms other than a feeling of fullness in the neck, or mild pain from the air movement caused by being touched by curious dive companions.

Recommended Treatment. Mild mediastinal and subcutaneous emphysema, even if unaccompanied by any evidence of other injury, require professional medical evaluation. If no breathing distress or other signs or symptoms of injury are present, divers suspected of these injuries should be carefully monitored and brought to a physician at the earliest opportunity. Breathing oxygen may help accelerate the absorption and elimination of subcutaneous air, and, if sufficient supply is available, can do no harm in the interim. A series of brief neurological examinations also is a wise precaution to help identify or rule out more extensive problems.

If the injury resulted from a rapid ascent for any reason, or if the incident included any period of unconsciousness underwater or on the surface, or if it is accompanied by any difficulty breathing, with or without chest pain, initiate immediate evacuation for professional assessment by qualified emergency medical personnel.

Major cases of emphysema almost invariably are only one of a group of life-threatening overexpansion injuries that will likely require life support, oxygen administration, and recompression therapy.

Pneumothorax

Pneumothorax ("air in the chest") results when any amount of air escapes, usually from a ruptured alveoli, and enters the space between the lungs and surrounding pleural membrane (the pleural cavity) (see Fig. 7-5). Even a relatively small amount of air can cause a partial collapse of the lung when free air expands on ascent and applies external pressure on the lobe.

If the air leak continues through the ascent or is initially of high volume, pressure around the lung continues to increase as the space between the lung and pleura fills with expanding air. Eventually the entire lung collapses, a condition termed tension pneumothorax. When this happens, the heart and attached blood vessels and other organs are displaced. Circulation and breathing are severely impaired and life-threatening shock ensues.

Signs and Symptoms. External signs of tension pneumothorax are various forms of respiratory distress: wheezing, choking, coughing, and difficulty catching one's breath. These may occur underwater or at the surface. Shock will be present and life support probably will be needed. There likely will be bloody sputum in and around the mouth. Breathing difficulty may result in cyanosis, a blue pallor to the skin and nail beds. Chest movement from respiration will be uneven and labored, with the affected side appearing stationary. The trachea (windpipe) also will be displaced towards the injured side, and the victim will favor the painful side.

The diver will feel sharp, sudden, possibly intense pain, especially in the case of tension pneumothorax, and distress associated with the problems noted previously.

Fig. 7-5. The chest cavity and lungs.

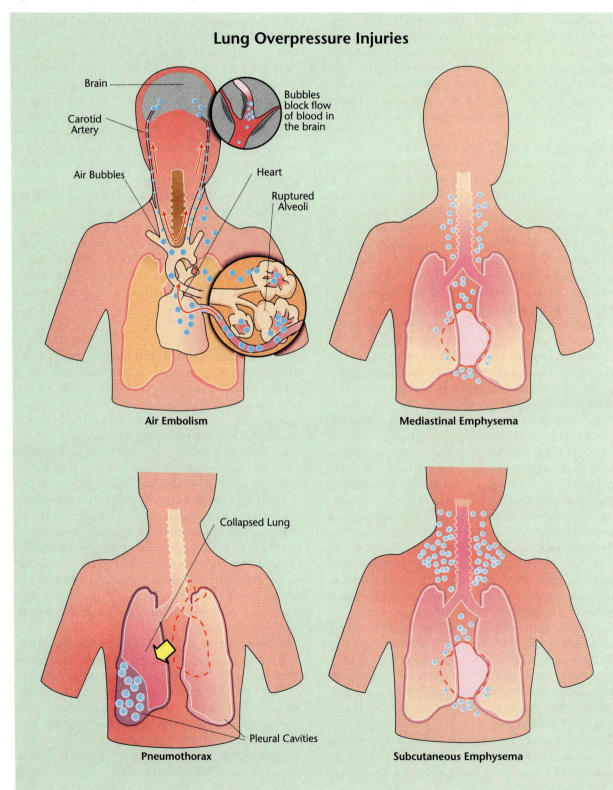

Recommended Treatment. Suspected pneumothorax, accompanied by life-threatening respiratory distress and shock, obviously requires immediate evacuation to an emergency medical facility. The offending air probably will be removed by insertion of a catheter, followed by a period of hospitalization and extended convalescence. Recompression therapy may be recommended to aid reabsorption of trapped air. On-site oxygen therapy, continuing through evacuation, may be extremely helpful.

Arterial Gas Embolism (AGE)

Arterial Gas Embolism (AGE) is the most immediately life-threatening result of lung overexpansion injury. It occurs when almost any amount of air escapes through lung perforation into the pulmonary capillary bed, the finest blood vessels that enclose the lungs and in which gas exchange occurs. This air is carried as bubbles through the venous system into the left chambers of the heart, where it is pumped along the arterial system carrying oxygenated blood throughout the body.

As the diver continues to ascend, these bubbles expand and may coalesce. Concurrently the bubble(s) are carried further into ever finer blood vessels. Eventually, driven by circulation and enlarging because of Boyle's Law, the air lodges. This creates a plug (embolus) beyond which the flow of tissue-nourishing arterial blood is severely restricted or even completely blocked. The trapped expanding air causes injury-driven changes in the interior structure of the blood vessel and blood chemistry. Clotting and swelling further restrict normal blood flow. Downstream of this blockage, tissues starved for nutrient-rich, oxygenated arterial blood, and unable to have waste products removed, begin to die.

This blockage can occur anywhere, but produces the most serious results when it occurs in the brain, the area where the blood vessels are finest and unimpeded circulation is most crucial to life.

Signs and Symptoms. The signs of AGE are virtually identical to those of stroke, another cerebral circulation trauma. Initially, signs can be extremely subtle, so that AGE may not be recognized until the victim's condition is significantly worse. Noticing subtle signs is difficult unless you are acutely aware of the possibility and especially observant. These can include difficulty walking or standing, speech impairment, agitation, anxiety-related behaviors, or personality changes. Signs of AGE may progress rapidly from mild to severe. Obvious signs can include sudden unconsciousness immediately upon surfacing or underwater, partial or complete blindness, or any combination of the previously mentioned problems. Since AGE is the ultimate result of a lung overexpansion injury, any of the previously detailed over-pressure injuries' signs can be present also, from breathing difficulty to coughing and choking with or without the presence of blood or chest pain.

AGE is generally revealed within 5 minutes of surfacing. Any diver found unconscious at the surface, or who becomes unconscious soon after a dive, or who has other signs of lung overexpansion injury may be a victim of AGE. Rescuers need to be alert at all times to the behavior and condition of dive companions, especially soon after a dive, for any unusual behavior that could be an early sign of AGE.

Symptoms can include visual disturbances, hallucinations, severe headache, nausea, dizziness, shortness of breath, numbness, weakness, tingling, lack of muscular control, and inability to concentrate. Difficulties are most likely to be confined to one side of the body. Symptoms of lung overexpansion injuries, including severe chest pain, also may be present.

Recommended Treatment. It is extremely probable that all manifestations of lung overexpansion injuries will occur in rapid succession or even concurrently in a victim. In any event, the treatment for AGE includes providing necessary life support and oxygen at as high an inspired rate as may be maintained throughout immediate evacuation for medical care and emergency medical care. Without timely recompression, the likelihood of survival is low and the chance of residual disability is high. Shock always will accompany AGE.

Rescuers are advised that the suspicion of AGE, even if dramatic signs are absent, is sufficient cause to administer oxygen, activate emergency medical services, and initiate immediate evacuation.

Decompression Sickness (DCS)

Decompression sickness (DCS) is the result of uncontrolled release of formerly dissolved inert gases (mainly nitrogen) into the tissues or bloodstream (Fig. 7-6). In diving, DCS is usually caused by some combination of exceeding recommended depth and time exposure limits and returning too quickly to the surface. Under these circumstances, nitrogen that has been absorbed into the tissues

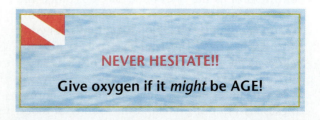

NEVER HESITATE!!
Give oxygen if it *might* be AGE!

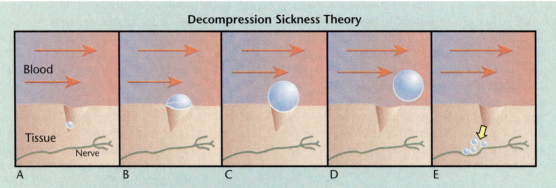

Decompression Sickness Theory

Nitrogen dissolved in tissue will form bubbles when the difference between the internal pressure of the diver and the ambient pressure increases too quickly or sharply. This may happen when a diver ascends too fast or has absorbed a large amount of nitrogen through prolonged or increased exposure, or due to environmental or individual physiologic factors. These bubbles are microscopic in size at first and are believed to originate from tiny gas pockets in the walls of tissues (A). Excess nitrogen during decompression dissolves into the microscopic pockets, causing them to enlarge and extend into the circulatory path (B) until they finally break free and become tiny bubbles (C-D), or they may continue to grow within the tissue itself (E). When they grow large enough to press on nerve tissue or disrupt circulation, pain or other symptoms result.

During an ascent, the volume of a microscopic bubble increases due to Boyle's Law. Gas pressure within the bubble decreases and the gradient (difference in pressure) between gas dissolved in surrounding tissue and the bubble increases. More gas is then drawn into the bubble causing it to grow larger. Therefore, bubbles not only grow because of Boyle's Law, but because of the inward diffusion of gas. Recompression, on the other hand, compresses bubbles and increases their internal pressure. Nitrogen then diffuses out of the bubbles back into solution in the tissues. Oxygen applied at increased pressures during recompression therapy augments the process by nourishing bubble-damaged tissues and helping to drive excess nitrogen from the system.

Fig. 7-6. Bubbles form in tissue surrounding joints and exert pressure on nerve sheaths.

at ambient pressure underwater, as explained by Henry's and Dalton's laws, can leave the tissues as gas. These nitrogen bubbles in tissue and blood will cause injury depending on where, and how much, nitrogen gas is released.

In theory, adequate time for gradual decompression provided by a normal ascent rate, and stage decompression, or limited exposures within recommended "no decompression limits," allows excess nitrogen to remain in solution until recirculated to the lungs via the venous system. There, the difference (gradient) between the amount and internal pressure of dissolved gas from the dive, and the amount of gas that can be held in solution under the decreasing ambient pressure of ascent, augmented by the normal pressure changes of breathing, causes nitrogen to return to the gaseous state and be exhaled normally. It is generally believed that disruptions in the process, from either the dive's events (depth, time, ascent rate) or unique physical factors of the diver, can result in DCS.

Certain physical factors have been revealed as contributors to the likelihood of DCS. Since the amount of gas that can remain dissolved in any liquid is limited by the amount of liquid, dehydration can increase the chance of DCS and may aggravate its seriousness. (Dehydration is more fully discussed in Chapter Three.) Other physical factors include any that affect circulation, normal in-gassing and out-gassing, or the ability of blood to reach and serve tissues (perfusion). These can include age, physical conditions such as previous injuries or circulatory diseases, or life-style choices such as smoking and drinking alcoholic beverages. Obesity may elevate the chance of DCS because nitrogen is more soluble in lipid (fat) tissues, and hence more nitrogen may be absorbed than accounted for in published exposure limits. (Most of these factors are discussed more fully in Chapter One.) Circulatory system changes from strenuous exercise soon after diving, immersion in very hot water, or exposure through high temperatures like spas or saunas can contribute to the incidence of DCS. Diving at altitude without making recommended adjustments to account for decreased ambient atmospheric pressure and fresh water as taught in altitude diving specialty courses can also result in DCS.

Other factors, such as diving in cold water or under arduous conditions, or diving while fatigued and thereby working harder, can increase the amount of gas absorbed under pressure, possibly invalidating some assumptions in published exposure limits such as the NAUI Dive Tables. This is why NAUI recommends that divers assess their own fitness before any dive, and plan and dive conservatively at all times.

For instance, NAUI advises divers to terminate a dive immediately when chilling occurs, and to increase their actual exposure time for planning a

> **When planning a repetitive dive:**
>
> If you became **COLD,** increase your time by one interval.
>
> If you worked **HARD,** increase your time by one interval.
>
> Increase **TWO INTERVALS** when **BOTH** apply!!

repetitive dive to the next higher table interval. (Hence, a 60 FSW (18 MSW) dive for up to 30 minutes in which a diver became chilled would be considered to have lasted 40 minutes for planning subsequent dives.) On strenuous dives also, divers are advised to use the next greater time interval as the starting point for planning a repetitive dive. The effect of these adjustments is to increase the amount of residual nitrogen that divers will have to account for in future dives, reflecting the (probably) increased absorption and retention of nitrogen caused by the dive's circumstances. Both adjustments are required for cold and arduous dives. (More complete information on dive planning, including underlying theories of dive tables and altitude adjustment is included in NAUI's text *Advanced Diving: Technology and Techniques.*)

DCS is divided into two types for purposes of academic discussion, though such distinctions are meaningless in the field. All suspected DCS requires medical evaluation. DCS Type I is decompression sickness in which the only symptom is pain, generally in joints, or which affects only the skin. DCS Type II may include joint pain, but mainly affects the central or peripheral nervous systems and usually is accompanied by shock and life-threatening respiratory distress. Unlike AGE, in which effects are usually confined to one side of a victim, DCS Type II can affect both sides of a diver at once, or can appear localized to a specific area like the arm or leg. Type II DCS is initially far more serious and dramatic, but all DCS is dangerous.

There are few studies of the long-term effects of decompression sickness or even of repeated diving exposures. Some studies have indicated that *even recommended exposures may cause bubbling in some people,* albeit without apparent signs or symptoms, *on nearly every dive.* These studies have also indicated that this bubbling (sometimes termed "silent bubbles," or "asymptomatic decompression sickness") can be reduced or eliminated by combining a slower ascent rate (around 30 FSW/minute (9 MSW)) with a precautionary decompression stop at a depth of 15 FSW (5 MSW) for a period of 3 minutes on every scuba dive in excess of 30 FSW (9 MSW) (Fig. 7-7). As a result, NAUI recommends that divers follow these procedures and plan air consumption to include sufficient supply to complete precautionary stops.

The wide range of human physiology and intricate relationships between various contributing factors makes DCS a problem that cannot be completely prevented. Some risk of DCS attends every dive, even those well within recommended no-decompression limits.

Type I DCS (Pain Only)

Pain-only DCS is believed to occur when a limited amount of nitrogen bubbles collect in the tissues in and around joints. The external pressure of these bubbles against nerves and (possible) internal tissue damage in the area causes pain.

Very mild DCS Type I may only affect the skin and/or lymphatic system, so-called "skin bends." Mild intermittent pains, colloquially called "niggles," may accompany this very moderate form of DCS. Such pains generally pass in a short time, usually within minutes.

Even so, all decompression sickness is serious. Pain only, or relatively pain-free "skin bends," are still evidence of uncontrolled nitrogen release. The possibility of increasing difficulty and a severely worsening condition always exists. The pain may mask neurological signs and symptoms that are difficult to detect without repeated, systematic examination.

Fig. 7-7. A precautionary stop at 15 feet (5 m) for 3 minutes at the end of every dive will significantly reduce the chance of decompression sickness.

Signs and Symptoms. A rash-type skin reddening after diving, usually on the torso, back, or arms, is a sign of DCS Type I. Such a rash would be especially indicative in areas that have been covered by exposure suits and therefore are not easily accessible to a sting or contact with allergic reaction-producing marine life. The symptoms of skin bends include burning and itching sensations, sometimes accompanied by mild and/or intermittent joint pains ("niggles") that pass within about 30 minutes.

Skin problems that occur with any joint pain—most often in the upper body, such as on fingers, wrists, elbows, and shoulders—are probably DCS. Pains can occur up to 24 hours or longer after diving, but they most likely begin from immediately upon surfacing to within about two hours afterward. Pain-only DCS Type I usually occurs without any skin indications.

Though there may be no apparent signs of pain-only DCS Type I, an observant rescuer may notice a diver favoring an arm or rubbing a shoulder or other area repeatedly, as if trying to deal with a strain or injury. Since DCS Type I is believed to be primarily caused by intrusive bubble pressure causing swelling that affects nerves, efforts to relieve it by rubbing will be unsuccessful. This can in fact provide a rescuer with a quick, rough tool for assessing such problems. If joint or limb pain after diving is unrelieved or unaffected by rubbing, it could well indicate DCS, especially if situational factors that might contribute to the incidence of DCS are present.

Recommended Treatment. Skin bends, or mild, intermittent pain that is completely gone after a short time ("niggles"), is still decompression sickness. Though these moderate instances of DCS Type I have little chance of apparent residual problems, only a qualified hyperbaric physician can make a thorough diagnosis. The diver should discontinue diving immediately. A victim of DCS Type I is best closely monitored for any other signs and symptoms of any decompression illness and assessed by a doctor at the earliest opportunity. In addition, any evidence of suspected DCS is ample justification for a rescuer to request that the diver submit to a series of brief neurological examinations as described below. These may reveal DCS Type II.

Divers experiencing any deep, aching, throbbing pains in the joints that are unaffected by changes in the limbs' position, or external pressure, especially if other factors that are implicated in DCS are present, are likely "bent." Any such pains may begin mildly but can escalate to incapacitating levels in a relatively short period. Progression in intensity, or movement along a limb, such as from hand to wrist to elbow to shoulder, help confirm the possibility of serious DCS.

Even pain-only DCS Type I requires immediate care and swift professional medical evaluation. Oxygen given at as high a partial pressure as possible for as long as necessary to transport the victim to the closest emergency medical facility for professional care is recommended. Oxygen may completely resolve or greatly relieve DCS Type I pain, further confirming the likelihood of DCS; however, relief is not cure.

Despite temporary relief, the possibility of more serious problems that can include permanent impairment still exists. As a result, NAUI recommends that *any diver with DCS be evaluated by a qualified diving physician as soon as possible.* A victim with joint pain only is fortunate if no other symptoms occur, but typically this is not the case.

DCS Type II (Neurological)

DCS Type II is any decompression sickness accompanied by serious functional impairment or respiratory distress. It is a life-threatening condition and can result in permanent residual neurological problems including blindness and paralysis. Unlike DCS Type I, in which bubbles are believed to affect only limited parts of the peripheral nervous system surrounding specific joints, or act on the skin or lymphatic system, DCS Type II affects the central nervous system (CNS) including the spinal cord and brain.

Despite the wide range of possible signs and symptoms, some characteristic types of DCS Type II have been identified. "Staggers" refers to DCS that affects balance and walking. "Chokes," though fortunately rare, describes DCS that includes pulmonary effects such as uncontrollable coughing and chest pain. Most frequently, DCS Type II will cause bilateral (two-sided) weakness and paralysis that appears in the upper or lower body, accompanied by areas of numbness and other neurological problems described below. The types noted can appear together. Any indication of DCS Type II is a life-threatening medical emergency. Act immediately.

Signs and Symptoms. DCS Type II can affect every function of a person, including the personality. Signs can include "staggers" or "chokes" as noted

ALL DCS IS SERIOUS!

Professional medical assessment is necessary for suspected victims.

Identifying the type of DCI a diver may have is less important than rapid treatment.

ACT IMMEDIATELY:

1. Call for evacuation.
2. Give oxygen.
3. Monitor constantly and reevaluate frequently.

above, unconsciousness, severe respiratory distress, loss of bowel and/or bladder control (either inability to control or perform normally), or personality changes like aggression or passivity. Sometimes mottled or marbleized skin in large patches that may rapidly change size, hue, and shape, precedes more serious effects. Do not confuse this with mild skin bends.

Any of these, or the symptoms below, may come and go in bizarre fashion and are likely to be accompanied by the signs and effects of shock detailed later. They are caused primarily when bubble incursion in the central nervous system and brain disrupts the normal transmission of neural impulses that control voluntary and involuntary functions. In short, nearly anything is likely to happen to a victim of DCS Type II, and none of it will be good. In addition to the direct bubble problems, secondary effects include damage to the nerve and brain tissues that can result in permanent disability for survivors.

Symptoms can include general and localized pain, especially chest, head, and neck pain, and severe respiratory or other distress such as anxiety. There may be dizziness, nausea, vertigo, visual disturbances, pronounced bilateral muscular weakness, paralysis, tingling, tinnitus (ringing in the ears), and loss or impairment of physical sensations such as touch, taste, sight, smell, and hearing. Rescuers should note the similarity of these signs and symptoms with those of AGE.

Recommended Treatment. DCS Type II, like AGE, is treated by immediate recompression under medical supervision, including interim administration of oxygen inspired at as high a partial pressure as possible throughout evacuation. Victims must be closely monitored because life support, including CPR or rescue breathing, likely will be required, especially if treatment is delayed.

Factors in the Recognition of DCI

DCI needs immediate treatment. Delay can lead to serious consequences that include permanent disability and death. Despite these facts, many divers are reluctant to admit to having DCI. Only one buddy of a pair may be affected, lending credence to the affected diver's claim that "I can't be bent!" Others may, through ignorance or bravado, refuse treatment. These factors place an additional burden on the rescuer.

Dealing With Denial

Denial is the term used to describe a person's refusal to believe unsettling or frightening information, despite facts or suspicions to the contrary. A rescuer may have to deal with a diver in denial in order to initiate treatment for DCI, though generally only in the earliest stages. The effects of delay, including unconsciousness or any of the other signs and symptoms, usually overcome or preclude the possibility of continued objections. Regardless, some of the worst effects of DCI may be prevented by timely administration of oxygen. Any delay in calling for evacuation or beginning transport to a recompression facility and professional emergency medical care can result in needless tragedy.

Denial comes from ignorance and fear, not only of the consequences of DCI, but also of disapproval because of the misconception the diver did something wrong. As noted, the diving community's current understanding of DCI is obviously incomplete. *People most frequently do get DCI from errors, but some divers just get DCI!* These facts, presented clearly, quietly, and privately, often will help a possibly afflicted diver to accept advice, evaluation, and treatment. This is no less true when the victim is yourself.

A Brief Neurological Examination

DCS Type I, or the earliest effects of AGE, is often difficult to detect or easy for divers to ignore or rationalize away. Sometimes a single complaint, such as a severe headache or a shoulder pain after diving, can have a number of possible causes, from a sinus squeeze to some form of DCI. Other divers may complain of great fatigue after a dive that was not particularly strenuous, or they may not feel like diving any more after an initial dive. Though most likely these are just normal feelings, they could be early signs of DCI.

Some diving events, such as any emergency or shared-air ascent, aborting a dive due to difficulty equalizing, or requiring assistance to return to a dive's exit point, are often precursors to DCI, though the diver(s) may have no immediate symptoms. Or DCS Type I-joint pain or skin rash may mask neurological-involvement DCS Type II until it becomes unhappily apparent, even resulting in permanent damage caused by delayed or omitted treatment. For all these reasons, NAUI recommends that rescuers administer brief neurological examinations to divers who have any signs or symptoms of DCI, have had underwater emergencies, or have been forced to terminate any dive in an unusual manner (Fig. 7-8).

Discovering neurological impairment takes subtle, systematic examination and keen observation and questioning. Learning to perform a complete field neurological exam that will yield useful information is an important skill that will take practice and coaching outside this course. Your NAUI instructor can recommend courses of additional training in this area.

Examining for Neurological Effects. A neurological exam is best conducted from the head down. The rescuer begins in position behind the supine diver, who is positioned comfortably so that the sun or other strong light source is behind the rescuer, if possible.

Checking for Sense, Senses, and Sensation. Simple direct questions about the events of the dive, the diver's identity, and current whereabouts will help determine if the victim is fully conscious and aware. Both the ability to answer questions appropriately and to articulate words without speech impairment or undue hesitation are important.

Fig. 7-8. A brief neurological examination can be performed on a seated diver.

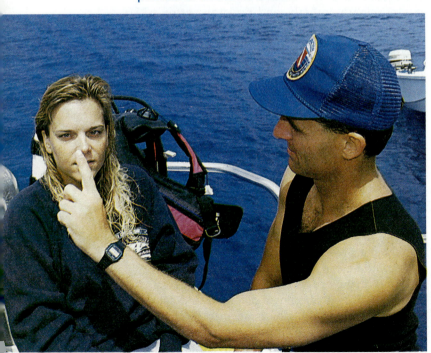

Check vision by leaning forward over the diver, watching the eyes, and moving from side to side while talking to the diver. The eyes should be responsive, following the rescuer's movements. Pupils should be evenly sized, and open and close appropriately when exposed to light. Both eyes should blink normally.

Check hearing by rubbing the fingers gently together out of the patient's peripheral vision, on either side, and ask the diver to describe what is heard, if anything. Repeat the test several times, alternating sides, testing both ears simultaneously, and asking the same questions with no sound being produced to rule out uncertainty or defeat efforts to fool you.

If possible, make the diver laugh and observe the facial muscles for normal movement. Asking the diver to smile or frown or grimace will produce the same results. Another check of facial muscles is to have the diver extend the tongue, moving it from side to side and up and down rapidly. This often will result in laughter. Ask the diver to swallow and observe the throat and Adam's apple move and neck muscles move appropriately and evenly on both sides. Check for symmetry in all facial movements.

Sensation is the ability to feel touch, and touching any diver must be done with the utmost care to avoid any semblance of inappropriate behavior. Despite having asked permission to conduct the exam, it is recommended that rescuers ask again before placing their hands on the diver.

Run the fingers lightly over the scalp and down the neck. Ask the diver to identify where the touch is felt, such as back of the head, top of the head, ear lobe, left side of the neck, etc. Repeat and alternate movements and ask the same questions when not touching the diver to avoid being fooled. Continue the examination from the side, with the hands preferably remaining outside the diver's vision. Examine up and down the insides of both arms and the chest and abdomen, then check the legs.

While examining, observe the diver's respiration for any signs of distress, noting the number of breaths per minute. Continue to monitor respiration rate and quality for any signs of developing problems. Also check the radial and carotid pulse while handling the head and neck and checking the wrists. Re-check vital signs at various points throughout the exam.

Examining for Strength and Function. Check the strength of the neck, hands, arms, and legs. Note any marked weakness, or uneven ability. Have the diver push the head up gently against a restraining hand on the forehead, and push down against a

DECOMPRESSION SICKNESS
or the effects of a
LUNG OVEREXPANSION INJURY
can rapidly become
life-threatening even if a diver
is on oxygen and regardless of the
lack of signs or symptoms!!

BE PREPARED TO INITIATE LIFE SUPPORT FOR ANY DIVER SUSPECTED OF DCI.

hand on the back of the head. Be careful not to drop the diver's head! Ask the diver to roll the head from side to side against resisting hands.

Have the diver squeeze the rescuer's hand in either hand, then pull against the rescuer's resisting arms. Have the diver clasp hands across the abdomen, and lift up, then pull down against the rescuer's resistance. Perform similar tests on the feet and legs, having the diver push and pull against the rescuer's strength. Rescuers are cautioned to use only enough strength to provide a test of the diver's function and ability. This is not a competitive test of strength. Effort should be appropriately moderate, particularly if you are dealing with a smaller or apparently weaker diver.

Checking Balance and Coordination. With the diver standing, have the diver stretch out the arms at shoulder height and quickly bring the index fingers together overhead. Ask that the movement be repeated two or three times to ensure accurate evaluation of ability.

Have the diver, still standing, lean back and close the eyes. Ask the diver to place the index fingers of either hand in turn on the tip of the nose. Ask the diver to walk heel-to-toe for a distance, turn sharply, and return. Conducting any of these exams may be difficult on a boat. The diver may be seated, if necessary, and checking gait may not be possible.

Assessment. If there is a physical reason to suspect DCI, for instance joint pain or any other signs or symptoms, the brief neurological assessment can be conducted while the diver is on oxygen to avoid treatment delay. If the examination is being conducted as a result of a diving incident, like an emergency ascent, it may reveal a diving malady, or may only increase the rescuer's suspicion that DCI is present. Suspecting DCI is ample reason to begin treatment. There is virtually no harm to beginning a diver on oxygen. Certainly begin treatment if there are any areas of apparent numbness, sensory or muscular disability, or pronounced asymmetrical ability, that are abnormal for the diver.

Additional Considerations. Any examination conducted on a conscious diver requires the diver's permission. Securing permission is the rescuer's first job, and it may be harder than actually conducting an examination.

Deciding how to approach a diver who may have DCI requires tact. The individual may be highly stressed or frightened. Denial may also be at work, making the task even harder. The wide variety of possible circumstances makes specific advice on approaches impossible, but there are some general issues rescuers can consider.

Time is Of the Essence. Generally speaking, giving a diver oxygen will not hurt; and delaying doing so, if needed, most certainly will. NAUI recommends that rescuers act immediately if DCI is suspected. Though confronting the diver is stressful, the rescuer has the responsibility to inform the diver that the examination ought to be conducted at once and treatment begun immediately if circumstances warrant it. Most of the time this is best done as soon as the diver is out of the water.

Present the request in a matter-of-fact way, joining it to the event that led to assistance, for instance, saying, "Now that we're back, let's make sure that everything's okay. I'd like to check you out with a simple exam." If the diver(s) agree(s), fine. If not, explain your qualifications and the need for the examination, including any signs noticed. This often will secure cooperation.

Diving leaders may have some advantages in securing permission for the examination and may have more responsibility to perform the examination, and begin timely treatment. It may be the diving operator's or leader's policy to conduct exams or give oxygen in some situations. This should be included in the diving event information so that divers are aware of it before participating. In any case, if an examination or oxygen is refused, diving leaders especially are advised to document the refusal, asking the individual(s) to state the refusal in writing.

Documentation is Important. Maintaining a record of the examination, which includes time of the exam, signs and symptoms discovered, time of any reexaminations, and any treatment begun, will enable subsequent treatment providers to assess the progress of a victim. Such a record includes all pertinent information, from the personal contact information about the diver, to the dive's profile or any unusual incident such as a rapid ascent that the diver experienced.

Privacy. Examinations should be conducted to protect the privacy of the diver. Curious onlookers add stress and distract rescuers. Use a sheltered area away from distractions whenever possible, such as a cabin on a dive boat, or a near area of the beach. Use assistants to help secure the area, if necessary.

Preexisting Conditions. Discussions of specific conditions beforehand are usually not wise because they may taint the examination; however, general questions such as simply asking "How are you feeling?" can reveal a great deal of useful information. There may be hearing loss in one ear, poor vision, or pronounced muscular weakness in one arm or leg that is perfectly normal for that diver. This type of information often is volunteered during the examination, but if not, discussion of any findings afterwards will avoid the embarrassment of unnecessary treatment or evacuation.

Repetitive Examination. There sometimes may be an inconclusive outcome to a neurological exam. Is pronounced weakness really present, or is it just normal function of a weak arm? The diver may have a preexisting condition that hampers accurate evaluation. Or there may be some DCI, and oxygen therapy has been initiated. In any of these cases, reexamining the diver after a brief interval of 15 to 30 minutes is recommended.

Having the baseline established by a previous examination will make subsequent examinations much more meaningful. If treatment was begun and symptoms are relieved, the original assessment is confirmed. If there has been no change after administering oxygen when uncertain, such as to a diver with a severe headache and nausea but no other symptoms, DCI may not be the problem.

Don't Forget the Buddy. People usually dive in pairs. If one buddy's dive profile, signs, and/or symptoms suggest the possibility of DCI, remember that the other buddy has made the same dive! Though there may be no early indication, a brief neurological exam and oxygen administration, if at all warranted and sufficient supply is available, cannot hurt. The same is true for any diver who may have helped another underwater, including qualified rescuers. Bringing another diver to the surface while sharing air, or just helping someone underwater, is stressful for both divers. Aiding another diver at the surface with a strenuous tow can result in injury to the rescuer, even DCI, if it occurs after a dive near the recommended limits or a repetitive dive.

RESPONDING TO DCI

Confirmed or strongly suspected DCI requires oxygen administration at as high a partial pressure as possible and immediate transport to a recompression facility for professional medical assessment and care (Fig. 7-9). Brief neurological assessment can aid in identification of subtle cases, but the presence of multiple signs and symptoms, which usually worsen rapidly, requires immediate action.

All cases of DCI, except for isolated instances of subcutaneous emphysema, skin bends, or "niggles," could be life-threatening emergencies. Life support including rescue breathing or CPR may be required, and rescuers who identify a victim should be prepared to initiate such measures. Careful, consistent monitoring of any DCI victim until passed on to emergency medical care personnel is mandatory.

Even without signs and symptoms of anything other than the mildest forms of DCI, field assessment alone cannot ensure that there are no more serious problems present, or that there will be no residual effect. The possible presence of any bubbles dramatically increases the probability of contracting serious decompression illness. Even if a diver is completely without signs or symptoms shortly after experiencing a possible DCI problem, returning to diving without professional evaluation by a qualified hyperbaric physician is unacceptably risky and foolhardy. A diver who has had any signs or symptoms of DCI, revealed through a series of brief neurological exams for suspected DCI, or who has received oxygen for a possible DCI problem, is also wise not to dive until having a complete exam for hidden ill effects.

Fig. 7-9. A, A multi-lock, multi-place recompression chamber with built-in breathing systems for oxygen therapy.

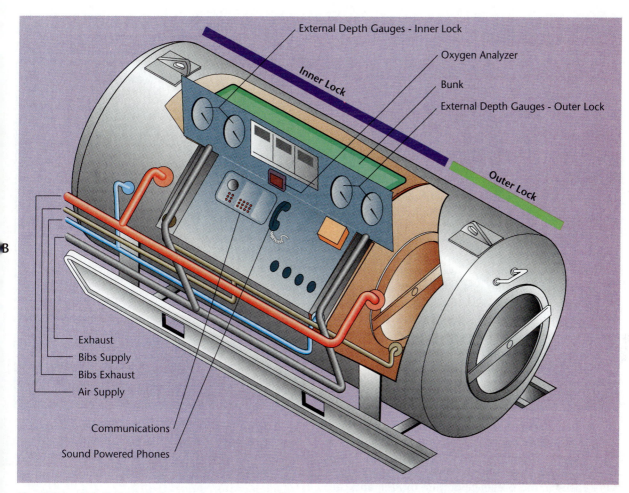

Fig. 7-9 cont'd. **B**, A typical recompression chamber suitable for treating an injured diver.

In fact, most DCI victims grow progressively worse. Even Type I DCS that is relieved by oxygen administration can worsen when the oxygen supply is depleted. This is what makes timely evacuation to professional care so important. Rescuers are advised to immediately activate emergency medical services for any but the mildest forms of DCI. In those cases, alerting emergency medical services of possible need and remaining in contact regularly throughout continuing assessment is suggested.

First Aid For Serious DCI

Unless they also are qualified medical personnel, rescuers are limited to providing DCI victims with first-aid support only. For most DCI problems, this means the ability to properly administer oxygen (Fig. 7-10), treat shock, and maintain life through rescue breathing and CPR until the victim is under the care of emergency medical personnel.

NAUI recommends having oxygen and a trained provider available for all diving events. Training and certification in oxygen administration is available from professional dive rescue-training companies, and from the Diver's Alert Network (DAN). All NAUI-certified rescuers should maintain appropriate current certification in first aid and cardiopulmonary resuscitation (CPR) from a recognized training agency such as the National Safety Council, Red Cross, or St. John's Ambulance.

The following is offered as an introduction to the field use of oxygen for diving maladies only. It is not intended to, nor can it, substitute for appropriate training and required certification in proper handling and administration techniques.

Oxygen Precautions

Though abundant in the atmosphere, pure oxygen, such as that used for DCI first aid, is a substance that must be handled carefully. An odorless, colorless gas, oxygen itself does not burn, but it is

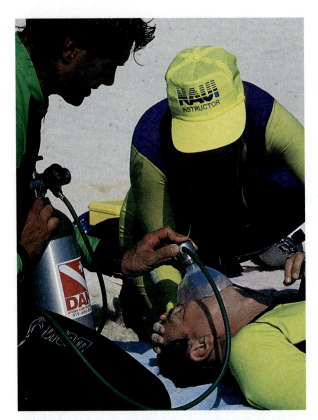

Fig. 7-10. A demand oxygen system gives a breathing victim the highest concentration of pure oxygen.

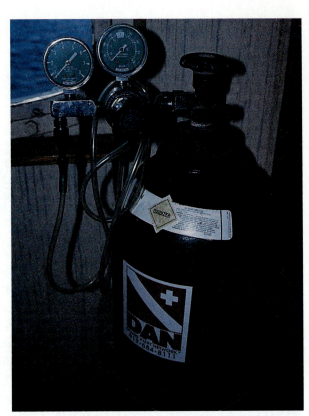

Fig. 7-11. A NAUI scuba center might have a large capacity oxygen cylinder, but the administration equipment will likely be identical to other demand systems.

one of the primary components of fire. Things burn very easily in the presence of pure oxygen and can seem to literally burst into flame when exposed to it. Any spark in an impure oxygen flow can cause a deadly explosion. The following precautions are recommended whenever oxygen is used:

1. Extinguish all flames and remove any other sources of ignition when using oxygen. NO SMOKING or OPEN FLAME!
2. Never shake, roll, or drop an oxygen cylinder. Handle all oxygen administration equipment as carefully as you would other life support equipment. Check cylinder contents by reading the gauge.
3. Use only "oxygen clean" equipment, including masks, tubing, regulators, etc., that is free of any grease or oils. All such items are preferably kept in similarly clean containers and only handled during an emergency. Petroleum products can ignite easily in the presence of pure oxygen. Normal body oils in high enough concentrations can, as well.

Oxygen Administration Systems

Oxygen administration systems consist of several components, each of which must be present and serviceable for a rescuer to initiate aid (Fig. 7-11). The basic parts of a system are a cylinder with a pin index valve and plastic o-ring, a "key" or handwheel for opening the cylinder to begin the flow, a dedicated, "oxygen-clean" (oil-free) regulator usually equipped with a pressure (contents) gauge and/or flow meter, sufficient oxygen-appropriate connecting hose, and an administration device. Suitable portable systems for diving first aid are available as components or complete, self-contained kits from various sources, including medical supply houses, rescue training companies, and DAN.

Most dive training facilities, dive resorts, and dive boats also have oxygen administration equipment on hand. These systems may be similar to what one might have in a personal O_2 kit, or they may include enough supply and administration gear to support several divers at once. Qualified rescuers are wise to request that they be allowed to familiarize themselves with available oxygen equipment whenever possible. Most trained providers working with divers will respond positively to such requests.

How Much Oxygen Is Necessary? The simple answer is, "As *much as you can carry!*" Oxygen is usually sold in standard-sized gas cylinders with volume measured in liters (approximately 1 quart), rather than the cubic-foot volumes with which divers are most familiar. See Table 7-1 for commonly available sizes.

Circumstances of the diving event will dictate how much is appropriate, but some guidelines will be useful. Under the best conditions, a victim will receive oxygen from the first sign of a problem until professional medical personnel take over. How long evacuation to such care is likely to take is a fundamental issue to consider when planning how much oxygen to have available. For most diving, at least an hour's supply is warranted. How much oxygen constitutes an hour's supply will depend on how it is administered.

TABLE 7-1 OXYGEN CYLINDER SIZES

CYLINDER TYPE	LITER VOLUME	APPLICATION
C	200	Portable (Often used in pairs)
D	350	"
E	626	Portable
M	3000	Boat or training facility

Freeflow Equipment. Many oxygen systems consist solely of freeflow equipment. Using a variety of face masks or a nasal cannula for administration, this gear ultimately delivers a relatively small amount of inspired oxygen to a victim because the pure oxygen mixes with ambient air before inhalation. As a result, it is less desirable for treating the breathing victim of DCI than other methods discussed below. Regardless of drawbacks, any amount of oxygen that a victim receives will be better than receiving no oxygen at all.

This type of system may have only an on/off valve (constant-flow system) with or without a cylinder contents gauge, or it may have a flow regulator that can be set to provide a chosen amount of gas release (adjustable constant flow), which is greatly preferred.

In some areas, only freeflow equipment is allowed for nonmedical professionals. Rescuers are advised to familiarize themselves with the local regulations under which they customarily operate by contacting the agency that provided them oxygen administration training, their instructor, or the local medical professional associations.

Nasal Cannula. Suitable for either type of freeflow system, a nasal cannula is essentially a plastic oxygen tube with two prongs that are inserted into a breathing victim's nostrils. Nasal cannulas are generally the least desirable means of providing oxygen to the breathing victim of a diving malady; however, when worn by a rescuer administering rescue-breathing to a victim ("oxygen-augmented rescue breathing"), they can greatly increase the amount of inspired oxygen the non-breathing victim receives.

A nasal cannula usually enriches the oxygen content of inspired air to the wearer to about 28% to 36%. Normally set at flow rate between 4 and 6 L per minute to avoid uncomfortably drying out the nasal passageways, simple arithmetic yields the corresponding times for the cylinders noted in Table 7-2.

Pocket Mask™. A pocket mask that includes a one-way valve between the mask and rescuer, equipped with oxygen inlet, is recommended for use on a non-breathing victim. With the flow rate set at about 10 L per minute, a well-sealed pocket mask can almost triple the amount of inspired oxygen that a nonbreathing victim would receive through rescue breathing with the rescuer wearing a nasal cannula (Fig. 7-12).

TABLE 7-2

CYLINDER AND VOLUME CAPACITY	TIME @ 5 LITERS/ MINUTE FLOW RATE
"C" Cylinder/ 200 L	40 minutes
"D" Cylinder/ 350 L	1 hour, 10 minutes
"E" Cylinder/ 626 L	2 hours, 5 minutes

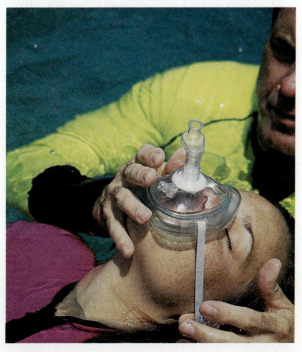

Fig. 7-12. Note the oxygen inlet on this pocket mask. A nonbreathing victim can receive a much higher concentration of inspired oxygen from oxygen-augmented rescue breathing with a pocket mask.

Standard Face Mask. This plastic mask fits loosely over the wearer's mouth and nose, allowing air to enter the mask and dilute the oxygen. Twin exhaust ports, usually on either side, allow exhaled air to exit freely. Suitable for breathing victims only, most face masks are used at a flow rate between 10 and 12 L per minute to ensure that excess CO_2 does not build up in the mask. At this rate, oxygen will last a little less than half the times shown above, making multiple "C" and "D" cylinders advisable, and an "E" cylinder a bare minimum, to achieve an hour's worth of oxygen.

Standard face masks boost the inspired oxygen content of a breathing victim's air supply to approximately 30% to 45% under ideal conditions. With the goal being to deliver as close as possible to 100% inspired oxygen for a diving malady, this amount is marginal. Furthermore, even achieving this relatively low percentage requires careful fitting of the mask in a well-sheltered, wind-free area, conditions that may be difficult to achieve at an accident site.

Partial Rebreather Mask. Equipped with a reservoir bag that must be primed (partially filled with oxygen) prior to being placed on a breathing victim, a partial rebreather mask allows some expired air to mix with incoming oxygen, increasing the effective oxygen administered. Under ideal conditions, a partial rebreather mask can enrich inspired oxygen to 30% to 50% for a breathing victim.

Non-Rebreather Mask. Also equipped with a reservoir bag that requires priming, the non-rebreather mask has a one-way valve between the mask and bag. As a result, each inhalation is nearly completely oxygen, with only a small amount of ambient air admitted, determined primarily by the mask's fit. This mask can provide a breathing victim with up to 75% inspired oxygen. As a result, it is the most useful type of freeflow oxygen administration equipment for a breathing victim.

Demand Systems. A demand oxygen system is a sophisticated piece of medical equipment. Working like a scuba system, except using oxygen instead of air, demand equipment delivers close to 100% oxygen on each breath, making demand systems the most preferable type for the treatment of DCI (Fig. 7-13). In some areas, possession or use of such systems may be restricted. Check your area.

Some demand systems are equipped with a positive-pressure second stage, making them identical to a common scuba regulator equipped with a second-stage purge valve. In the hands of a medical professional, a positive-pressure demand oxygen system can provide a nonbreathing victim with close to 100% inspired oxygen, even under field conditions. However, without special training and certification, using a positive-pressure oxygen system entails a chance of causing or exacerbating a lung overexpansion injury.

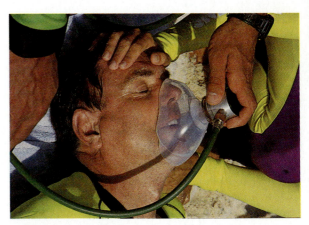

Fig. 7-13. A demand system can be used on an unconscious diver as long as the victim is breathing.

Rescuers should note that positive-pressure oxygen administration equipment exceeds the usual definitions of first aid. However, many diving excursions include medically trained and certified personnel. New systems with pressure relief mechanisms to prevent overinflation are also becoming available. In qualified hands, a demand oxygen system equipped with a positive-pressure second stage is a versatile tool for supporting life in a non-breathing victim.

Shock

DCI almost always includes serious tissue damage. Such injuries almost always lead to life-threatening shock, gravely diminished efficiency of the circulatory (blood) system. Some type or degree of shock occurs when there is any disruption of the normal blood supply to tissues. In diving situations, these disruptions can result from a blockage, such as air or nitrogen bubbles in the circulatory system (AGE or a possibility of DCS Type II), or the result of any severe tissue injury, from lung overexpansion injury to major wounds or burns. Whatever its cause, if untreated, shock can lead to death.

> A **Demand Oxygen Delivery System** comes closest to achieving the goal of administering *as high a partial pressure of inspired oxygen as possible* to the breathing victim of a diving illness.

Signs and Symptoms. Recognizing shock is easy for a careful observer, but rescuers are advised that waiting for signs and symptoms may be waiting too late to prevent rapid deterioration. A person in shock will feel cool and clammy to the touch, difficult signs to discern after diving. As shock advances, and blood supply to the exterior of the body diminishes, a victim's skin will appear grey, and the nail beds will be slightly blue. Respiration will be shallow and rapid in an attempt to stimulate better oxygen delivery to the tissues. The victim may be incoherent, giddy, or faint from diminished circulation to the brain. The pulse will be weak and erratic, may grow stronger and faster, and then begin to fade as shock becomes worse. The pupil's reaction to light will grow progressively more sluggish, dilating in advanced stages. Repeated pulse, pupil, and vital-sign assessment can help a rescuer determine how rapidly shock is advancing.

Symptoms of shock include lightheadedness, blurred vision, nausea, and vomiting. Anxiety and general uneasiness are early symptoms of shock. Rescuers should note the similarity between these signs and symptoms and those of DCI.

Recommended Treatment. It is wisest to presume that an individual with any injury or DCI is in shock and begin immediate treatment, rather than waiting for shock to grow apparent. Shock has an emotional component and it is therefore impossible to predict what an individual's reaction to injury will be. First aid for shock includes dealing with any obvious wound or injury to stop bleeding that is contributing to shock. (Appropriate techniques are covered below.) In addition, oxygen administration at as high a partial pressure as possible is recommended. Oxygen can help alleviate the tissue death that results from seriously impaired circulation. Shock victims should be kept horizontal or on their left sides if no breathing distress is present and CPR is not required. Life support including rescue breathing or CPR may become necessary at any time.

Reduced circulation impairs the body's ability to maintain thermal balance. Shock victims are best kept loosely covered in a sheltered area, if available, but not made overly warm. Use two layers of blankets or similar material beneath shock victims and one covering. Wet decks or ground can draw heat more quickly than air. Wet suits or other diving dress should be removed; dry suit underwear may be left on, if dry and not constricting. No fluids should be administered, even to a conscious victim in shock. Complaints of thirst are best dealt with by moistening the victim's lips. Divers in shock need immediate evacuation to professional medical care that likely will include blood transfusion.

> Life support skills such as rescue breathing and CPR, and recommended first aid procedures, are best learned by hands-on practice under the professional coaching and evaluation of instructors trained and currently certified to teach them by nationally recognized agencies. Standards and protocols for these techniques change with ongoing medical research. The following are included for review purposes only.

Providing Life Support

Any DCI can lead to respiratory or cardiac arrest. Divers who may have, or are treated for, DCI require constant monitoring for these possibilities.[1]

Rescue Breathing Out of the Water. Any victim who has received in-water rescue breathing should be re-evaluated immediately upon removal from the water. Techniques for performing a standard check for unobstructed airway, breathing, and circulation are included in all first aid courses.

If the victim is still not breathing, rescue breathing must be continued. The rescuer should administer two full, deliberate breaths to the victim if there has been any interruption to the respiration cycle as a result of getting the diver out of the water. At that point, the rescuer should again check the carotid pulse for approximately 5 to 10 seconds and, finding it, continue rescue breathing at the recommended rate of one breath every 5 seconds.

Oxygen-augmented rescue breathing, administered via freeflow equipment set at 4 to 6 L per minute to a nasal cannula on the rescuer will greatly enrich the amount of inspired oxygen a non-breathing victim receives. Using a pocket mask and a freeflow system set to 15 L per minute as described earlier will further increase oxygen delivery to the victim. Either will help to forestall tissue hypoxia and alleviate some effects of shock, but more oxygen is always better. A somewhat slower breath rate may be advisable to allow better ventilation (exhalation), and prevent CO_2 from accumulating in a tight-fitting mask. The victim's pulse should be rechecked for 5 to 10 seconds

---

[1] Training and certification in CPR and First Aid may be available through your NAUI instructor, or may have been a prerequisite for course attendance. In any case, proficiency in these skills, shown by practical demonstration and achieving certification from a recognized source like the National Safety Council, is a condition of receiving NAUI Scuba Rescue Diver or Advanced Scuba Rescue Diver certification. See Appendix A for further information.

every ten to twelve breaths, about once every minute. If there is a pulse, a 5 to 10 second-breathing check is recommended. Rescue breathing should continue, preferably augmented with oxygen as available, as long as there is a pulse and breathing has not resumed.

Rescuers are further advised to monitor carefully any patients being aided with masks. It may be difficult to discover an airway obstruction when using rescue aids. Rescuers must observe for chest movement as an indicator that breaths are having the desired effect. Masks must be displaced during necessary pulse and breathing checks to make sure of reliable assessment.

Dealing With Airway Obstruction. An obstructed airway defeats life support efforts. Visual inspection and finger sweeps for debris,[2] followed by the Heimlich maneuver if the former are ineffective, can usually force obstructions out (Fig. 7-14).

A Heimlich maneuver uses the victim's diaphragm as means of expelling any blockage in the airway. The Heimlich maneuver can be performed on a standing, conscious adult, or, as is more likely in the case of DCI or diving-related injury, an unconscious, prone victim. In this case, abdominal thrusts are used.

The rescuer's hand is placed with the heel of the palm located just above the navel. The other hand is placed on top of the first, and all fingers point upward toward the victim's head. Thrusts should be made directly up the midline of the body, in distinct, sharp movements. Each is a separate attempt to dislodge the obstruction. After five attempts, if there is no evidence of the airway having been cleared (breathing begun or an item flying from the victim's mouth), the rescuer is advised to again try to see and remove foreign objects in the mouth or airway by finger sweeps. If the airway is clear, attempt breaths again. If the airway remains obstructed, repeat the series of thrusts.

Cardiopulmonary Resuscitation (CPR). If there is neither breathing nor a pulse, a victim will die quickly without immediate aid. This is an important point for rescuers fearful of causing injury by CPR to remember. Such injuries, if any, are the least of a victim's problems.

Timely, effective CPR can save lives. Maintaining the skill to perform CPR properly requires practice, not only for refining technique, but also to develop the stamina prolonged efforts require. NAUI members are required to demonstrate practical ability and to have recognized certification in both one- and two-rescuer CPR. Other NAUI-certified rescuers are advised to seek that level of training as well. The following procedures are reviewed for informational purposes only.

One-Rescuer CPR. The rescuer kneels alongside, facing, and perpendicular to, the victim, who should be lying on a flat, hard surface. A pad, such as a wet suit jacket, beneath the rescuer's knees is highly recommended. After checking for an obstructed airway and breathing, by looking, listening, and feeling (Fig. 7-15) for 5 to 10 seconds, and finding neither, the rescuer extends the airway and gives two full, deliberate breaths.

At this point, the rescuer carefully checks the carotid pulse. The victim may have responded to the breaths and resumed breathing, or there may

---

[2] Finger sweeps are not recommended for clearing a child's obstructed airway unless the debris is visible.

Fig. 7-14. Performing CPR on a victim with a blocked airway is futile. Clear the airway obstruction first.

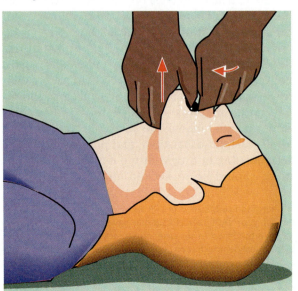

Fig. 7-15. Look, listen, and feel for breathing.

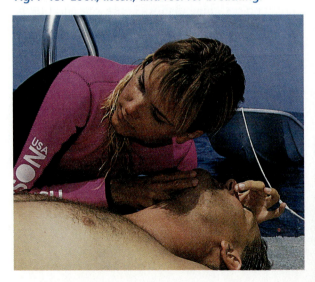

be a pulse. (Chest compressions should never be performed on a victim with any detectable pulse.) If there is no sign of a pulse after checking for about 5 to 10 seconds, CPR is started.

Locate the recommended compression point by first using the middle finger of the hand closest to the victim's legs to trace the line of the rib cage from the lower point to its center notch in the middle of the chest. Place the heel of the other hand the distance of two fingers (middle and index fingers) on top of this point on the victim's breastbone. Place the other hand on top of the hand on the chest, and lock the fingers together to make certain that there will be a firm compression with the palm of the hand.

Compressions are made by leveraging down on the victim's chest from the rescuer's hips with the rescuer's arms rigid above the hands. The chest is compressed in adults 1½ to 2 inches (4 to 5 cm) (Fig. 7-16). Smooth, piston-like compression movements will most closely simulate the natural activity of the heart that normally drives circulation. Compression strength comes from the rescuer's body weight, not arm strength or wrist movement. The fingers do not touch the chest.

Adult victims are best aided by compressions at a rate of about 90 per minute, faster than one compression per second. Two full, deliberate breaths are given after each 15 compressions. Each compression and breath cycle takes about 11 to 18 seconds. The hands should be carefully repositioned after each cycle (Fig. 7-17), and the airway extended to make sure that air enters when breaths are administered.

After about a minute, or four cycles, rescuers are advised to recheck the carotid pulse for about 5 to 10 seconds. The initial group of compression and breath cycles may well restart the pulse and breathing. If not, begin CPR again with two full, deliberate breaths. Check for pulse for 5 to 10 seconds every few minutes.

Two-Rescuer CPR. Having an additional trained, qualified person, if not several more, available, greatly aids any rescue efforts and definitely extends the time that CPR can be continued. Performing CPR as a team, two rescuers divide the responsibilities for compressions and giving breaths, maintaining a higher rate of breathing. They also may exchange places at intervals, and the person giving breaths (ventilator) can keep a frequent check on effectiveness by monitoring the "false pulse" as compressions are done. This flexibility, increased air delivery, and better assessment capability makes two-rescuer CPR preferable whenever possible.

Two-rescuer CPR compressions are performed exactly the same way as when one rescuer administers aid. However, the breathing cycle is increased to the rate of one breath for each five compressions. Full, deliberate breaths of 1 to 1½ seconds are given at the end (upstroke) of the fifth compression. (Giving breaths slowly helps prevent filling the abdomen with air.) Check the pulse again for 5 seconds after the first compression cycle (five strokes). Cease compressions when any pulse is detected. If there is no pulse, begin CPR again with a full, deliberate breath. After the first minute, check the pulse every few minutes.

Fig. 7-16. Compressions should be straight up and down. Allow the chest to rise before applying pressure again, and maintain a steady rhythm.

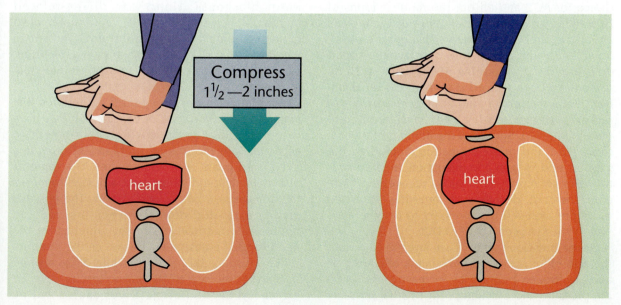

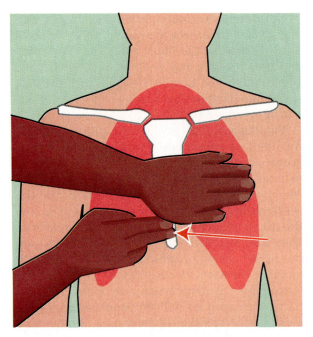

Fig. 7-17. Position the hands carefully for compressions to avoid serious internal injuries caused by the xiphoid process, a small cartilagenous projection located below the apex of the sternum. Relocate the compression point if the hands are removed from the chest.

Procedures for switching rescuer positions, joining one-person CPR in progress, or replacing one or both rescuers with fresh, trained personnel are part of all recognized CPR certification courses for professional rescuers. For your NAUI Scuba Rescue Diver or Advanced Scuba Rescue Diver certification, completing a CPR training class is required (Fig. 7-18).

Recompression Therapy

Recompression therapy is the treatment of choice for AGE and all but the mildest forms of DCS. With quick aid from qualified technicians under the direct supervision of hyperbaric physicians, its results can be truly spectacular. Apparently dead, nonbreathing AGE victims with no pulse have been revived in recompression chambers. DCS victims in similar states of arrest or racked with excruciating pain have been completely relieved. Speedy recognition, professional treatment, and proper transport, including life support and oxygen administration, are the keys to these seemingly miraculous recoveries. More often than not, despite such measures, repeated recompression will be necessary to resolve completely the symptoms of most DCI.

Recompression therapy is an attempt to reduce the size of, or completely eliminate, offending air and/or nitrogen bubbles by increasing the ambient pressure and providing a high partial pressure of oxygen. It is believed that the ambient pressure increase within the therapy chamber will help drive the gas back into solution and help shrink bubbles to the point where they will be passed through even an obstructed vessel, recirculated to the lungs, and exhaled normally.

In addition, by administering oxygen to patients in recompression at the ambient pressure (significantly greater than one atmosphere), excess nitrogen is driven from the system more quickly, and oxygen-starved tissues are abundantly nourished. (Oxygen administration periods are given at carefully controlled intervals depending on the treatment protocol for the suspected injury, and they are monitored by on-site emergency medical personnel for any adverse reactions caused by so-called oxygen toxicity.)

Timely therapy is essential for effective recompression. Life support and oxygen administration during transport to recompression facilities enhance victims' chances of recovery. Without such aid en route, even recompression cannot ensure recovery, and severe permanent damage, even death, are nearly inevitable.

FIRST AID FOR COMMON DIVING-RELATED INJURIES

Divers not only are at risk of injury from diving-specific causes such as squeezes and DCI but also face some other unique risks related to diving. Injury from inappropriate handling of or blundering into marine life, for instance, is not a risk during land-based recreation. Neither is drowning, seasickness, or hypoxia underwater (shallow-water blackout). Along with diving-related injuries, the strenuous activity that is integral to diving combines with the water environment to increase usual risks of exercise or overexertion, such as heart attack, stroke, or even simple muscle cramps.

Standard first-aid procedures for injuries like major wounds, fractures, or concussions may have to be modified in the diving environment to accommodate the unique problems of providing aid aboard boats or at remote sites. The contents of a diving first-aid kit are best adjusted to reflect the demands of the site and activity. The possibly greatly extended delay between first aid and appropriate medical treatment underscores the need for this adjustment, as well as the need for skilled, resourceful rescuers. While diligent effort and attention in a NAUI Scuba Rescue Diver or Advanced Scuba Rescue Diver course will be

CHAPTER 7 DECOMPRESSION ILLNESS AND DIVING INJURIES 145

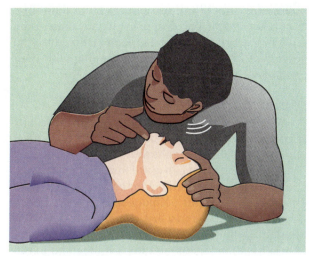

1. Check for breathing by looking, listening, and feeling for 5—10 seconds.

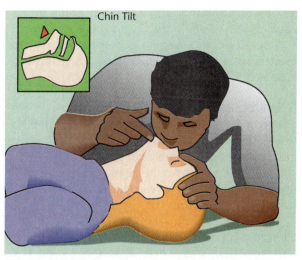

2. Make sure that the airway is clear; tilt head back as shown. Give two full, deliberate breaths.

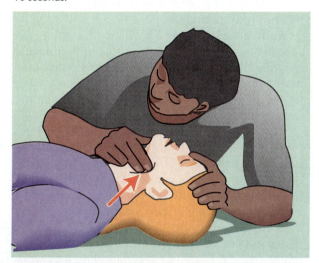

3. Check carotid pulse for 5—10 seconds. If no pulse, proceed to next step, otherwise continue with mouth-to-mouth respiration.

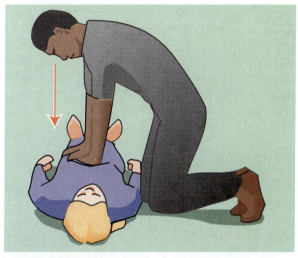

4. Position shoulders over hands, locating the compression point (see Fig. 7-17).

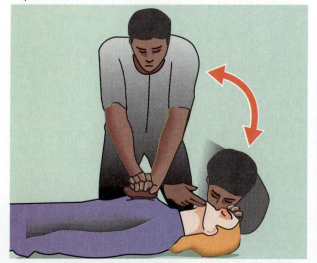

5. Do 15 compressions and two breaths. Repeat this cycle 4 times for about 1 minute.

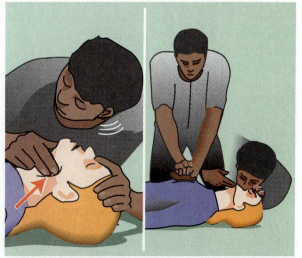

6. Check for breathing and pulse for 5—10 seconds; continue with more sets of compressions and breaths if necessary.

Fig. 7-18. CPR certification from a nationally recognized organization is required for any NAUI *Scuba Rescue Diver*.

rewarded with important skills and useful knowledge, the necessity of dealing with even "ordinarily" injured persons under such extraordinary circumstances adds additional risk to the victim and the rescuer.

Overview of First Aid Principles

First-aid training organizations have codified a set of standard principles for emergency action. At the heart of these is preserving the health of, and reducing the risk to, would-be rescuers. No rescue that results in harm to a rescuer can be considered completely successful.

Survey the Scene

A survey of the scene is first dedicated to answering the question "Is it safe for me to intervene?" In diving, the ever-present risk of drowning must be reduced as much as possible by careful attention to buoyancy and a cautious approach to any in-water distress incident. The details and necessities of transport come next. Finally, the rescuer is advised to consider the most appropriate aid for the specific problem. Details of rescue planning and management are included in Chapter Eight.

Primary Survey

The primary survey is conducted to discover a life-threatening injury. This is done with a conscious victim by a combination of knowledgeable questioning and detailed observation and may include a brief neurological examination, as discussed above. Obvious life-threatening injuries or conditions, such as cessation of breathing, major bleeding, or other wounds or burns that may result in shock require immediate attention. Discovery of any of these conditions or DCI is cause to alert emergency medical services immediately of the need for assistance, including evacuation.

Secondary Survey

After determining the primary problems, initiating first aid treatment, and calling for professional help in the case of life-threatening conditions, a secondary survey is done to discover any other injuries. Secondary surveys include interviews with any witnesses to the events, particularly the victim's dive buddy and other participants, and a head-to-toe exam with recording of vital signs. (This may be part of a brief neurological exam.) These signs include pulse, respiration rate, and the general appearance of the victim, such as skin tone, color (i.e., pallor, flush, or cyanosis), and external and internal temperatures.

Common Injuries in the Diving Environment

Though not an exhaustive list by any means, the following typical injuries occur frequently to divers. All rescuers should be familiar with their recommended first aid.

Wounds

Wounds can happen anywhere, but those that occur while diving need particular care to prevent infection. Salt- or freshwater environments can harbor bacteria that can make infections more serious. Organic material may enter the wound, as in the case of coral cuts or injury on encrusted underwater debris. Wounds that remain wet over long periods of time, or that begin to heal and are softened by reimmersion in water can become infected more easily. Much diving takes place in remote locations where professional medical help may not be readily available.

Wounds accompanied by major bleeding can cause shock. The delay in acquiring further necessary medical treatment, such as suturing, also may contribute to shock's onset. Though each wound is unique, certain basic procedures apply to all wounds.

Control and, if possible, stop bleeding. Direct pressure and elevation will work for small wounds, but arterial bleeding or major injuries, such as a deep cut from a boat propeller or similar trauma, definitely will require stitches and professional care. In these cases, applying pressure at the appropriate pressure points—places where an injured major vessel crosses a bone between the injury and the heart—to stop bleeding may work. Packing such wounds with gauze and/or sugar may hasten clotting. The wound should be cleaned first and, once packed, left so until removed by emergency medical services.

Tourniquets to control bleeding generally are not recommended unless loss of blood is so massive that without one, death is assured. If used, the tourniquet should be applied only tightly enough to curtail bleeding from the wound, permitting normal circulation to surrounding tissues. Constant monitoring for shock is recommended. The tourniquet is best left in place for removal by a physician.

Cleanliness prevents infection. Flush minor wounds with potable water to clean out organic and inorganic matter, and apply a suitable disinfectant like hydrogen peroxide to kill germs and bacteria that may be left. An anti-bacterial ointment may also be used before dressing the wound. Bandages should protect wounds from dirt but be loose enough to allow clotting, normal movement, and, above all, circulation. Larger wounds are best covered by clean, moist bandages and the victim should be evacuated to the closest emergency medical facility. Monitor all wound victims' vital signs carefully until qualified medical personnel take over. Follow-up medical assessment to help prevent serious infection is wise for all wounds incurred in a diving environment.

Fractures

Fractures can occur if a diving cylinder falls on a hand or foot, or a diver loses footing on a boarding ladder or deck while wearing gear. Any slip and fall around a dive site can cause a fracture. Standard first aid for simple fractures is immobilization of the injured bone, usually by splinting and bandaging that includes the closest adjacent joints, and then professional treatment (Fig. 7-19). Ice applied intermittently to the wrapped site limits swelling, helps prevent further tissue damage, and reduces pain.

Compound fractures, those in which the broken bone pierces the skin, require immobilization of the bone and treatment of the wound. All fractures require medical treatment, which will include x-ray evaluation, setting, and immobilization. Rib fractures, or any possible fracture to the rib cage, can cause damage to tissues surrounding the lung or to the lung itself. Spontaneous (partial) or tension pneumothorax may result. Even the most minor fractures, such as a toe stubbed while walking around barefoot, are probably best left to heal before continuing diving activities. Internal damage to blood vessels and bone may increase the likelihood of DCS since normal circulation and perfusion are hampered.

Concussion

Head trauma, possibly accompanied by soft-tissue injury of the neck, which may include spinal injury, is essentially a problem of diving entries and exits, especially in surf. If gear rides up and the valve strikes the diver on entry, concussion can result. Twist-and-fall accidents can cause spinal injury and concussion. Swimming up under a ladder that is riding the swell and being struck can knock a diver senseless, and even result in unconsciousness underwater (Fig. 7-20). A diver falling from a ladder onto another while exiting, or landing on another diver upon entry, may also cause a concussion. All concussions are serious, may include spinal injury, and are best treated by emergency medical personnel. If a diver with a head injury becomes unconscious, or if there is any chance of spinal injury, immediate evacuation is recommended.

Even without spinal injury involvement, many of the usual signs and symptoms of concussion, such as unconsciousness, dizziness, nausea, ringing in the ears, disorientation or visual disturbances, especially after diving, may be caused by DCI. This possibility makes a brief neurological examination and constant monitoring of concussed divers mandatory until medical treatment is obtained. Ice may be used to relieve pain and swelling. Associated wounds should be treated appropriately.

Cramps

Cramps can afflict any diver (Fig. 7-21). In the water, muscle cramps in the legs or feet can be so disabling that the diver requires rescue or assistance. Techniques for self-rescue include extend-

Fig. 7-19. Bandaging and splinting are first aid procedures. Fractures need immediate, professional care.

Fig. 7-20. Stay away from boarding ladders until they are clear. Then approach cautiously with the arm extended to avoid being hit.

Fig. 7-21. Leg cramps can be common if diving infrequently or wearing fins that are too stiff. Regular exercise with fins will prevent most leg cramps and build tolerance.

ing the toes downward for cramps in the quadriceps (forward thigh muscles) and shins, and pulling the toes back for calf and hamstring cramps. Foot cramps can sometimes be relieved by removing the fin, rolling the ankle, and wiggling the toes. Assistance for leg cramps includes helping the victim perform all of the above actions.

Abdominal cramps are more serious, especially underwater. They may be from an intestinal block on ascent (gut squeeze), or they can be a sign of DCS. Dealing with gut squeeze is covered earlier in this chapter. If abdominal cramps are in fact a symptom of DCS, other signs and symptoms invariably will be present. Appropriate treatment for DCS is covered in detail earlier.

Some female divers may experience increased menstrual cramping as a result of pressure changes and normal diving stress, though this is unusual. It is first a personal decision as to whether such cramps impair your fitness to dive. There is a clear distinction between discomfort and debilitating pain. The former may annoy, but the stress of the latter can increase risk to the diver and companions. Sitting out a particular dive until severe cramps are relieved is a wise choice.

After a dive or underwater, cramps may be diving-related, particularly if they begin suddenly on ascent and are unusually severe in the diver's experience. A series of brief neurological exams can help rule out or reveal DCI.

Burns

Burns are commonly typed by degrees from first, the mildest, to third, the most severe. All burns are painful and carry the risk of infection caused by tissue injury and lack of circulation in the injured area. Burns over large areas (around 10% of the body's area), whether from flames, hot objects like cooking utensils or engines, cooking grease, or chemicals like wet-cell battery acid, can be life-threatening, especially since they invariably will be accompanied by shock.

Burns to a hand (1% of your body area) or a similar section of the body, so long as there is no accompanying open wound, are best cleaned with cool, potable water, lightly patted dry, and covered loosely. Blisters and reddening that accompany relatively mild burns should be left alone. More serious or extensive burns require medical treatment, often including hyperbaric oxygen therapy in a recompression chamber if there has been any smoke inhalation. Depending on the burn and the victim's reaction, evacuation may be required.

Sunburn is a radiation burn with symptoms like any other overdose of dangerous rays. Depending on severity and extent, the victim can experience heat exhaustion, heat stroke, circulatory distress (shock), and dehydration, any of which can be life-threatening. Any signs or symptoms of these problems preclude further diving until completely resolved. Many diving excursions and prolonged dive vacations have been ruined by inadvertent sunburn or careless efforts to tan. Sunburn is an injury that is easily avoided.

Marine Life Problems

Though usually not a danger to divers, fish do bite. Other underwater animals have some very effective means of active and passive defense against larger animals, including divers (Fig. 7-22). Avoid molesting, threatening, or seeking direct contact with marine animals and organisms. A combination of common sense and practicing careful diving procedures, including using Minimal Impact Dive Skills, will prevent most problems. Also refusing to participate in "fish-feeding" dives and other thrill-seeking underwater adventures that include interactions with wild creatures prevents injuries. Even so, through bad luck or carelessness, injury can happen.

Stings. Sea urchins, stingrays, and some other tropical fish such as stonefish and lionfish (Fig. 7-23) are examples of marine animals better left alone. Unfortunately, many divers, particularly when entering the water from a sandy shore, blunder into basking rays while crossing the shallows on foot, or touch urchins, stonefish, or lionfish accidentally while diving.

Stingrays have a bony spine that will snap upward causing a nasty wound even through a fin or neoprene bootie's sole. Such tearing wounds are called avulsions and carry great likelihood of severe infection, as well as a possible immediate life-threatening reaction to poisonous venom, and shock. Cleaning the wound thoroughly and then soaking it in the hottest water that the rescuer can stand may help prevent the worst effects. (Victims may have lost sensation as a result of the injury. Test the water yourself to prevent burns.) Medical treatment with antibiotics and pain killers is advised. Shuffling into the water particularly in warmer waters, as opposed to stepping down hard, probably will scare any rays away.

Urchins' spines are brittle and break off on contact. Even so, they are strong enough to pierce most wet suits and can cause painful wounds. Some sea urchin spines also secrete venom that can cause neurotoxic or other severe allergic reactions. A sea urchin sting causes immediate pain and a burning sensation. Vinegar (dilute acetic acid) and hot water soaks can neutralize stinging and may hasten healing. Spines left deep in the

Fig. 7-22. Wild animals are always unpredictable.

Fig. 7-23. Marine animals are only dangerous if a diver touches or molests them.

wound will dissolve over time, but removal is preferred to prevent permanent nodules of scar tissue from developing around remnants. Urchin stings over a large area, as might happen to a diver who falls from a dock into a patch of them, can cause shock that may require medical treatment.

Other venomous marine creatures generally only sting if touched. Don't touch them. A sting, depending on the animal, may require immediate medical treatment. Some stings can result in neurological effects, discussed below.

Bites. Fish bites on divers are unusual, but the proliferation of "Shark-Feeding Experiences," "Cage Dives," "Fish-Feeding Dives," and the like will undoubtedly result in major injuries (Fig. 7-24). Divers are advised to remember that signing an additional waiver to participate in these underwater events only relieves the operator from liability for their injury. It neither ensures a wild animal's cooperation, nor the creature's ability to discriminate between professional feeder and the amateur as food. In any case, such bites can be potentially life-threatening wounds.

Panicked flight can result if someone is bitten underwater. Even after a successful ascent, bleeding on the surface or underwater in the vicinity of hungry or aggressive beasts creates an uncomfortable situation. Most of the time, further attack can be deterred if the wounded diver or healthy buddy approaches the animal threateningly. Wounds from the bites of large fish such as sharks, groupers, or great barracuda, from aquatic mammals such as seals or sea lions, or, from aquatic reptiles such as turtles are likely to grow infected and result in major tissue damage. This can include injury to irreplaceable connective tissue like tendons and ligaments and result in permanent disability and disfigurement. Life-threatening shock is certain. Medical treatment for the wound and its results is required.

Sea snakes, usually found in the Pacific or Caribbean side of the Panama Canal can carry deadly venom. Octopuses have sharp beaks, and at least some species, including the deadly Blue-Ringed Octopus of the Great Barrier Reef, also inject potent venom when biting.

Smaller fish also bite. Bluefish or other voracious feeders operating in large groups can injure an unlucky diver. Territorial animals such as moray eels may bite a diver who unwittingly or purposely encroaches on their lair. The threat of infection and panicked flight are the chief dangers of such encounters. They are avoided easily by leaving aquatic animals alone. All bite wounds should be evaluated by a physician as soon as possible. Usual first aid for major wounds, bleeding, and shock is recommended in all cases.

Allergic Reactions. Some divers have extreme, life-threatening reactions including respiratory and circulatory distress, even cardiac arrest, as a result of contact with some organisms in the marine environment. Such organisms include stinging jellyfish like the Portuguese man-of-war, venomous cone shells (Fig. 7-25), poisonous octopuses, and some types of sea snakes.

Jellyfish are a large class of animals, only some of which are harmful to people. Those that are, however, can cause grave harm to the diver unlucky enough to encounter them. Jellyfish tentacles have small stinging cells called *nematocysts* that uncoil and eject a toxic substance when disturbed. If the wound is extensive enough, shock results.

Small injuries are best treated carefully. "Unfired" cells may be on a victim's flesh. Underwater or on the surface, scraping a dive tool carefully over the area to remove any residual matter and then flushing it with sea water is recommended. A paste of water and baking soda may help to denature any toxin present on the skin's surface, but avoid rubbing. In some cases of jellyfish stings, shaving the affected area will prevent problems from stinging mechanisms left on the skin.

Most other allergic reactions are from neurotoxins, injected venoms that act directly on the central nervous system. Without immediate medical aid, including, in some cases, the injection of appropri-

Fig. 7-24. Large pelagic creatures are thrilling to see, but can be very dangerous to feed.

Fig. 7-25. Some species of cone shells have deadly venom. It is best to look, not touch, when diving.

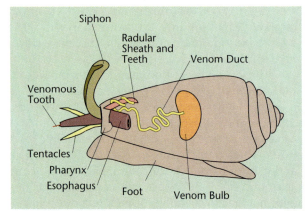

ate anti venin serum, death can result from progressive paralysis of the mechanisms of circulation and breathing. In remote areas, prolonged efforts at life support have been known to save victims paralyzed by neurotoxin. Fortunately, encounters with deadly animals are extremely rare and almost wholly avoided by careful diving practices.

Individuals with sensitivities to marine organisms, either known from specific experience, or surmised from allergic reactions to bee stings or the like, would do well to make diving companions aware of the fact. It is advisable for these divers to carry appropriate medication, including prescribed, one-time use, prepared antihistamine injections, to prevent the onset of anaphylaxis, a life-threatening hypersensitive allergic reaction with symptoms similar to shock.

Fish Poisoning

Many more divers are injured from biting into fish than vice versa. Serious illness can result from ingesting some types of fish or from eating fish that has been stored or handled improperly. The signs and symptoms of common fish poisoning can range from the usual problems of food poisoning—nausea, vomiting and diarrhea—to the same as those of allergic reactions and reactions to neurotoxins, which can include death.

First aid for the mildest form of fish poisoning is to keep the victim well hydrated to deal with the effects of vomiting, etc., and to monitor the sufferer regularly. This type of fish poisoning usually passes within about 24 hours, but a victim can be seriously weakened during this time. A visit to a physician may be wise. Diving is certainly not recommended until the victim is free of symptoms and functioning normally.

Serious cases of fish poisoning can resemble DCI, particularly decompression sickness. Though oxygen will not hurt, neither will it help. Professional medical care is necessary in any case. Keep the victim comfortable, monitor vital signs, and activate emergency services.

Fish poisoning and many other problems can be avoided by confining your diet solely to vegetables and grains, but it is more frequently prevented by avoiding eating fish that may be tainted. This is unfortunately difficult to do since no raw fish looks especially poisonous. Local advice, if you are fishing (or dining) in an unfamiliar area, can help prevent being poisoned.

Gas Toxicity

Some divers, through ignorance, neglect, or bad luck, unexpectedly wind up with other than pure air in their scuba cylinder. They may fill their cylinders from an impure source, such as a poorly operating, inadequately filtered, petroleum-powered compressor, or a common non-breathing-air facility such as a gas station. These may result in the introduction of oil or oil combustion by-products such as carbon monoxide into the breathing gas. Carbon monoxide poisoning or lipoid pneumonia from inhaling oil droplets can result. Other divers mistakenly fill scuba cylinders with oxygen instead of air. This leads to oxygen toxicity in a short time underwater at even shallow depths. Any of these conditions can occur when you are purchasing air or renting filled cylinders.

Carbon Monoxide Poisoning. Carbon monoxide is much more attractive to the body's main oxygen-delivery cells, hemoglobin, than is plain oxygen. Even a small amount in air can lead to death because tissues die when CO instead of O_2 is delivered to the cells. Signs include bluish skin color, vomiting, instability, confusion, and memory loss. Dead, or nearly dead, victims of CO poisoning may have deeply flushed "cherry red" lips.

Symptoms include headache, difficulty focusing, breathlessness, perspiration, and unconsciousness. Carbon monoxide poisoning is easy to mistake for DCI. Fortunately, the same response is called for: oxygen inspired at as high a partial pressure as possible, and immediate evacuation for emergency medical treatment, which will probably include recompression and hyperbaric oxygen treatment. Life support is likely to be needed in the interim, and, like DCI victims, a CO-poisoned diver requires constant monitoring.

If caught in time, medical treatment may completely relieve CO poisoning. However, given the swiftness with which crucial brain cells die when deprived of oxygen, survival without residual deficit—from its onset underwater, usually accompanied by hypoxia-induced unconsciousness that can lead to drowning—is highly unlikely. Know your air sources (Fig. 7-26).

Oxygen Toxicity. The effect of too high a partial pressure of oxygen for too long a time, such as when breathing pure oxygen at any depth, can be seizures and convulsion with little or no warning

---

Never dive with a questionable air cylinder, or if air tastes or smells. Check for a current visual inspection and hydrostatic test.

KNOW YOUR AIR SOURCE!

Fig. 7-26. Dive only with freshly filled cylinders from a reputable air source like a NAUI scuba center to reduce the chance of impure breathing air problems.

Fig. 7-27. Diving with breathing mixtures other than normal air requires special training.

(see Chapter Three). Only pure air is recommended for most recreational diving applications; however, many divers are adopting "enriched air" or "Nitrox" as their primary breathing mixture. Using such mixtures requires special training and certification by recognized authorities, as well as a diligent search for gas-providers and dive operators that are careful in their mixing and testing procedures (Fig. 7-27).

Removal from the source of pure oxygen is mandatory; but underwater, a convulsion can lead the victim to drown before being returned to the surface. This is another problem for which the best treatment is simple prevention.

Seasickness

Severe seasickness is a temporary contraindication to diving, as discussed in Chapter One. Having to deal with its effects, however, is likely for any rescuer, possibly even for yourself. Other than removing the victim from the source of motion, and attempting as well as possible to maintain hydration and comfort, there is little that can be done.

Shallow-Water Blackout

The associated problems and prevention of shallow-water blackout are covered in Chapter Three. First aid will include in-water rescue, surface transport, and life support to prevent drowning.

Near Drowning

Near drowning is defined as narrowly missing dying by suffocation underwater, by breathing fluid or from aspirating fluids of any kind. In saltwater environments, it can include a relatively mild event called "saltwater aspiration syndrome." In any case, it can be a life-threatening emergency that requires immediate medical attention (Fig. 7-28).

Signs of near drowning or saltwater aspiration syndrome include blue lips, unconsciousness underwater or at the surface, chest pain, shortness of breath, no breathing, or no pulse (apparent death). Symptoms are dizziness, disorientation, and breathing difficulty.

Oxygen at as high a partial pressure as possible and immediate life support, if required, may rapidly relieve some effects; but the chance for death from secondary effects, including pulmonary swelling and fluid retention in reaction to the invading fluid, loss of lung function and elasticity, and shock is great.

Near drowning is often the result of a panicked ascent, possibly precipitated by an out-of-air emergency, or coughing or choking underwater. DCI may be present, and the similarity of some signs and symptoms, again, fortunately requires the same first aid and treatment.

Heart Attack or Stroke

Underwater, heart attacks and strokes are usually fatal. At the surface, survival will depend on swift rescue and appropriate life support until medical evacuation for professional treatment.

Heart attack as the result of diving with heart disease, an absolute contraindication to participation, is discussed in Chapter One. Nonetheless, a heart attack can happen to a diver underwater or at the surface. Victims will have signs and symptoms similar to serious lung overexpansion injuries, including sudden severe chest pains, radiating pains, particularly on the left side, breathlessness or difficulty breathing, profuse sweating, anxiety, and shock. Life support, including oxygen at as high a partial pressure as can be maintained, until evacuation is recommended.

Stroke will have nearly identical signs and symptoms as AGE, discussed previously. First aid and treatment are identical. In the field, distinguishing either from the other is impossible, and it may remain so even after professional evaluation and testing.

Seizures or Convulsions

Whatever their cause, underwater and probably at the surface, seizure or convulsion will likely result in near-drowning. See the recommended treatments above.

At the dive's exit, the victim of convulsion needs protection from traumatic injury that is likely to result from random, violent movement, falling down, etc. The head in particular should be protected from striking hard objects, which can result in concussion. Seizure or convulsion may be a sign of AGE or DCS. The same first aid and treatment for suspected DCI, including repeated brief neuro-

Fig. 7-28. Positioning a diving accident victim face-up is a critical step in effective care. What may seem an obvious step is often overlooked and suffocation results.

logical examinations and careful monitoring, is recommended. Wounds that may result also will require treatment. Severe head injuries or unconsciousness, whether or not related to diving, require immediate professional medical evaluation and treatment.

A Final Word

By now you have discovered that pure oxygen is probably the most useful first aid item that you can have at any dive site. Its use is standard treatment for many of the common injuries associated with diving, as well as serious DCI. Having sufficient supply available and being proficient and unhesitating in its application is the hallmark of a prepared and knowledgeable rescue diver.

> **NAUI recommends that all divers make sure that there is sufficient oxygen supply, appropriate administration equipment, and a trained provider available for all diving events.**

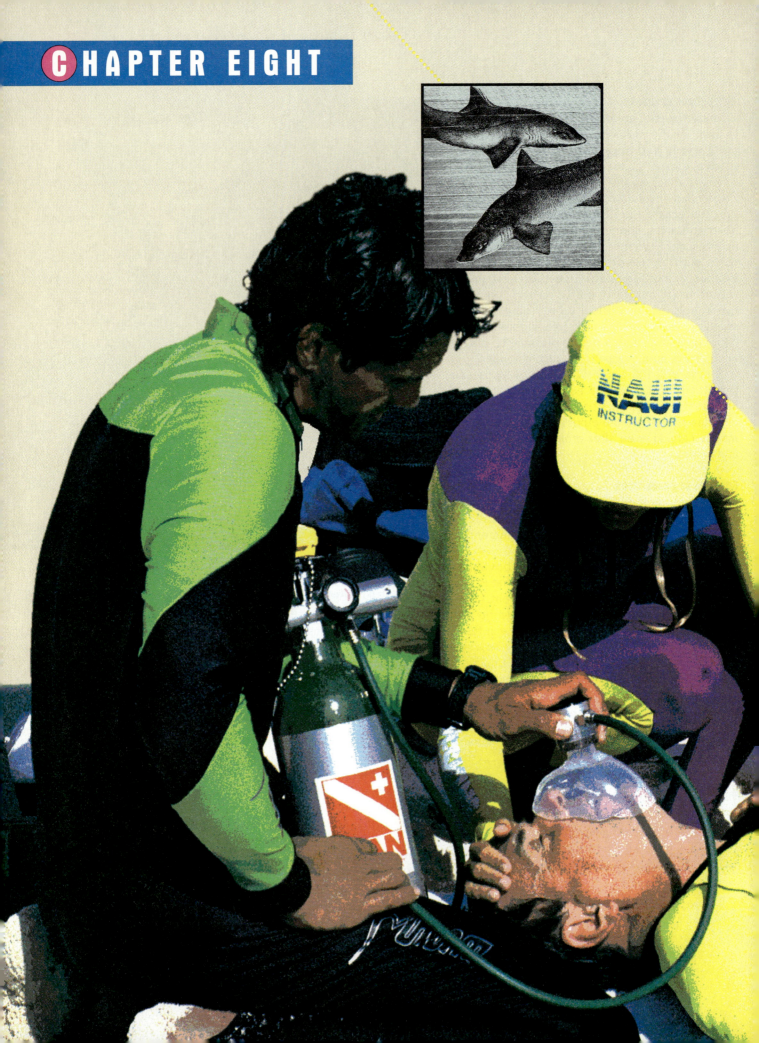

CHAPTER EIGHT

ACCIDENT MANAGEMENT

Advance planning and preparation are as crucial to reducing the risks of rescue as they are to enjoyable diving (Fig. 8-1). Uncoordinated rescue efforts, no matter how skilled or heroic, are likely to fail. Would-be rescuers without a plan or effective leadership can themselves become victims. Vital equipment may be unavailable, unusable, or even ignored in haste. Evacuation may be delayed needlessly by lack of information and foresight. Confusion caused by improvising under stress instead of choosing between well-thought-out options can hamper any part of the process.

Moreover, an accident is a complex, unusual event. At its most basic level, a person or persons are unexpectedly injured, sometimes seriously. No matter how or why accidents occur, even successful rescues can result in blame rather than gratitude. As noble as it is to risk yourself to help another, failure or incomplete success almost always will result in recrimination. Victims or their families may seek compensation from rescuers regardless of the victim's own responsibilities for the problem, its possible random nature, or the appropriateness or quality of the response. Careful documentation of the actual events of any accident and dealing properly with its aftermath are other critical parts of a rescuer's task.

PLANNING FOR EMERGENCIES

Emergency planning is the act of creating a detailed, carefully organized directory of response options to deal with possible diving accidents. This includes identifying the personnel on hand or readily available to respond, being confident of the availability of necessary equipment, and understanding how those people and that gear best can be deployed to achieve success.

Emergency Personnel and Services

Qualified, dependable people, whether volunteers or professional rescuers, are necessary for dealing with an accident. As a rescue-certified diver, identifying what resources are available—not the least of which is you, your training, and your skill—can significantly improve emergency responses.

In Advance

Virtually every part of the globe has emergency medical services available, though the quality and accessibility of such services varies greatly. Whether for a routine weekend excursion or for a group's vacation to a foreign resort, emergency planning includes identifying and evaluating available outside resources and ensures the ability to access it in a timely manner (Fig. 8-2).

Sources of aid include local emergency medical services and rescue organizations. Among these are professional and voluntary ambulance corps and fire and police departments. Municipal marine services such as harbor patrols or police, local harbormasters, or even commercial towing companies may be able to help a rescuer dealing with a diving emergency. The Federal Park Service often has waterborne rangers at popular dive areas in

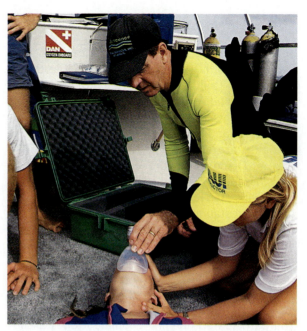

Fig. 8-1. Having trained personnel and a thoughtful emergency plan in advance ensures a quicker and more effective response to any dive accident.

Fig. 8-2. Highly trained, specially equipped water rescue experts are prepared to respond to emergencies in most recreational dive areas of the world.

national parks. The U.S. Coast Guard will invariably respond for evacuation of any diving casualty in navigable waters within their jurisdiction, and their usual offshore patrol area is even more extensive. U.S. Navy bases, particularly those that deal with submarine or ship maintenance and submariner training, all are equipped with fine recompression facilities and have highly skilled medical personnel and technicians on call.

Similar public and military rescue organizations exist outside the United States. NAUI, DAN, and other diving service organizations can provide divers with listings of knowledgeable diving leaders and facilities worldwide (and locally) that can be helpful in recommending rescue support services. This includes the locations of recompression chambers and emergency medical facilities that are attuned to the needs of injured divers. Discovering these resources will take research but is usually no more time consuming or difficult than learning about the best dive sites and area restaurants.

It is important for all divers to remember that no matter who may be organizing or leading a dive, independent knowledge is as valuable as self-sufficient ability. Creating a contact list of local services for your usual diving activities and a similar list for vacations and remote diving in which you participate is highly recommended. Rescue-certified divers in particular should be prepared to assume full control of an emergency situation. Diving leaders themselves may be victims, or a leader coordinating rescue or life support efforts may have to delegate contacting emergency services or other parts of the rescue to you. Crucial time is saved when you are completely prepared.

At A Dive Site

Making activity leaders aware of your rescue ability and certification, and willingness to help if needed, is always appreciated. This enables leaders to organize better, even if only mentally, the people that can help in an emergency. Sharing this information often will result in more detailed questioning by the leader and perhaps a role in the activity plan. It could result in a request that you voluntarily pair with a specific diver about whom the leader may have some concern. Unless you are leadership-certified, your actions are limited to acting strictly as that person's buddy, as discussed in Chapter Two.

> **Always dive within the most conservative assessment of your ability.**
>
> **It is irresponsible and dangerous to make any dive beyond your skill level or for which you are not fully trained and prepared.**

Conversations with diving companions not only are enjoyable social interactions but can help you identify possible help and potential sources of problems in advance. Speaking with unfamiliar dive companions, a usual assessment practice of diving leaders, will help you learn which participants in an activity may be medical professionals or may have other qualifications that would be helpful in an emergency, and which others may be uncomfortable about the coming dive. Even if not rescue-certified, any diver can have skills and knowledge that may be invaluable in caring for a victim.

Professional dive-boat crew and captains can be integral to an effective rescue, and they probably have contingency plans in place. As a diving leader, coordinating your rescue plan with the boat's crew is routine procedure. A certified rescue diver who customarily dives on a particular boat eventually may become part of the boat crew as the captain and staff grow familiar with that person's ability. Even if they are not specifically qualified to aid a diving victim, a boat crew usually has complete knowledge of the vessel and its equipment. Their background in seamanship, boat-handling, and emergency communications will undoubtedly be needed in any rescue attempt and certainly in affecting rapid evacuation.

Equipment

What rescue equipment any diver carries will depend greatly on the dive's location, the planned activity, the group involved, and the individual diver's role, as discussed in Chapter Six. You should also remember that almost any item imaginable can be useful to a specific rescue, but all dives are best conducted with oxygen administration equipment, a trained provider, and a suitable first-aid kit on hand. Other useful items can include common things like change for public telephones or any of the rescue equipment previously mentioned.

Preparation

Whatever gear you may carry, knowing in advance that it works and that you are qualified and able to use it properly is mandatory (Fig. 8-3). This includes being absolutely certain that you have what you think you have!

Conduct an inventory of emergency gear before any dive. Checking the contents of your first-aid kit, noting expirations for any medications you may carry, and making sure that all items are present, organized, and easily accessible is a good practice. This is especially true if the kit was opened at all during the last dive, even for a simple Band-Aid. Things may have shifted or been misplaced. Someone may have used the last ban-

Fig. 8-3. High-tech equipment is only as good as its user. Become proficient with any gear you carry.

dage of a needed type, or the kit may have gotten water in it that has compromised supplies. Making certain that all is complete, organized, and ready for use is a common-sense preparation technique.

Oxygen kits in particular should be checked, including a reading of the remaining pressure with the valve turned on. A small leak over time can empty the cylinder, rendering it useless in an emergency. If used at all, the cylinder is best completely refilled, with medical-grade oxygen only, and the date and filled pressure recorded on an attached tag. Checking kits periodically, every two or three weeks, is recommended, but certainly enough in advance of any dive so that the cylinder can be serviced and filled, if required. If you are diving on consecutive days, oxygen gear is best checked before beginning and after completing each day's diving.

Just as with personal dive gear, a preparatory inventory of emergency equipment that includes checking the function of crucial items will provide peace of mind. It also will help a rescuer mentally prepare. Seeing and touching the items is a good way to maintain complete familiarity with their use.

Typical Dive First-Aid Kit

After oxygen and associated gear including a pocket mask, a dive first-aid kit best includes items that will deal with your specific needs and the unique demands of the diving you do. On a personal level, any prescription medications that you normally take should be included. Non-prescription items, such as eye washes, contact lens fluids, ear drops or favorite analgesics (painkillers like aspirin or stronger compounds), should be present.

The usual ingredients of a first-aid kit, from elastic bandages, gauze, swabs, and Band-Aids, to tools like scissors, tweezers, a needle, sharp knife, and magnifying glass are wisely included. In addition, vinegar (dilute acetic acid), as well as hot and cold packs, local anesthetic ointment, disinfectants, topical antibiotic creams, or iodine paint, can help deal with wounds, coral and live-rock cuts, marine-life stings, and the like. Extra adhesive tape is always useful, as is spare sun-block or tanning lotion. (The latter also is very effective for removing tar from skin and gear! If it is used for this purpose, make sure to wash the gear before storing it because some suntan creams can harm rubber if left on for an extended period.) Decongestants for use after diving, if needed, whether in pill or inhaler form, and seasickness medication can be useful. If there is room, a lightweight blanket or pad can be included, as well as water or appropriate juice.

A good first-aid kit also includes a basic manual, pen and paper to facilitate documentation of efforts and record other important information, waterproof slate and pencil for "wet" notes, a flashlight, and coins to use to call for help. If telephones are likely to be unavailable, a rescuer, particularly at the leadership level, might consider including a portable marine VHF radio and a cellular telephone, with fresh batteries in the kit. Flares and other attention-getting devices like signal mirrors have their place in a rescuer's first-aid kit, as well as personal dive gear.

These recommendations are only a beginning. Additional medical qualifications, such as EMT certification, will increase the medications, life-support, and emergency response equipment you may choose to carry. Assuming a leadership position may increase how much of anything is required and used. (Keeping a first-aid kit stocked can add significant expenses to your diving if you become the regular source of Band-Aids, gauze, and tape for groups of divers. This can lead to not having needed items on hand. Make sure *you* maintain control over *your* first-aid kit.)

Other Gear

A throw bag, described in Chapter Six, and any other floating lines and surface assistance gear like inflatable floats, can be extremely helpful in an emergency. They are also easy to carry and pack in your gear. A flexible or rigid cervical collar and a backboard or similar transport device are other important items to have. Though possibly available on many dive boats and as part of local lifeguard services at popular areas, checking to be certain they are, and (especially if in a leadership role) bringing them if they are not, is wise. Three or four divers, or a pair of buddies who dive together regularly, may acquire such items jointly, bringing them as a group or individually, depending on the circumstances.

Know how, and be prepared to use any emergency equipment you carry!

TRAIN AND PRACTICE WITH IT OFTEN.

Responding To An Emergency

Seeing a diver in trouble is disturbing and frightening, whether you are rescue-trained or not. When distress includes a major injury or a real threat to life, you may have an extreme reaction. To be an effective rescuer, you must find the strength to put aside normal feelings, from physical revulsion to fear, and concentrate solely on rescue (Fig. 8-4). Advanced planning can make single-minded effort easier and will help when coordinating the efforts of others.

Taking charge of a rescue operation places great responsibility on a diver, regardless of the diver's certification. Everyone's willingness to help, the heightened sense of urgency, and the excitement of an unusual event can lead easily to more problems. The presence of victims' (or rescuers'!) friends, family members, or loved ones increases the stress. In any case, unless the rescue coordinator exerts strong, rational control, success is doubtful.

Nearby divers who see another struggling at the surface may respond unthinkingly only to find themselves under attack and in similar distress. A diver who surfaces without a buddy, and then redescends without notifying anyone else of the problem, may well become a second missing diver, or even the only one if the buddy follows recommended procedures. Helpful divers without effective direction have embarked on underwater searches with less than full cylinders of air, or with air turned off, or they have become victims themselves by pushing their own exposures beyond reasonable limits.

Planning appropriate actions in advance, considering what you have learned in this course, will help you coordinate a successful rescue. The best plan will be easily modified to accommodate the actual circumstances of any emergency, the nature of the accident, and the resources available to deal with it.

The Four "A's" of Effective Response

From the standpoint of an individual rescuer, or the needs of a rescue coordinator, every emer-

Fig. 8-4. No diver expects to have an accident, but a rescue diver must always be prepared to respond.

gency can be divided into four distinct phases. Neglecting any of these likely will contribute to a rescue effort's failure.

With good prior planning and preparation, the first two A's, "Assess" and "Appoint," will be accomplished rapidly. The third A, "Account," will begin as soon as the first note is made and continue through the entire incident, documenting all "Actions," the fourth A, connected with the event.

Assess

Assessment—careful evaluation of options for risk and results—is the first phase of any emergency plan and the first response to any incident. Thinking about what will best achieve the goal of protecting accident victims from further harm with the least risk to rescuers continues throughout the incident because each step in a rescue will include new options and new risks (Fig. 8-5).

Sometimes, figuring out what needs to be done and the most appropriate method can be more difficult than actually doing it. This underscores the importance of planning for emergencies. Knowing what options are recommended and thinking in advance about how they may be put in effect under the circumstances you face will help shorten the assessment phase. A list of emergency resources, as detailed earlier, will certainly help should outside assistance and evacuation be required. Knowing who is qualified to provide aid at the scene will help. Deciding on boarding options for an unconscious diver, if you are on a boat, or assessing the shore for water removal before you may actually have to transport an injured victim, are smart rescue practices.

Water rescue is dangerous. Rapid response can add more danger, unless rescue gear and person-

ASSESS
APPOINT
ACCOUNT
ACT!

nel are coordinated, familiar with procedures, and cognizant of the overriding need to keep themselves from harm. NAUI recommends that rescuers follow the hierarchy of methods below when deciding on what action will best help get a diver in distress from the water.

It is better to be able to reach to a diver in distress, or deliver buoyancy from a secure position, than to enter the water. If you are near a conscious distressed diver, it is better to coax the person back to the exit than to grapple with a distressed diver and risk injury or death. If a diver is unconscious, using a rescue float (Fig. 8-6) or rescue barrel and line to help return the diver to the exit point is preferred to towing the person on your own.

Even if it is necessary to administer in-water rescue breathing, having help available to get the diver more quickly to treatment will be less risky for the primary rescuer and more efficient than attempting to do it alone. Divers or other rescue personnel that can meet a rescuer between the site of the incident and the water's exit are surely welcome. Their assistance will greatly reduce the chance of harm that can befall an exhausted, highly stressed rescuer.

Once victims are out of the water, assessment continues throughout care. Treatment must be initiated, information recorded, examinations performed, and outside resources kept informed of the progress. Keeping everything on track and progressing smoothly ultimately is the rescuer's job, whether you are coordinating a team effort or working on a buddy alone. Following a pre-arranged plan and using all available aid and equipment identified before the incident will make things easier and more efficient.

Appoint

Identifying helpers that may be available to you at a dive site before an emergency will help you coordinate their efforts when you need them. You may be lucky enough to have someone medically trained at the site, whether a nurse, doctor, or emergency medical technician. Having that

Fig. 8-5. Rescue begins at the first sign of a diver in trouble and ends only when all persons are out of the water and receiving appropriate care.

Fig. 8-6. Throwing a handy float to a distressed diver is better than going in after the person and better still if the line is attached first! Prepare and check all rescue equipment thoroughly.

person dedicated to life support, by administering rescue breathing or CPR or by supervising care, certainly increases a victim's chances. However, as coordinator and as a rescue expert, you retain responsibility to make sure that personnel appointed to carry out parts of the plan are qualified and able to do so.

What to do First . . .

CALL

REACH

THROW

WADE

ROW

SWIM

COAX

TOW

"If you don't write it down, it didn't happen."

Document all rescue events and treatment you initiate for any injury.

It is entirely possible that a medical professional will be less competent at handling the victim of a diving accident than you or another rescue-trained diver. Some medical professionals' training and background, even if they are divers, may not include dedication to maintaining important first-aid skills such as CPR. They even may be unfamiliar with the benefits of oxygen or with techniques for its administration in the field for diving ailments. (This may also be the case with responding emergency medical servicers that may have no training in diving accidents.) Nevertheless, qualified assistants willing to help expedite rescue and treatment for an injured diver are invaluable.

Account

Some would say that the most important facet of coordinating or conducting any rescue, apart from physically aiding the injured diver, is creating a detailed account of an incident that includes a complete record of the actions taken on another's behalf.

Parts of the account will be needed as soon as emergency medical personnel take over the victim. Being able to supply pertinent information regarding the patient's identity, the incident, care, and condition can help responding persons provide appropriate treatment. Because timely response is so important, this is a serious rescue responsibility. And it is wise to remember that if some event is not written down, it did not happen; and if it did, it was probably not the way you recall it.

If you are coordinating a rescue effort, it is recommended that a recorder be appointed, or that you begin the account as soon as the incident happens. Other people used to document a rescue need not be rescue-certified, but they should be careful, responsible persons who can take notes, and your direction, well.

It is just as important to keep track of what is happening at all times when conducting a rescue on your own. Unfortunately, this may be quite difficult to do while dealing with a victim, particularly if life support is required. Under these circumstances, anyone who can pick up the job of recording for you, even a willing bystander, should be welcome. If there is nobody available, at least jot down the time you began the effort and any other salient events, such as beginning oxygen administration and calling for evacuation. Creating a detailed form for this purpose in advance will help ensure that the information you will need is recorded.

It is helpful if more than one copy of at least parts of the account is available. For instance, the principal rescuer or rescue coordinator will need complete information, particularly if in a leadership role, since an accident report must be filed under the terms of NAUI's *Standards and Procedures*. A rescue diver also may be required by the circumstances of the accident to file similar reports with the United States Coast Guard or other law enforcement agencies, as discussed below. A complete, detailed account of what happened, to whom, when, and what you or anyone else working with you may have done about it, will definitely make complying with these requirements easier, and it can help prevent future legal complications.

If the incident happens aboard a boat, the captain will probably require an account of what occurred. (All information that a rescuer provides anyone else, orally or in writing, should be confined to the bare events and facts of the incident.) The following details should be part of any rescue account:

Victim Information. Victim information includes the name, address, and telephone number, as well as age and next-of-kin contact, if available. This information often can be found in the dive master's event log, or in a diver's personal logbook. If you are not on a professionally organized dive, divers are advised to provide these details, as well as medical and diving insurance information, to buddies. Keeping this information, including insurance identity cards, certification cards, and other identification documents, in a shared, secure place like a dry box, is a wise practice. Having this information and a valid passport readily available can be critical to getting care outside of the United States.

Event Information. It may be difficult to take time to record everything that happens when you are dealing with an incident alone. But as soon as it is possible, a written account of what happened, when, to whom, and what was done about it, is required. This account should begin as soon as any accident occurs.

Whether creating your own account, or having someone do it while events unfold, note the time of any significant actions, such as dispatching a rescue diver to tow an unconscious diver back to the boat, or being notified when a diver is missing or when a person falls or is accidentally cut. Doing so will help make your subsequent account more accurately reflect the actual sequence of events.

This becomes extremely important because so many things can happen almost at once. For instance, seeing an unconscious diver on the surface, a rescuer simultaneously might be entering the water with a rescue float and line and telling a bystander or the boat's captain to alert emergency services that evacuation is needed. All three events—sighting, response and notification—are important for documentation.

Treatment Information. Treatment information includes any efforts made to deal with a victim's symptoms, from rinsing debris out of someone's eye to placing a diver on oxygen. It includes the results and times of any brief neurological examinations that are conducted and vital signs noted. This information will be extremely valuable to responding emergency medical personnel, and it will be considered in their treatment of the victim.

Rescuers are advised to request the names and other identifying data of anyone who responds to a diving emergency. If a diver is evacuated, the name of the rescue service and, if possible, the names, badge numbers, or license plates (if applicable) of responding emergency service personnel should be recorded for future reference. Recording case or incident numbers assigned by emergency workers will make acquiring documentation you need later easier.

Location Information. Location information includes the name of the place if it is a well-known dive site, and, if applicable, the nautical chart or map coordinates. Include the body of water, name of the beach or vessel, and notes on the environmental conditions. Note the weather, water, and air temperature, sea and current conditions, wind direction and strength, and air and water visibility. Such details are especially important because they may have been factors that contributed to the accident or affected the rescuers' efforts.

Witness Information. Record the names, addresses, and phone numbers of anyone who has seen the event, witnessed the rescue or treatment, and who is willing to provide you with information. This includes other people at the dive, in particular anyone who may have helped in the rescue and the victim's dive buddy(ies). If possible, have them write an independent account of what they observed, or tape-record their narrative with their recorded (oral) and written permission. (Such information is for you alone, as we will discuss.) If it is impractical at the time of the accident, contact these people soon afterward to request it, perhaps at a meeting that evening.

Rescuer's Identity. The last part of the account is your own personal contact information, including name, address, telephone number, and certification level if requested. Emergency response personnel, law enforcement officials, and, if on a boat, the vessel's captain will need this for their records. The victim is entitled to know who you are, as well as anyone else directly involved in the rescue or any treatment administered.

Action

Action—what response you make or coordinate to relieve a diver's distress or remove the person from the chance of further harm, including any treatment possibly required—is the fourth "A." It is most important to the well-being of any victim. Your timely actions, based on judicious assessment of the situation, appropriate intervention techniques, and skillful use of the personnel and other resources on hand, can save a life or prevent a person from suffering gravely diminished capacity and ability.

More typically, your actions will make a diver think twice in the future, learning from the mistakes that led to your intervention. Most divers never have a serious problem or dive accident. Few ever even see one. In fact, most rescues are far less dramatic than some of those you have studied in this

---

The best dive accidents are the ones that never happen!

PREVENTION BEATS INTERVENTION!

course. This is because rescue training, like dive training, is based on the principle that one "plans for the best, but is ready for the worst."

Even so, your actions to aid another diver, even if they are as minor as disinfecting and bandaging a small cut, must be as considered and well done as they would be if you were faced with an unconscious, nonbreathing victim. Exactly the same emergency response principles apply to any action taken on another diver's behalf. In that sense, no rescue, no intervention, is minor.

Evacuation Procedures

Evacuation—speedy removal to professional care—is necessary for any life-threatening condition. As with other facets of rescue, assessing whether or not such measures are required should be done before calling for aid. But if evacuation is the right choice, choosing the quickest, most direct method is vital. The right choice might sometimes be the boat you are on or a personal vehicle parked at or near the site.

The time it may take emergency services to make the round trip between a dive site and medical center by ambulance can be longer than it would take for you to go one way in your own vehicle. Though a dive boat's home port can be far from the site of an accident, there may be a much closer point for victim transfer. Weather, other emergencies, and factors like traffic patterns, time of day, and holiday schedules can delay professional response.

Emergency services will invariably provide callers with an ETA (estimated time of arrival). If response time is longer than you might take to get there on your own, going yourself is clearly a better choice. On the other hand, if your field life-support efforts will be interrupted by transport, evacuation by professionals who will be able to better aid the victim is preferred, even if it means waiting a little longer. No matter what the method of evacuation, life-support efforts must continue.

Send An Account

Emergency service providers will need an account of the incident and information on what treatment was provided to the victim and any results of the treatment. Along with this, the identifying information covered above is necessary. Medical insurance information, if available, can be included. (In some areas, despite acute needs, treatment is delayed if patients have no payment guarantees or proof of appropriate medical insurance. Knowing this before foreign travel can make a real difference in receiving timely emergency care.)

Accompany the Diver

The rescuer or a designated assistant familiar with the diver's problem should accompany the evacuee to answer questions so that emergency care will go forward smoothly. This person may be in charge of handling the written record. It usually is not wise to expect a victim's buddy, friend, or loved one to perform this role, unless there is no other option.

Diver Transfer

Having to rerescue a diver mishandled in transport is entirely possible unless the rescuer is scrupulously careful. Whether from boat to boat or dock, or from land or boat to air, there are many things that can go wrong. For the most part, it is better to let the responding professionals direct this phase of a rescue effort and to follow their directions exactly. This is why excellent communications, by radio, telephone, or hand signals, are fundamental to all evacuations.

Calling for Evacuation. The traditional boating radio distress call, "MAYDAY," should be used for any life-threatening accident that occurs on a boat. The vessel's captain will broadcast this message over VHF Channel 16 (156.8 MHz), including the name and position of the vessel, its description (size, color, and type), number of persons aboard, and the nature of the distress and aid requested. The rescue agency, usually the Coast Guard in United States waters, will maintain contact with the vessel from that point until aid arrives. Offshore more than 25 miles (40 km), however, a boat's radio distress message may not get through. If you are diving that far out, especially in less populated areas where there is less likelihood of another boat receiving and relaying your message, more powerful radio transmitters, such as single-sideband units, are suggested.

SSB radios are aboard most offshore commercial vessels, especially those engaged in international trade. Many of these radios (as will all in the future) automatically sound an alarm notifying the operator of receipt of a distress call on their standard hailing frequency, 2182 kHz. These sets are capable of operating at great distances and, with

---

Evacuate victims as quickly as possible to the closest emergency medical facility. Unnecessary delay can cost lives.

relays or through land-based communication links, can be used to call for assistance from almost anywhere. Getting that assistance quickly enough to do any good, however, is less assured. Diving in remote areas requires great caution and especially conservative planning and execution, for this reason. Even inshore within sight of land there can be times when radio communication is difficult to establish or maintain.

For shore-based diving, the telephone is usually the best choice for getting help in a hurry (Fig. 8-7). Many places use "911" as an emergency calling number. Calls to this number may not even require coins. Trained operators will provide knowledgeable assistance for most emergencies, but they may be unfamiliar with diving. It may be necessary to explain what the problem is and the kind of aid you will need to resolve it. In any case, once reaching an emergency operator or other operator, stay on the line throughout the time it takes for aid to arrive. The connection can prove invaluable in directing personnel to your location. Most phone companies can directly connect an emergency response unit's radio with a telephone, or they will gladly relay messages back and forth.

Coordinating an Evacuation

There may be times when there is no one better qualified than the rescuer or rescue coordinator to direct the transfer from the site. As a result, knowing about the general procedures of such operations can help rescuers reduce risk to themselves, emergency response personnel, and victims.

Most evacuations include several delicate moments when small distances between large machines and vulnerable people can lead to mishap. Environmental conditions, especially at sea, can introduce other problems, some that may even preclude transfer. Victims receiving life support can be lost by even brief delays in care that occur during movement into a rescue vehicle. Despite knowledge of accepted procedures, and perhaps the urging of on-scene professionals, rescuers are advised to use their own judgment before committing themselves or any victim to transport.

Boat-to-Boat Transfer. Boat-to-boat victim transfer is relatively unusual since the risk and delay of transfer can equalize the speed difference between most dive boats and responding vessels. There are times, however, when emergency medical personnel and equipment may need to move between boats to help support victims on their way back to shore.

Maneuvering two vessels near enough each other to transfer anyone, especially an injured person, takes enormous skill and no little amount of

Fig. 8-7. Cellular telephones may be a useful, direct link to emergency medical services in some areas.

Stay within your abilities.

USE SPECIALISTS TO ACHIEVE YOUR GOALS!

luck. Poor weather and rough surface conditions add difficulty. The many forces involved when even relatively small boats shift and touch each other can cause damage or injury. Haste increases danger, but speed is essential. Getting the boats together, transferring personnel, and then maneuvering apart quickly cannot be done without planning.

Most of the time a rescuer will operate under the boat captain's instructions—the captain coordinating efforts with the responders. But there are times when the diving leader, usual rescue coordinator or rescuer, captain, and victim can be the same individual. Under these circumstances, you may be required to handle the operation.

In calm conditions, stopping the boat and letting the response vessel come alongside is easiest. Have fenders (boat bumpers) deployed along the widest point of the boat and, if available, line-handlers stationed at the bow (front) and stern (back) of the boat. The rescue craft's crew will direct these persons' activities, advising them where and how tightly to tie off the lines sent out.

Transfers will take place at the least active, most closely aligned point of both vessels. In transferring someone to a larger vessel, very long lines may be needed to secure a small boat to its side. A crane and sling may have to be used to lift the diver from the much lower deck. In this case, a litter basket, similar to a metal-wire stretcher, may be placed aboard the dive vessel so that the victim can be secured in it before transfer.

Whatever the exact circumstances, it is important that everyone aboard the boat keep clear of the edges, and preferably the entire side used for transfer, unless they are actually involved. An observer can be hurt just as easily as a rescuer when two vessels, even momentarily, collide.

Boat Transfer-to-Shore. At a dock, transfer to land is relatively easy if a stretcher or other device to move the victim is available. If you are diving from a small boat with a group, however, it may sometimes be preferable simply to land the vessel at the closest beach if aid can be arranged to meet the boat there. If you are using a boat for your diving activities, make sure that you can handle it properly. Seek training from volunteer boating-safety groups such as the U.S. Coast Guard Auxiliary, and practice handling your boat under different conditions. The midst of an emergency is no time to start learning.

A suitable beach area will be unencumbered by rocks, surf, or steep banks. Easy access to the road for an ambulance or other transport is an important criterion. If the boat is not flat-bottomed and relatively small, such as an inflatable or run-about, damage almost certainly will result when running it aground. It may be possible, if there is a stretcher or backboard in the boat, to bring the vessel into chest-deep water without damaging it and then float the victim ashore.

Air Evacuation

Removing a victim to care via aircraft—by airplane or, more frequently, by helicopter—often is the fastest method available. Most professional rescue services rely on helicopters to circumvent the traffic problems and extra distance of road transport (Fig. 8-8). Many emergency medical centers have air-ambulance landing facilities and may even keep a specially equipped helicopter and medically trained flight crew on standby. Some of these coordinate in offering rescue training with volunteer or public service agencies. Taking these courses is highly recommended.

Fig. 8-8. Many areas rely on military personnel to provide evacuation services. Know how to contact them in an emergency where you dive.

Conventional Aircraft. Though much less commonly used for emergency evacuation, conventional aircraft may be part of a rescue. If transporting a DCI victim, however, such aircraft must be capable of operating at one atmosphere internal cabin pressure. If not, as in the case of unpressurized planes, transport altitudes less than 800 feet above sea level must be maintained. Any greater reduction in ambient pressure undoubtedly will worsen a DCI victim's condition.

Helicopter Evacuation. Since their invention, rotor-driven aircraft have established themselves as workhorses of rapid response and rescue in otherwise inaccessible areas. Their abilities to land and take off vertically in areas limited only by their own rotor span and length, hover in place, and operate directly between points at high speeds and low altitudes make them especially suitable for transporting dive casualties from shorelines or boats offshore. But capable as they are in the hands of a highly skilled pilot, helicopters are relatively fragile craft. Mishandling the bottom side of a rescue that includes an airborne helicopter can lead quickly to tragedy.

Land Pick-up. With space to land, a helicopter evacuation is a straightforward affair. Stay well clear of turbulent propeller wind and the fuselage's landing gear, and remain far from the overhead and tail rotors until signaled to approach by the crew.

More often than not, the pilot will pick the landing area and, after a surveying fly-over that can include dropping a smoke marker to help indicate prevailing wind, will set the craft down. At that point, emergency medical personnel on board will immediately leave the craft and begin their care of the victim. Approach any helicopter from the front only in full view of the pilot.

However, it may be necessary, especially at night, to indicate a suitable landing area to the helicopter. Even in daylight, especially if you are diving at a remote site that may be free of significant landmarks or obscured by overhanging trees, you may need to help the helicopter find you. Having flares or a smoke marker on hand will greatly facilitate this. A powerful dive light or several lights together also can be used to mark an area at night. Setting these up horizontally around the perimeter of the landing zone, with one straight up in the center, will signal aircraft.

If landing is impractical, some of the precautions and procedures below for directing a flying pick-up from a boat are appropriate.

Boat Pick-up. Getting a victim from the deck of a boat into a helicopter in flight is a particularly hazardous operation for the boat, the helicopter, and for any persons on either. Despite their remarkable abilities, helicopters are far from invincible. A stray flock of birds can damage or destroy their engines or crucial tail rotor. If their lifting gear, litter basket, or attached line is snagged, they can be dragged down onto the boat or into the sea. The following procedures are recommended. Though this type of evacuation in particular is likely to be under the supervision of professional captains and pilots, it is wise for a rescuer to understand the process.

The boat will be directed to power ahead at a moderate speed into, or slightly off, the wind. This will enable the aircraft to use some forward speed to maintain strict control, and it will usually make the boat more stable. All removable masts, antennas, and rails should be lowered, and any loose gear should be tied down or stored below. The tremendous rotor wash can move surprisingly large items that will injure anyone in the way or may be drawn up into the blades or aircraft.

The helicopter will probably make a test pass over the vessel to make sure that there is nothing in the way and to determine an appropriate altitude for the lift. A litter basket with an attached cable or line will be lowered to the vessel's deck. It is extremely important that the cable be allowed to touch the deck before anyone handles it. The rotor's movement through the air builds up tremendous static electricity and this charge is grounded through the boat to the water through the tag-line cable. *Anyone touching the cable before it touches the boat will become a link to the electrical ground, possibly with fatal results.*

Once on the deck, however, the cable is best hand-tended as the basket is lowered. Never make this line fast to the boat. A sudden updraft, wave, or swell can literally pull the helicopter from the sky if it is so attached. Be prepared to clear any persons from the cable or basket by simply letting go. You most often will be instructed to release the basket when it is on deck, allowing the helicopter to stand by out of position adjacent to the boat while the victim is strapped in, or the lift master at the helicopter end may release it. Usually, however, once the basket is on deck, the helicopter will maintain position above the vessel until the basket and victim are lifted clear. (Remember, if the basket is disconnected the cable must be allowed to ground again before it is touched.) Conversation on deck beneath a helicopter usually will be impossible. Fortunately, diving hand-signals can be used effectively for any routine communications.

In either case, the victim, with appropriate information pinned inside an enclosing blanket or to the clothing, should be secured by the straps on the litter. Use all straps provided, making them snug but not unduly tight. When you are finished, signal the liftmaster or pilot to commence the lift. *The tag line should be controlled to prevent the basket from swinging, possibly further injuring the victim or anyone else on deck.* Once clear of the deck, and above the heads of persons on deck, the line tender makes sure the line will leave smoothly without catching anything and then lets go.

All personnel involved in the lift should be equipped with eye protection. Dive masks or sunglasses may be used for this purpose, but unbreakable, shatterproof plastic goggles are preferred. Sound-deadening ear muffs like those worn around loud machinery also are a good idea. At least one pair of these, if not more, can be found in most commercial boats' engine rooms.

Rescuers should bear in mind that any or all of these suggested procedures may need to be modified by the actual conditions of a rescue. Weather or the dive vessel itself may make evacuation difficult. Only moderately poor weather and sea state may make it impossible to land a litter basket on a small boat. Other boats, like sailboats, may have no suitably clear deck area. Under some circumstances, a small auxiliary boat or life raft may be a better pick-up point. Other times, evacuation may require the victim, suitably buoyant and usually accompanied by professional rescue swimmers from the aircraft, to be lifted from the water itself.

Most of the time air evacuation is a job for professionals only! If you are present, stay out of their way. If you are involved, follow their directions exactly.

Dealing with the Aftermath of a Diving Rescue

Whether providing simple first aid to an injured diver at the site, or performing a complete water rescue that ends in evacuation to recompression, the rescue actions may be only the beginning of a rescuer's involvement with the event. Serious responsibilities remain after the victim has left. These responsibilities are directly proportional to the aid you provided and to the eventual outcome of the incident.

Additional Documentation

After the situation has been resolved, the rescuer is advised to document as much information as can be accurately recorded. This information is best detailed in a strictly factual narrative statement that is organized chronologically. Personal feelings, conjecture, or speculation have no place in the statement. Record facts only.

In addition to your narrative, gather as much supporting information as is available. This can include, but is not limited to, photographs of the incident scene and victim and statements from witnesses and other participants, especially the victim's dive buddy and professional rescuers that completed the evacuation. When gathering information, secure the names, phone numbers, and addresses of witnesses and bystanders in case you need them later.

All information gathered should be kept secure and discussed only with your attorney before it is released for any other purpose. Although this information is your personal property, it can be subpoenaed in a court of law. Diving leaders insured through NAUI should consult with NAUI's attorney as soon as possible after any involvement in a rescue or diving accident.

An Injured Diver's Gear

An injured diver's equipment is best sent with the diver. In a serious accident or death, this dive gear may be needed as evidence. If it was left at the site, a rescuer is obligated to see that the gear is delivered to the appropriate law enforcement authorities.

Cylinder pressure and the number of turns necessary to turn the cylinder off should be recorded. The assembled equipment should, if possible, be placed in a bag and sealed in front of witnesses. N*o disassembly or modification should be made or allowed.* The gear, and any other possessions of the victim(s) should be identified by tagging and photographs or at least a description that includes brands, appearance, and serial numbers of all items.

Whether required by law enforcement personnel or, as is more usual, to be returned to the divers or their families at some point in the future, this detailed inventory made and witnessed at the site will eliminate any question about missing items. When passing the equipment on to authorities, request that the agent inventory the items and obtain a receipt that includes the name, date, time, and signature of the receiver.

Notifications

A rescuer's final responsibility is to make certain that appropriate notifications are made. In some cases, particularly those involving serious injury or death, notifications will be made by local emergency medical and law enforcement authorities.

NAUI leaders are required to submit an Accident Report Form to NAUI's attorneys as soon as possible after any diving accident in which they have any part. Injured divers' families must also be notified about where divers have been taken after an accident. Rescuers are wise to record when and to whom notifications about an accident are made, as well as to keep copies of any official reports they may be required to file.

All notifications should be limited to the facts of the incident and the identities of those involved only. No discussions of blame or guilt, or conjecture on causes or possible outcomes, should be offered.

Local and Other Authorities. Local authorities probably will know about any serious diving accident since they will be among the first contacted to help affect evacuation. Even so, a separate report usually is required. It is a rescuer's responsibility to find out about and comply with any of these requirements. Failure to do so, particularly if a death is involved, could be considered criminal negligence.

Diving accidents that result in any treatment beyond simple first aid and that occur in U.S. waters must be reported to the Coast Guard in writing within 24 hours, or as soon as possible after the incident. Failure to do so can result in fines and/or imprisonment.

NAUI. As a professional association, and through its individual members, NAUI is dedicated to the goal of eliminating all diving accidents. Reporting any rescues that you are involved in to NAUI provides valuable information that can be used to improve diver training and further reduce risk.

NAUI leaders must make sure that NAUI and its attorneys are notified immediately of any accident in which they may be involved. These reports are privileged communication when sent directly and only to NAUI's attorneys. Failure to send a report can compromise a member's insurance coverage.

DAN. The Divers Alert Network (DAN) maintains a database of diving-accident information. Statistics and other information are used to help make diving safer. Filing one of their brief Diving Incident Report Forms for any diving injury or rescue in which you are involved contributes to diving safety and helps expand diving knowledge. These forms are available from DAN affiliates or directly from the organization (see Appendix E).

Family. Whatever the circumstances or outcome of a rescue, the diver's family must be notified if the diver is taken or sent anywhere except home. This is a task that usually falls on responding authorities or local law enforcement officials, but sometimes a rescuer or diving professional may be present.

Speaking with the loved ones of an injured or deceased diver is a difficult, stressful experience. The family often has little understanding of diving, and their feelings of grief can make them angry and resentful towards you. They may even feel that the rescuer is to blame. Because of this, rescuers should make family notifications only as a last resort. If it is necessary for you to contact the family, limit conversation to notification that there was an accident and the victim's current location. Avoid any discussion of cause, blame, or responsibility, giving necessary information and a simple expression of sympathy. This takes tact and preparation.

All important details are best given to the diver's family in writing, with a copy that indicates when and to whom the information was given retained by the rescuer. Besides where the diver was taken and by whom, include pertinent information concerning the diver, such as accident-report numbers assigned by emergency services, the name and address of the organization (dive boat or store) that may have organized the trip, and your identity. If you are in a leadership position, include your certification level and membership number. (Leaders are advised to give NAUI Headquarters or NAUI's attorneys as their contact number, unless appointing a spokesperson to handle inquiries as suggested in *Mastering NAUI Leadership*.)

It is wise to have someone else present during any discussions. Having a witness present can prevent later misunderstandings. Though specific circumstances will vary, never let anyone's assertions that whatever happened was your fault pass unchallenged. It also is generally best to avoid discussions with an injured diver's legal representatives, even if they are in the diver's immediate family, unless you have your own attorney present.

Legal Aspects of Diving Accidents

Rescue-certified divers have no legal obligation to use their skills to aid another diver, particularly since doing so may place them at risk. Despite this, most divers—most people, whether specifically trained in rescue or not—will feel morally obligated to respond to another person in distress. Rescue divers who do respond to divers in distress because of their rescue training and knowledge, then assume legal responsibility, a duty, to perform in accordance with a reasonable standard of care.

This standard includes not doing anything that worsens the condition of an injured diver and doing everything possible to help that might be expected of any similarly trained person (Fig. 8-9). The fact that rescuers' participation is voluntary in no way changes this obligation once they have intervened. This is entirely reasonable, and it is doubtful that any persons attempting to help another person would suddenly change their minds, or purposefully do something to harm the person in distress. However, once the duty has been created, errors or omissions, regardless of rescuers' good intentions, may be considered a breach of duty if examined by a court. This might happen if a diver or the diver's heirs sued.

If that breach resulted in some harm to the diver, even if only a minor part of the overall problems, the rescuer may be found negligent—"careless" or "irresponsible." (The same liability may apply for any individuals you appoint to necessary tasks who are injured, or who may cause unwitting harm to another diver in the course of a rescue you coordinate.)

Fig. 8-9. Once you begin to aid an accident victim, you have a duty to perform to the best of your ability and to leave the person no worse than when found.

If a rescuer is found to have been careless, acted improperly, or not done everything that could be reasonably expected, the rescuer (and any assistants) may be liable for damages to the diver and the victim's family, even to the point of having to pay for all or part of the injured diver's care, as well as an additional amount to help relieve the victim's additional pain and suffering.

Since these decisions are made in court, rescue divers will need expert help, at least a lawyer and possibly outside expert witnesses, to defend themselves if a claim is made. This process in itself, regardless of its outcome, will be extremely time consuming and expensive. A liability judgment can be catastrophic, resulting in substantial financial loss. *Even if you have nothing of significant value at the present time, a judgment of liability can follow you throughout your life, requiring you to pay part of any future income you earn or otherwise acquire.* Such problems are best avoided in advance.

Fig. 8-10. Maintain a complete record of your rescue training and related skill certifications in your log book.

Avoiding Negligence

Anyone can be sued for anything, but being found negligent and liable usually can be avoided if you have acted to the best of your ability and training, and you can prove it. Proof is best achieved by maintaining your rescue skills and ability, continuing your diving education, and carefully documenting any actions you take in connection with aiding or rescuing another diver (Fig. 8-10). Following the procedures outlined in your rescue course and this book will assist you.

Maintaining Your Skills and Ability. Remaining fit to dive, and ensuring your own diving fitness by diving and through regular exercise, will help you maintain your ability to rescue another diver in distress. But rescue skills, like other diving skills, will become rusty without your work to refresh and refine them. NAUI recommends that you participate in rescue classes at least every other year. Many NAUI instructors are glad to have some experienced divers in any Scuba Rescue Diver or Advanced Scuba Rescue Diver course. They provide peer-learning opportunities and rescue-trained divers to simulate victims of diving injuries. Instructors usually will give discounts on course fees or may give credit in other ways to rescue-certified divers, as part of their commitment to encouraging continuing education for divers.

Good CPR and first-aid skills demand regular practice and annual re-certification from a recognized authority. Many organizations like the National Safety Council make these classes available for nominal fees. Without valid certification, it may be possible to aid another diver as a "Good Samaritan," as explained below; however, taking a refresher course annually is preferred and highly recommended. Professional coaching and evaluation of your skills will keep them effective and maintain your confidence in your ability.

The "good Samaritan Law". A "good Samaritan" is one who aids another, by providing first aid for an injury or attempting rescue, though no legal duty to do so exists. Some states have enacted laws to protect from liability for negligence people who voluntarily help others. Some of these laws include non-leadership-certified rescue divers who aid an injured diver. Their actions often occur in remote areas, and without their timely help more substantial injury or even death might occur. Rescue divers should discuss laws such as these in their diving areas with competent legal authorities.

Legal Information for Leadership Divers

NAUI members are recreational diving professionals. As professionals, they have greater responsibilities than other divers. These responsibilities include a duty to aid any divers with whom they work according to the standard of care expected of a professional diving leader. That standard is established by NAUI, other recreational diving associations, and divers themselves. These concepts and more detailed information on liability are discussed in Chapter Twelve of *Mastering* NAUI *Leadership*, but the following are included for review purposes.

Duty, Assumption of Risk, and the "Prudent Professional".

A duty exists when there is an implied or express (oral or written) contract between parties. In organizing a diving excursion, leaders have a duty to use their best judgment to reduce the risks of injuries that divers will face. Any risks that remain must be carefully and thoroughly explained to participants. Given this information, divers or students can decide whether they wish to assume the risk of participation. If so, they signify that assumption by signing an appropriate waiver, preferably at the dive itself.

In the event of an accident, despite the fact that the divers have assumed the risk of their participation, a diving leader has a duty to be reasonably prepared to help, consistent with what a "prudent professional" would be expected to do. These standards are higher than those that a rescue-certified diver would be expected to meet. For instance, a diving leader is probably obligated to make sure that suitable oxygen administration equipment and a trained provider are readily available to treat injured divers at any events they organize. Rescue-certified divers may bring an oxygen supply and have the required training; however, they are not obligated to treat any diver unless they choose to.

A leader's duty also extends to any assistants employed to help in a rescue whether or not aides are paid or volunteer their services. If assistants are harmed by their participation, the leader can be held responsible. If other divers are hurt by the actions of designated assistants, the diving leader in charge will also likely be considered responsible.

Insurance

There are two types of insurance that are specifically connected to dive rescue. The first is accident insurance. Available from DAN and other sources, this insurance is designed to help provide a diver with the costly medical care that can be required to treat a diving injury, such as recompression therapy and follow-up treatments. This kind of care is not always included in normal medical insurance. In fact, some insurance plans specifically exclude diving-related injuries from their usually covered events. Some diving insurance programs also provide coverage for the costs of evacuation from an accident site and emergency transportation back to the diver's home area for continuing medical treatment. All divers should investigate and subscribe to one of these programs.

The second type of insurance connected with rescue is liability insurance. This insurance is designed to protect rescuers if a lawsuit is brought as a result of a rescue in which they participated. Diving leaders with NAUI Professional Liability Insurance are already covered for this possibility so long as they remain members in good standing, maintain insurance coverage, and comply with the terms of the policy in effect.

Non-leadership rescue divers may be covered for liability arising from a rescue under other insurance programs they may have. Sometimes homeowner's, automobile, or boat insurance has extended protection for the actions of the policy holder. If not, rescue divers are urged to find out how they can obtain coverage through these sources or to discuss their involvement in diving with their insurance agents. Your NAUI instructor or local dive shop may also have more information about appropriate liability insurance you may purchase.

The National Association of Underwater Instructors (NAUI) exists to support dedicated diving professionals in their goal of making underwater recreation less hazardous. NAUI members provide the public with quality dive training and education and with the opportunity to participate in well-organized diving events. Enjoyable recreational diving is the result of careful planning, preparation, and superior training, rather than luck. Though the chance of diving accidents will continue to exist, NAUI's motto "Safety Through Education" will likewise continue to define succinctly the association's mission and approach.

THE ZERO-ACCIDENT GOAL

Accident-free dive training is one aspect of NAUI's commitment to the Zero-Accident Goal. Providing individual structured learning experiences, NAUI instructors challenge students to develop physical skills and abilities at the same time they increase their knowledge of complex diving information. Acting freely within the strict parameters of NAUI's published *Standards and Procedures*, members focus on helping each student become the best diver possible as they work hard first to meet, and then exceed, minimum requirements. The simple truth is that this works. Although training accidents are not yet completely eliminated, NAUI teaching professionals have created a safety record that is unsurpassed by any other training association.

Though more difficult to achieve because of the wide variety of divers and diving conditions, accident-free recreational diving is the other aspect of NAUI's commitment to eliminating diving accidents. This book, and the Scuba Rescue Diver and Advanced Scuba Rescue Diver courses for which it is written, are important parts of NAUI's efforts to achieve this.

Better prepared, more knowledgeable divers will have fewer accidents because they will understand the risks of their participation, and they will understand what can be done to reduce them. If accidents do occur, NAUI rescue-certified divers, through swift intervention and appropriate treatment, can effectively limit the injuries that can result to other divers.

Your NAUI Rescue Training Options: Scuba Rescue Diver and Advanced Scuba Rescue Diver

NAUI offers two levels of rescue training to certified divers. They are distinct options, though either will help divers reduce their chances of becoming victims of diving mishaps and increase their abilities to aid other divers.

NAUI Scuba Rescue Diver

The NAUI Scuba Rescue Diver program is a specialty course for certified divers who wish to acquire the skills and knowledge of dive rescue primarily for their own and their dive buddies' benefits as recreational divers. It is open to any certified divers and is a logical next step from NAUI Scuba Diver or Advanced Scuba Diver certification. There are no other prerequisites, except the willingness to work hard to improve your diving skills and knowledge.

Building upon the foundation of the self-rescue and assisting techniques taught in basic certification courses, Scuba Rescue Diver helps divers better understand the causes and prevention of common diving accidents. Its goal is for divers to develop the ability to recognize and deal with potential diving problems in themselves and in their dive buddies.

Divers also learn and practice recommended emergency-ascent techniques for out-of-air situations and assisting techniques for dealing with a dive buddy in distress at the surface and underwater. These include airway-control techniques, diver-assisting techniques, in-water rescue-breathing techniques, and procedures for rescuing breathing and non-breathing divers found underwater. Surface skills include performing in-water rescue-breathing and exit techniques for an injured diver, and providing routine first aid and elementary principles of accident management.

NAUI Advanced Scuba Rescue Diver

The NAUI Advanced Scuba Rescue Diver program includes all the rescue skills of Scuba Rescue Diver, but it goes further since it is dedicated to preparing future diving leaders to manage all aspects of a dive rescue for a single buddy or a group of divers. Recognized certification in CPR and first aid, as well as diving experience and swimming ability are prerequisites. Prior certification in oxygen administration from an approved training organization also is required. (Required skills instruction and certification may be included in the course.) Unlike NAUI Scuba Rescue Diver, Advanced Scuba Rescue Diver certification expires after 3 years and must be renewed by successful demonstration of all skills to an Advanced Scuba Rescue Diver-qualified NAUI instructor.

Advanced Scuba Rescue Diver training includes use of lines and floats, missing-diver procedures, exhausted-diver assists with and without the aid of a float, skin-diver rescue of a submerged scuba diver, and shore or beach and boat or dock rescue exits. As prospective diving leaders, Advanced Scuba Rescue Divers are trained in some aspects of diving supervision, including learning how to direct rescue assistants, prepare local accident management plans, and present a diving accident management plan (briefing) to a group of divers. Demonstrations of first aid and life support skills to the level of a professional rescuer, including two-person CPR and CPR techniques for infants and children, oxygen administration, patient survey techniques, accident management through evacuation, and preparation of a sample accident report are also part of the program.

Successful completion of an Advanced Scuba Rescue Diver program is highly recommended for any divers who wish to enter leadership training courses for Assistant Instructor, Divemaster, or Instructor, or who wish to achieve recognition as Training Assistant Specialty Scuba Divers. Many of the rescue, management, and planning skills also are highly useful for Skin Diving Instructors.

Prerequisites for Entering the NAUI Advanced Scuba Rescue Diver Course (from the NAUI Standards and Procedures Manual). Divers should note that the following are included for informational purposes only. NAUI Headquarters should be consulted for the current standards in effect for any course. Updates and modifications may affect any of these performance objectives, minimum requirements, or certification standards.

A. Minimum age for entry into training is 17.
B. Minimum-entry scuba certification is *Naui Advanced Scuba Diver*, or equivalent training (at least nine training dives).
C. Training and current certification in first aid and CPR to the Professional Rescuer level are required if not offered as part of the Advanced Scuba Rescue Diver course. The training must be sanctioned by the National Safety Council, Red Cross, the American Heart Association, St. Johns Ambulance, or similar national organizations approved by the NAUI Training Department.
D. Training and certification in lifesaving or lifeguarding techniques are strongly recommended.
E. Completion of training within the past two years of a Divers Alert Network (DAN)–oxygen administration course or equivalent is required (in countries where sanctioned oxygen training is available), if such a course is not offered as part of the Advanced Scuba Rescue Diver course. Oxygen administration training must include the assembly, use, and basic maintenance of constant-flow and demand-valve oxygen delivery systems.
F. Participants must perform the following skills satisfactorily, i.e., without undue stress, before entering the course. The instructor is to use these skills as preentrance evaluation criteria:
   1. Swimming skills (no equipment):
      a. Swim 220 yards (201 m), non-stop, any stroke, in 6 minutes.
      b. Survival-swim for 15 minutes.
      c. Recover 10 lb of weight (4.5 kg) from 8 to 12 feet (2.4 to 3.7 m) of water.
      d. Transport another person of equal size 25 yards (22.9 m).
   2. Skin-diving skills (mask, fins, snorkel, BC or vest, exposure suit, and weights, as appropriate):
      a. Demonstrate proper techniques for entries, exits, swimming, and surface dives.
      b. Demonstrate adjustment of weights and buoyancy control to achieve and maintain neutral buoyancy.
      c. Demonstrate the ability to make a buoyant recovery by diving to a depth of 8 to 12 feet (2.4 to 3.7 meters) while wearing an exposure suit without a weight belt [buoyant by approximately 10 lb (4.54 kg)] and remaining at that depth for a minimum of 20 seconds.
   3. Scuba skills (skin diving equipment [see 2 above] plus scuba equipment):
      a. Assemble equipment, make adjustments, don equipment, and perform predive equipment inspections.
      b. At the surface, as separate demonstrations, remove and replace mask, snorkel, fins, weight belt, and scuba unit.
      c. Underwater, as separate demonstrations, remove, replace, and clear mask and regulator; buddy-breathe; and share air using an alternate air source.
      d. Demonstrate buoyancy control at the surface and underwater.
      e. At the surface, transport another scuba diver 100 yards (91 m) within 4 minutes. The person being transported may not assist. Both divers are to wear scuba gear, and weight belts are to be retained. Breathing from the regulator is not permitted.

BLOOD-BORNE PATHOGENS

To date, there is no known case of disease transmission through sharing a scuba mouthpiece during training or under the conditions of a diving emergency. The possibility of exposure to any blood-borne pathogen from another diver through sharing air underwater is virtually nonexistent, however, since both HIV and HVB cannot live long outside the host body, and both are readily killed by saltwater contact. Other microbes, bacteria, and viruses generally cannot survive in the water environment. If concerns still exist, using an alternate second stage or redundant scuba system is highly recommended and will eliminate all chance of contamination. Rescuers may, however, be exposed to disease by handling injured divers on the surface and by providing first aid treatments, from cleaning and bandaging wounds to administering rescue breathing and CPR. Protecting yourself against these possibilities is prudent.

Your NAUI instructor has taught you several methods for handling injured divers with this in mind. Using surgical gloves when working with victims, carefully cleaning and disinfecting any areas where spilled blood or other bodily fluids may have accumulated, and using face shields or pocket masks with one-way valves during rescue breathing and CPR are among these techniques. Mouth-to-snorkel rescue breathing is another effective technique that also protects rescuer and diver from disease.

CHANGES TO NAUI STANDARDS AND PROCEDURES 1994

(THIS UPDATE REPRESENTS CHANGES TO STANDARDS AND PROCEDURES SINCE THE ADDENDUM TO THE 1991 S&P WAS SENT TO THE MEMBERSHIP IN LATE 1993)

The NAUI Board of Directors adopted the following changes to NAUI Standards and Procedures at its meetings 4–8 April 1994. The changes may be implemented upon receipt. All NAUI sanctioned diving activities and courses must comply by 1 January 1995. These changes will be incorporated in the next revision of the NAUI Standards and Procedures Manual.

OXYGEN POLICY

"An oxygen supply and personnel trained to provide oxygen in the event of a diving accident or emergency to breathing and non-breathing victims are to be accessible at all NAUI sanctioned diving activities unless otherwise prohibited by law or legal code."

Oxygen first aid should be available to anyone who needs it. The language of the policy was crafted to achieve that goal while recognizing the implicit practical and logistical concerns.

- The type of oxygen supply is not specified because first aid that results in an increase of oxygen in the air inspired is desirable.
- Training requirements are not delineated because in-service training with the available equipment should be completed and not be deferred until an oxygen first aid certification course can be completed.
- Stating that the equipment and personnel, "are to be accessible", allows for reliance on paramedic and/or lifeguard services where appropriate. Its recognized that equipment may require securing in a vehicle at some sites.
- Local laws or operational guidelines are allowed for in the language of the policy. For example commercial airline rules that would prevent one from bringing oxygen supplies to a diving activity via air. Participants should be advised of the absence of an emergency oxygen supply and allowed to make an informed and responsible decision regarding their participation. The same advice and decision process would apply when oxygen supplies are depleted during an extended diving excursion.

BUDDY BREATHING

Change
NAUI Credo # 14. "NAUI believes that proficiency in the skills of *sharing air* buddy breathing (sharing a single regulator) and making an emergency swimming ascent is essential for diver safety."

This language is consistent with the change to the Openwater I Scuba Diver standard regarding buddy breathing made in December 1993 – as follows:

VII. Skill Performance Objectives

D. Open Water – Scuba diving skills; open water scuba gear appropriate for the area.

11. Buddy breathe *Share air* with another diver. Be the donor of the air and the receiver of the air. To be performed in a stationary position at a depth of approximately 15 to 25 feet (4.6 to 7.6 meters).

DRY SUIT TRAINING

Change

Add the following language to NAUI Standards and Procedures Manual, Standards Applying to All NAUI Diving Courses and NAUI Openwater I Scuba Diver Course Standards:

VI. Equipment
   C. *When dry suits are used during open water training activities the instructor must assure the student has had adequate training or experience in the use of dry suits prior to participating in open water activities. This may be done by verifying experience through a training or diving log or by specialty certification. If dry suits are to be used during Openwater I training courses the minimum additional curriculum on page 2.19 must be completed prior to open water activities.*

Renumber paragraphs "C, D, E, to D, E, F respectively.

Insert the following in the Openwater I Course Standard page 2.19 VII. A.
   4. *If dry suits are to be used, the student must complete the following skills in confined water before participating in open water training activities:*
      a. *demonstrate the use of suit controls*
      b. *recover from an inverted position while buoyant.*
      c. *recover from a simulated stuck suit valve*
      d. *demonstrate a procedure for a jettisoned weight system*
      e. *select a compatible buoyancy compensator.*
      f. *maintain a minimum volume of air in the suit to prevent suit squeeze*

DIVING LEADERSHIP SPECIALTY STANDARD
—NOW TRAINING ASSISTANT SPECIALTY

- See the July/August 1994 issue of Sources for a xample course outline.

PURPOSE AND SCOPE

The purpose of this change to the Diving Leadership Specialty Course standard, henceforth called the Training Assistant Specialty Course, is to establish the minimum standard of training **for the specific tasks of:**

- temporarily overseeing remaining students while the instructor conducts a skill with other students or…
- escorting diving students at the surface and on underwater tours at a ratio not to exceed two students to one training assistant.

While standards have required active-status members for this role, actually it has been fulfilled to a varying degree by so-called "Safety Divers" or "Teaching Assistants" without the benefit of a legitimate standard of training. An individual who completes this specialty course and acts in a training assistant capacity has **no impact on supervisory ratios** in confined or open water. This individual is **not** qualified to perform in any capacity other than those conforming to the approved standard.

CONFIDENTIAL **CONFIDENTIAL**

NAUI ACCIDENT REPORT

Date of Accident _____ Name of Victim _____

Location of Accident _____

Address of Victim _____ Sex _____ Age _____

Was this an instructional or supervised dive? ☐ Yes ☐ No

Check all applicable: ☐ Fatality ☐ Bodily Injury ☐ Bends ☐ Embolism ☐ Non-Injury ☐ Other

Briefly describe the diving experience of victim, if known, was he or she a student, novice diver, experienced diver, or whatever best describes the level of competence of the victim. Describe the accident and the events leading up to it, including the damages to the victim as known at the time of preparing this report. Please give all details as to safety personnel, divers, assistant instructors, water conditions, rescue methods, equipment failures, if known, length of time to effect rescue, emergency procedures employed, first aid administered, and other agencies responding to the accident, if any. In general, please give your best narrative as to the events involved in the accident. Use additional pages if needed to give a complete account of the facts:

Narrative Report: _____

_____

_____

_____

_____

_____

_____

_____

_____

_____

_____

_____

Your Name _____ Your NAUI Number _____

Your Address _____

Telephone Number: Day _____ Evening _____

Please describe your current diving status, i.e., Instructor, Assistant Instructor, Divemaster, Certified Diver, whatever best describes your current certification and skill level. Also describe your relationship to the accident, i.e., were you a witness?, were you actively involved with the victim?, were you called on to attempt a rescue?, whatever best describes your relationship to the events described in this report:

_____

_____

Please list the names and addresses and telephone numbers of all witnesses that you are aware of. Use a separate attachment, if necessary, to insure a complete list.

Names	Addresses	Phone Numbers

Please use additional sheets to insure completeness of report.

89-0014(1)

DIVING INCIDENT REPORT FORM

Please return this completed form to:
Divers Alert Network, Attn: Medical Division, 3100 Tower Blvd., Suite 1300, Durham, NC 27707 USA. Phone (919) 684-2948; fax (919) 490-6630.

All the following questions relate to the particular dive involved in the incident. They do not, however, have to be filled out by the diver involved, but by **the person observing the incident.**

THE INCIDENT

1. On the back of this form, please briefly describe the incident. To report more than one incident, you may photocopy this form.
2. Whose incident was it?
   ❑ yours   ❑ your buddy's   ❑ someone else's
3. When was it detected?
   ❑ preparation   ❑ during dive   ❑ descent   ❑ entry   ❑ ascent   ❑ after exit
4. Did any harm result to anyone?   ❑ Yes   ❑ No
5. Do you think any of the following factors contributed to the incident (you may need to check more than one):
   ❑ none
   ❑ anxiety about the dive
   ❑ inexperience in diving
   ❑ weather conditions
   ❑ poor physical fitness
   ❑ failure to check equipment
   ❑ haste
   ❑ inattention
   ❑ poor dive planning
   ❑ poor servicing of equipment
   ❑ sea sickness
   ❑ insufficient training
   ❑ not familiar with diving conditions
   ❑ error in judgment/incorrect decision
   ❑ poor communication
   ❑ lack of a buddy check
   ❑ drug or alcohol intake
   ❑ failure to understand equipment
   ❑ lack of medical clearance to dive
   ❑ inadequate supervision
   ❑ failure to understand dive table
   ❑ poor maintenance of equipment
   ❑ malfunction or failure of equipment
6. Did the incident occur while under training?   ❑ Yes   ❑ No
7. What influence did the incident have on the dive plan?
   ❑ none   ❑ delayed the dive   ❑ aborted dive   ❑ changed the plan
8. Did the incident involve (you may need to check more than one):
   ❑ none
   ❑ out-of-air situation
   ❑ rapid ascent
   ❑ omission of decompression stops
   ❑ misreading of decompression tables/computer
   ❑ multiple ascents/descents
   ❑ bounce diving
   ❑ loss of buddy contact
   ❑ marine animal
   ❑ equalization problem on ascent
   ❑ equalization problem on descent
   ❑ giddiness/vertigo
   ❑ flying/altitude after diving
   ❑ problem at safety stop
   ❑ buoyancy problem at decompression stop
9. Was the diver involved: ❑ a diving student   ❑ untrained   ❑ certified diver
10. Diver certification level: ❑ basic   ❑ open-water   ❑ advanced   ❑ not known
    ❑ instructor   ❑ divemaster   ❑ commercial
11. Sex: M   F   Diver's age: _____ years   ❑ not known
12. Which country did the diver train in? _____ Phone no. _____ (Please include country & area codes.)
13. Please indicate geographical location of incident. Country _____ Phone no. _____

AIR SUPPLY

1. Air consumption: ❑ ran low   ❑ out of air   ❑ not a problem
   ❑ octopus used   ❑ not known   ❑ buddy breathing
2. If there had been an alternative air source (i.e. a Pony Bottle, "Spare Air"), would it have helped in the situation?
   ❑ Yes   ❑ No   ❑ Not known
3. Regulator and air supply:
   ❑ didn't check contents gauge regularly   ❑ contents gauge inaccurate/failed   ❑ problem w/regulator despite frequent servicing
   ❑ air supply not turned on   ❑ unable to read contents gauge at depth   ❑ hose rupture
   ❑ second stage problem   ❑ first stage problem   ❑ not involved

City where normally serviced: _____ Phone no. _____
Air consumption this dive greater than previous dives: Yes   No

BUOYANCY

1. Buoyancy problem: ❑ Yes   ❑ No
   ❑ overweighted   ❑ air used frequently to maintain buoyancy
   ❑ underweighted   ❑ weight belt problem
2. Buoyancy jacket:
   ❑ not worn   ❑ vest leaked   ❑ incorrect use
   ❑ inflation device failed   ❑ vest provided inadequate buoyancy   ❑ not involved
   ❑ inflation device not connected correctly   ❑ vest uncomfortable to wear
   ❑ unable to vent vest to slow down   ❑ unfamiliar with its use   Name/model of vest: _____

DIVE TABLES/COMPUTER

1. Dive tables used:
   ❑ None   ❑ USNavy   ❑ RN   ❑ BSAC/RNPL   other (specify) _____
   ❑ NAUI   ❑ DCIEM   ❑ BASSETT   ❑ PADI
2. Was a dive computer used?   ❑ Yes   ❑ No
   If so: ❑ stopped working   ❑ unable to read number
   ❑ inaccurate   ❑ forgot to activate it
   Make: _____   Model: _____

REFERENCES AND RECOMMENDED READING

Alaska Department of Health and Social Services. *State of Alaska Hypothermia and Cold Water Near Drowning Guidelines.* Juneau: Emergency Medical Services Section, Division of Public Health, 1982.

Allport, Gordon. *Study of Values.* Boston: Houghton Mifflin, 1960.

American Academy of Underwater Sciences. *Proceedings of Special Session on Coldwater Diving.* Seattle: University of Washington, AAUS, 1987.

American Red Cross CPR *For The Professional Rescuer.* St. Louis: Mosby, 1993.

American Red Cross. *Lifeguarding Today.* St. Louis, MO: Mosby, 1994.

Appley, M. D. and R. Trumbull. *Psychological Stress.* New York: Appleton-Century-Crofts, 1967.

Audubon Society. *Field Guide To North American Fishes, Whale and Dolphins.* NY: Alfred A. Knopf, 1983.

Auerbach, Paul S. A *Medical Guide To Hazardous Marine LIfe.* Jacksonville, FL: Progressive Printing, 1987.

Auerbach, Paul S. "An Introduction to Stinging Marine Life Injuries." *Alert Diver.* January/February, 1994.

Bachrach, Arthur J. and Glen Egstrom. *Stress and Performance in Diving.* San Pedro, CA: Best Publishing Co., 1987.

Barocas, Ira M. (Ed.), et al. *Mastering NAUI Leadership.* Montclair, CA: National Association of Underwater Instructors, 1993.

Barsky, Steven M. *The Dry Suit Diving Manual.* Santa Barbara: Steven M. Barsky, 1988.

Bascom, Willard. *Waves and Beaches.* Garden City, NY: Anchor Books, 1980.

Bennett, Peter B. and Richard E. Moon. *Diving Accident Management.* Bethesda, MD: Undersea and Hyperbaric Medical Society, 1990.

Bennett, Peter B. and David H. Elliott, (Eds.). *The Physiology and Medicine of Diving.* San Pedro, CA: Best Publishing Company, 1982.

Berne, Eric. *Games People Play.* New York: Grove Press, 1976.

Boehler, Ted. *The Divemaster Manual 2: A Guide To Facilitating the Joy of Diving.* Crestline CA: DeepStar Publishing, 1981 (Rev.).

Bookspan, Jolie. "Things That Stings." *Alert Diver.* January/February, 1994.

Bove Alfred A. and Jefferson C. Davis. *Diving Medicine.* Philadelphia: W. B. Saunders, 1990.

British Sub Aqua Club. *Seamanship for Divers.* London: BSAC, 1986.

British Sub Aqua Club. *Instructor Handbook.* Ellesmere Port: BSAC, 1992.

British Sub Aqua Club. *Safety and Rescue For Divers.* London: BSAC, 1991.

Code of Federal Regulations, Title 33: Navigation and Navigable Waters. *Subchapter P: Ports and Waterways Safety.* Washington, D.C.: Government Printing Office, 1990.

Code of Federal Regulations, Title 46: Shipping. *Subchapter C: Rules and Regulations for Uninspected Vessels.* Washington, D.C.: Government Printing Office, 1990.

Combs, A. H*elping Relationships.* Boston: Allyn And Bacon Company, 1977.

COMDTPUB P16754.7. *Boating Statistics 1993.* Washington, DC: United States Coast Guard, D.O.T., September, 1994.

Coren, E. Steven., et al. *The Law and the Diving Professional.* Santa Ana, CA: PADI, 1986.

"Diabetes and Diving." *Alert Diver,* January/February, 1995, pp 6-7.

Divers Alert Network. 1991 *Report on Diving Accidents and Fatalities.* Durham, NC: DAN, 1993.

Divers Alert Network. *Oxygen First Aid in Dive Accidents.* Durham, NC: DAN, 1993.

Divers Alert Network. *Oxygen First Aid in Dive Accidents Instructors Manual.* Durham, NC: DAN, 1992.

Douglass, Darren. "Better Boat Diving." *Pacific Diver.* May/June, 1991.

Douglass, Darren. "Beach Diving Made Almost Easy." *Pacific Diver.* April, 1991.

Edmonds, C. *Diving Medicine for Scuba Divers.* Carnegie, Victoria, Australia: J. L. Publications, 1992.

Edmonds, C. and C. Lowry and J. Pennefather. *Diving and Subaquatic Medicine.* Mosman, New South Wales, Australia: Diving Medical Centre, 1980.

Egan, G. *The Skilled Helper.* Monterey, CA: Brooks-Cole Incorporated, 1980.

Farmer, Joseph. "The Most Common Diving Accident: Middle Ear Barotrauma." *Alert Diver,* November/December, 1990.

Federal Communications Commission. *Bulletin No. FO-33: Study Guide and Reference Material for the Marine Radio Operator Permit.* Washington, D. C.: 1987.

Girdano, D. A. and G. S. Everly. *Controlling Stress and Tension: A Holistic Approach.* Englewood Cliffs, NJ: Prentice-Hall, 1979.

Graver, Dennis. "Scuba Diving First Aid Supplement." The National Safety Council (In Press). 1994

Graver, Dennis. *Scuba Diving.* Champaign, IL: Human Kinetics, 1993.

Grenard, S., G. J. Beck and G. W. Rich. *Introduction to Respiratory Therapy.* Monsey, NY: Glenn Educational Medical Services, Inc., 1971.

Griffiths, Tom and D. Steel and P. Vaccaro and M. Karpman. "The Effects of Relaxation Training on Anxiety and Underwater Performance." *International Journal of Sport Psychology.* Vol. 12, pp 176-82, 1981.

Halstead, Bruce W. *Dangerous Marine Animals That Bite, Sting, Shock are Non-Edible.* Centerville, MD: Cornell Maritime Press, 1980.

Hazzard, J. *Diving Officer's Handbook.* London: BSAC, 1986.

Heine, John, N., et al. *Advanced Diving: Technology and Techniques*. Montclair, CA: NAUI, 1994.

Hendrick, Walt Butch and A. Zaferes. *The Field Neurological For Diving Emergencies*. Hurley, NY: LifeGuard Systems, 1990.

Hendrick, Walt Butch and B. Thomson. *Oxygen and The Scuba Diver*. Hurley, NY: LifeGuard Systems, 1988.

Jennett, J. *Skin Diving For Everyone*. Montclair, CA: NAUI, 1991.

Klinck, Meyer P. "Risk Management for the Dive Boat Operator." SOURCES, *The Journal of Underwater Education*. Sept./Oct. 1991

Klinck, Meyer P. "Boating and Nuisance First Aid." SOURCES, *The Journal of Underwater Education*. Sept./Oct. 1991.

Leone, Nicholas C. and E. C. Phillips. *The Cruising Sailor's Medical Guide*. NY: David McKay, 1979.

Lippmann, John. *Deeper Into Diving*. Carnegie, Victoria, Australia: J. L. Publications, 1990.

Lippmann, J., Bugg, S. *The DAN Emergency Handbook*. Carnegie, Victoria, Australia: J. L. Publications, 1991.

Maloney, Elbert S. *Chapman Piloting, Seamanship & Small Boat Handling (60th Ed.)*. New York: Hearst Marine Books, 1991.

Meyer, Peter. "Risk Management for Underwater Educators and Supervisors —Program Overview." Rev. October, 1992. Montclair, CA: NAUI, 1992.

Miles, S. and D. E. MacKay. *Underwater Medicine*. Philadelphia: J. P. Lippincott, 1976.

National Association of Underwater Instructors. *Leadership Course Instructors Guide*. Montclair, CA: NAUI, 1992.

National Association of Underwater Instructors. *NAUI Course Directors Guidelines*. Montclair, CA: NAUI, 1990.

National Association of Underwater Instructors. *NAUI Openwater I Scuba Diver Instructor Guide*. Montclair, CA: NAUI, 1987.

National Association of Underwater Instructors. *NAUI Professional Liability Insurance and Risk Management Recommendations, 1993-1994*. Montclair, CA: NAUI, 1993.

National Association of Underwater Instructors. *NAUI Standards and Procedures Manual*. Montclair, CA: NAUI, 1994 (Rev.)

National Association of Underwater Instructors. *The Best of SOURCES, Volume I*. Montclair, CA: NAUI, 1993.

National Association of Underwater Instructors. *The NAUI Textbook II*. Montclair, CA: NAUI, 1990.

National Association of Underwater Instructors. *Advanced Diving Technology and Techniques*. Montclair, CA: NAUI, 1991.

National Safety Council. *First Aid and CPR Level 2*. Boston: NSC, 1994.

Naval Sea Systems Command. *US Navy Diving Manual, Vol. I (Air Diving)*, (NAVSEA 0994-LP001-9010 Rev. 3). Flagstaff, AZ: Best Publishing Co., 1993.

Pierce, Albert. *Scuba Life Saving*. Champaign, IL: Leisure Press, 1985

Pilmanis, Andrew A. *Emergency Management of Diving Accidents and Hyperbaric Chamber Operations (Course Notes)*. Catalina, CA: USC, 1988.

Radio Technical Commission for Maritime Services. *Marine Radiotelephone Users Handbook*. Washington, D.C.: Federal Communications Commission, 1987.

Rogers, Carl. "Empathy: An Unappreciated Way of Being." *The Counseling Psychologist*, 1975, Vol. 5, No. 2, pp 2-10.

Rogers, Raymond E. *DCS and the Traveling Diver: How to Avoid the Bends*.

Sausalito, CA: Insightful Newsletters, LLC, 1995.

Rutkowski, Dick. *Nitrox Manual*. Key Largo, FL: Hyperbaric International, 1990.

Shindell, Lawrence, M. "The Good Samaritan." *Alert Diver*, January/February, 1995, pp 19-23.

Singer, R. *Myths And Truths In Sports Psychology*. New York: Harper And Row, 1978.

Sleeper, Jeanne B., et al. *Legal Aspects of Underwater Education*. Montclair, CA: NAUI, 1976.

Smith, R. and R. Allen. *Scuba Lifesaving and Accident Management*. Key West, FL: National YMCA Underwater Activities Program, 1978.

Strauss, R. H. *Diving Medicine*. Orlando, FL: Grune and Stratton, 1976.

Talge, Helen. "Impact of Recreational Divers on Coral Reefs In The Florida Keys." *Diving For Science*-AAUS Proceedings 1990, pp 356-373.

Telford, Hans W. *Diving Rescue Techniques and Diver First Aid Manual*. Queensland, Australia: NAUI Australia, 1988.

U.S. Coast Guard. *U.S. Coast Guard Auxiliary Boat Crew Manual* (COMDTINSTM16798.8). Washington, D.C.: U.S. Coast Guard, Department of Transportation, 1983.

U.S. Coast Guard. *U. S. Coast Guard Auxiliary Manual* (COMDTINST M16790.1C). Washington, D.C: Department of Transportation, U. S. Coast Guard, 1992.

U.S. Coast Guard. *Navigation Rules, International*, (COMDTINSTM16672.2). Washington, D.C.: U.S. Coast Guard, Department of Transportation, 1982.

U.S. Coast Guard Auxiliary. *Boating Skills and Seamanship*. Washington, D.C.: U.S. Coast Guard Auxiliary, U.S. Coast Guard, Department of Transportation, 1988.

U.S. Coast Guard Auxiliary. *Boating Skills and Seamanship, Instructor's Guide*. Washington, D.C.: U. S. Coast Guard Auxiliary, U.S. Coast Guard, Department of Transportation, 1988.

U.S. National Oceanic and Atmospheric Administration, Office of Undersea Research. *NOAA Diving Manual, Diving for Science and Technology*. Washington, D.C.: U.S. Dept. of Commerce, 1991.

U.S. Divers, Inc. *Snorkeling Fun Guide*. 1990.

Van Dorn, William G. *Oceanography and Seamanship*. New York: Dodd, Mead and Company, 1974.

A

Abdominal cramps, 148
Academic Video Series, 48
Accident, diving, 34-59
   environmental hazards and, 41-51
   equalization difficulties and, 53-54
   equipment problems and, 35-41
   judgment problems and, 55-59
   problem breathing patterns and, 51-53
Accident insurance, 171
Accident management, 156-171
   avoiding negligence and, 170-171
   dealing with aftermath of diving rescue, 168-169
   duty, assumption of risk, and prudent professional in, 171
   emergency personnel and services and, 157-158
   equipment and, 158-159
   evacuation procedures and, 164-167
   event information and, 163
   Good Samaritan law and, 170-171
   insurance and, 171
   legal aspects of, 169-171
   legal information for leadership divers and, 171
   location information and, 163
   planning for emergencies and, 157-171
   rescuer's identity and, 163
   responding to emergency and, 160-164
   treatment information and, 163
   victim information and, 162-163
   witness information and, 163
Accident prevention, 4-17
   contraindications to underwater activities and, 5-12
   diving fitness and, 12-13
   diving medical examination and, 5, 6-7
   planning and preparation in, 13-17
Accident report form, 168
Account as response to emergency, 160-164
Action, rescue and, 72-73, 163-164
Active relaxation as response to stress, 65, 66
Advanced Diving: Technology and Techniques, 25, 46, 131
Advanced Scuba Rescue Diver course, NAUI, 12, 144
Adventures in Scuba Diving, 27
AGE; *see* Arterial gas embolism
Aggressiveness as sign of stress, 64-65
Air consumption calculations, 25
Air consumption problems, dry suits and, 38
Air hunger, 24, 52, 79
Aircraft, evacuation by, 166-167
Airway obstruction, decompression illness and, 142
Alcohol
   as contraindication to diving, 10-11
   dehydration and, 43
   heat exhaustion and, 43

Allergic reactions, marine life problems and, 150-151
Alpha, code flag, 50-51
Alternate air sources, 21-31
   alternate second stage and, 22
   multiple scuba cylinders and, 23-24
   planning for, 28-31
   pony bottles and, 23
   tiny tanks and, 24
Alternate second stage, 22, 26, 29-31, 40, 82, 83
Altitude, diving at, 46, 130
Antibiotics, wounds caused by stingrays and, 149
Antihistamines as contraindication to diving, 9-10
Appoint as response to emergency, 161-162
Arterial gas embolism (AGE), decompression illness and, 129, 131, 133, 140, 144, 153
Ascent, emergency; *see* Emergency ascent
Ascent squeezes, 125-126
Aspirin, heat exhaustion and, 43
Assessment, rescue and, 72, 85-87, 160-161
Assisting; *see* Towing, assisting, and surface rescue
Asthma, 8, 127
Asymptomatic decompression sickness, 131
Attitude, judgment problems and, 55-56
Auxiliary rescue equipment, surface rescue and, 104-109

B

Backboard, spinal cord injury and, 109-110, 111, 159
Backscatter, underwater dive lights and, 44
Backwash, wave, 48, 49
Balance, assessment of, decompression illness and, 135
Bandaging, first aid and, 146-147
Bank drag, surface rescue and, 116-117
Barodontalgia, 124
Barotrauma, 53, 122-126
Barracuda, 150
BC; *see* Buoyancy compensator
BC carry, surface rescue and, 113, 114
Beach toys, surface rescue and, 108
Behavior, obsessive, as sign of stress, 65
Bends, skin, decompression sickness and, 131, 132, 136
Bites, marine life problems and, 150
Blackout, shallow-water, 51, 52-53, 152
Blankets, surface rescue and, 117
Bleeding, first aid for, 146
Blocks
   equalization difficulties and, 53, 54
   reverse, 125-126
   reverse sinus, 124
Blooms, visibility and, 45
Bluefish, 150
Blue-ringed octopus, 150

Boat fenders, surface rescue and, 108
Boat pick-up, air evacuation and, 167
Boating traffic, environmental hazards and, 50-51
Boats
   getting victim aboard, 111-112
   motor, 105
   power, 104-105
Boat-to-boat transfer, accident management and, 165-166
Boat-to-shore transfer, accident management and, 166
Body boards, surface rescue and, 107-108
Bolting, out-of-air emergencies and, 77
Boogie boards, surface rescue and, 107-108
Booties, drags and, 116
Bounce lift, surface rescue and, 114, 115
Boyle's law, 122, 129
Breath holding, 51, 52-53, 126-127
Breathing
   rescue; *see* Rescue breathing
   skip, 51, 53, 68, 93
   stabilizing, 72
   stress and, 68
Breathing problems, 51-53
Broken nose or jaw as contraindication to diving, 9
Bronchitis as contraindication to diving, 9
Bubbles, excessive, underwater distress and, 68, 85
Bubbling, decompression sickness and, 131
Buddy breathing, 28-29, 30
Buddy system, 20-31
   alternate air sources and, 21-31
   depth indicator and, 67
   emergency shared-air ascent and, 82-83
   in-water distress at surface and, 71
   leader in, 25
   neurological examination and, 136
   planning for emergencies and, 27-31
   predive activities and, 24-27
   stress and, 66-67
Buddy-breathing ascent, emergency shared-air ascent and, 82-83
Buoyancy
   freshwater and, 46
   in-water distress at surface and, 71-72
   neutral, 38, 88
   problems with, underwater distress and, 68, 70
   underwater distress and, 86
Buoyancy compensator (BC), 22, 71
   buoyancy failure and, 36
   low pressure inflator problems and, 36
   problems with, 35-36
   spinal injury and, 110
Buoys, inflatable, surface rescue and, 108
Burns, first aid for, 148-149

C

Caffeinated beverages
   dehydration and, 43
   heat exhaustion and, 43
Calming response, stress and, 65, 71, 78
Canoes, surface rescue and, 106
Captains, dive-boat, accident management and, 158
Carbon dioxide excess, 37, 53, 68, 70, 93, 140
Carbon monoxide poisoning, 151
Cardiac disease as contraindication to diving, 8-9
Cardiopulmonary resuscitation (CPR), decompression illness and, 137, 142-144, 145
Carotid sinus, 37
Carries
   multiple person shore, 115-117
   surface rescue and, 112-114
Carry mats, surface rescue and, 117
Caves and caverns, overhead environmental hazards and, 44, 50
CB radio; *see* Citizen's band radio
Ceiling of caves and caverns, 50
Cellular telephone, emergency communication and, 17, 159, 165
Central nervous system oxygen toxicity, 44
Cervical collar, spinal injury and, 109, 110, 111, 116, 159
Cervical injury; *see* Spinal cord injury
Charles' law, 22
Chest cavity, lung expansion injuries and, 128
Chilling, 41, 42, 130-131
Chokes, decompression sickness and, 132-133
Choking, 51, 126
Chronic obstructive pulmonary disorder (COPD) as contraindication to diving, 5
Citizen's band (CB) radio, emergency communication and, 17
Cleanliness, first aid for wounds and, 146-147
Clearing problems as contraindication to diving, 9, 123
Coast Guard, 16, 72, 157, 162, 164, 166
Cold water
   decompression illness and, 130
   environmental hazards and, 41-42
   surface resting in, in-water distress and, 71
Cold weather, environmental hazards and, 41-42
Colds as contraindication to diving, 9
Communication, buddy system and, 27
Compound fractures, first aid for, 147
Computers, dive, 24-25, 46
Concussions, first aid for, 147, 148
Cone shells, 150
Consumption; *see* Tuberculosis
Continuing education
   diving fitness and, 12-13
   judgment problems and, 59

Convulsions, 44, 151-152, 153
Coordination, assessment of, decompression illness and, 135
Coughing, 9, 51, 52, 126
Counseling as response to stress, 66, 67, 73
CPR; see Cardiopulmonary resuscitation
Cramps, first aid for, 35, 147-148
Current, 41
   geographic, 48-49
   longshore, 48, 49
   oceans and, 47-49
   removal of diver to shore and, 114-115
   rip, 48, 49
   rivers and, 46
   tidal, 48
Current charts, 48
Current lines, surface rescue and, 115
Cushions, surface rescue and, 108
Cyanosis, pneumothorax and, 127

D

Dalton's law, 130
Dams
   low-head, 47, 48
   river diving and, 46-47
DAN; see Diver's Alert Network
DCI; see Decompression illness
DCS; see Decompression sickness
Debilitating stress, 63
Debris, visibility and, 45
Decompression illness (DCI), 25, 31, 37, 46, 77, 96, 97, 109, 126-136, 153
   air embolism and, 128
   air evacuation and, 166
   airway obstruction and, 142
   arterial gas embolism and, 129
   carbon monoxide poisoning and, 151
   cardiopulmonary resuscitation and, 142-144
   denial and, 133
   factors in recognition of, 133-136
   first aid for, 137-144
   lung overexpansion injuries and, 126-129
   mediastinal emphysema and, 127, 128
   near drowning and, 152
   neurological examination and, 31, 87, 133-136
   oxygen administration and, 137-140
   pneumothorax and, 127-129
   providing life support and, 141-144
   recompression therapy for, 144
   rescue breathing out of water and, 141-142
   responding to, 136-144
   shock and, 140-144
   smoking and, 11
   subcutaneous emphysema and, 127, 128

Decompression injuries, 120-153
   barotrauma and, 122-126
   common, first aid for, 144-153
   signs and symptoms of, 121
Decompression sickness (DCS), 28, 38, 44, 80, 89, 120, 126, 129-133, 144, 153
   asymptomatic, 131
   dehydration and, 10
   fish poisoning and, 151
   theory of, 130
   type I, 131-132, 133, 134, 137
   type II, 131, 132-133, 134, 140
Decompression stop
   mandatory, 23
   precautionary, 25, 28, 31, 52, 79
Decongestants, 9-10, 43, 124, 159
Defensive position in approaching panicked diver, 95
Dehydration, 10, 43
Demand oxygen system, 140
Demand setting, too high, regulators and, 40
Denial, decompression illness and, 133
Density, nitrogen narcosis and, 44
Depth
   nitrogen narcosis and, 44
   problems with, drysuits and, 38
Depth indicator, buddy system and, 67
Diabetes as contraindication to diving, 8
Dinghy, surface rescue and, 106, 114
Distress, 67-73
   definition of, 67
   in-water, signs of, 67-70
   rescue of responsive diver in, 85-87
   responding to, 70-72
   stress and; see Stress
Dive computers, 24-25, 46
Dive flag, 51
Dive shops, planning and preparation and, 14
Dive site, emergency personnel and services at, 158
Dive Tables, NAUI, 15, 16, 24-25, 28, 41, 46
Dive-boat crew, accident management and, 158
Diver
   accompanying, accident management and, 164
   responsive; see Responsive diver
   transfer of, accident management and, 164-165
   unconscious; see Unconscious diver
Diver's Alert Network (DAN), 5, 16, 137, 168-169, 171
Diving
   at altitude, 130
   contraindications to, 5-12
   elevator, 68, 70, 86
   ice, 42, 50, 51

Diving, cont'd.
   repetitive, decompression sickness and, 131
   river; see River diving
Diving accident; see Accident, diving
Diving courses, 59
Diving hand signals, 68, 69
Diving Incident Report Forms, 169
Diving injuries
   common, first aid for, 144-153
      burns and, 148-149
      concussions and, 147, 148, 153
      cramps and, 147-148
      fish poisoning and, 151
      fractures and, 147
      gas toxicity and, 151-152
      heart attack and, 153
      marine life problems and, 149-151
      near drowning and, 152, 153
      seasickness and, 152
      seizures and, 153
      stroke and, 153
      wounds and, 146-147
   and decompression injuries, 120-153
Diving medical examination, accident prevention and, 5, 6-7
Diving publications, 13-14, 59
Diving skills, judgment problems and, 57
Documentation
   aftermath of diving rescue and, 168
   of neurological examination, decompression illness and, 135
Doors, surface rescue and, 117
Do-si-do tow, surface rescue and, 102
Drags, surface rescue and, 116-117
Drift-diving, 46, 48
Drug abuse as contraindication to diving, 10-11
Dry suit squeeze, 125
Dry suits
   depth, time, or air consumption problems with, 38
   improper fit of, 36-37
   leaks and tears in, 36
   over-weighting and, 38
   problems with, 36-38
   puncture in, 37
   removal of, surface rescue and, 117
   seal failure in, 37
   trim problems with, 38
   valve failure in, 37-38
Duty, accident management and, 171

E

Ear, structure of, 122
Ear infection as contraindication to diving, 9
Ear muffs, air evacuation and, 167
Ear squeezes, 54, 122-123
Earaches as contraindication to diving, 9
Earplugs, outer ear squeeze and, 123
Education
   continuing; see Continuing education
   safety through, 55, 84
Eels, moray, 150
Elevator diving, 68, 70, 86
Embolism, arterial gas, decompression illness and, 129
Emergencies
   buddy system and, 27-31
   dealing with aftermath of diving rescue and, 168-169
   evacuation procedures and, 164-167
   out-of-air; see Out-of-air emergencies
   planning for, 157-171
      accident prevention and, 16-17
      emergency personnel and services and, 157-158
      equipment and, 158-159
      rescue and, 72, 73
   responding to, 160-164
   separation underwater, 27, 28
   sharing air procedures and, 28-31
Emergency ascent, 31, 76-89
   independent; see Independent emergency ascent
   independent rescue procedures and, 78
   out-of-air emergencies and, 77-78
   shared-air, 80-83
   underwater rescue and, 84-89
Emergency buoyant ascent, independent emergency ascent and, 79, 80
Emergency Medical Services (EMS), 16, 73, 157
Emergency personnel and services, accident management and, 157-158
Emergency swimming ascent, independent emergency ascent and, 79, 80
Emphysema, 127
   as contraindication to diving, 8
   mediastinal, 127, 128
   subcutaneous, 127, 128, 136
EMS; see Emergency Medical Services
Enriched air, breathing, 152
Entanglement, visibility and, 45
Environmental hazards
   boating traffic and, 50-51
   cold water and, 41-42
   freshwater and, 46
   general underwater, 44-46
   hot weather and, 42-44
   oceans and, 47-49
   overhead, 49-50
   rivers and, 46-47

Epilepsy as contraindication to diving, 8
Equalization difficulties, 53-54, 122-123, 126-127
Equipment
   emergency, inventory of, 158-159
   fumbling of, as sign of stress, 64
   injured diver's, aftermath of diving rescue and, 168
   predive checks of, buddy system and, 25-27
   problems with, 35-41, 85-86
   rejection of, underwater distress and, 70
   shore transport, surface rescue and, 117
   specialized, accident prevention and, 14-15
   towing and assisting and, 101
Equivalent depth, dives at altitude and, 46
Escape from panicked diver, 95-96
Estimated time of arrival (ETA) of emergency services, 164
Evacuation, rescue and, 73, 164-167
Evaluation, rescue and, 73
Event information, accident management and, 163
Excessive talking as sign of stress, 64
Exercise, diving fitness and; *see* Fitness
Exhalations, forceful, lung squeeze and, 124
Exhaustion, heat, 43
Exposure suits; *see* Drysuits; Wetsuits
Eyes
   protection of, air evacuation and, 167
   stress and, 68

F

Face mask; *see* Mask
Face-down diver, unconscious, surface rescue of, 97
Face-up diver, unconscious, surface rescue of, 97, 98
Facial injuries as contraindication to diving, 9
Facial muscles, assessment of, decompression illness and, 134
Family, notification of, aftermath of diving rescue and, 169
Federal Park Service, 157
Fin loss, 35
Finger sweeps, airway obstruction and, 142
Finkeepers, 38
Fireman's carry, surface rescue and, 113
First aid, 73
   for common diving-related injuries, 144-153
   primary survey in, 146
   secondary survey in, 146
   for serious decompression illness, 137-144
First-aid kit, 15, 158-159
Fish poisoning, first aid for, 151
Fish-feeding dives, 149
Fitness
   accident prevention and, 12-13
   judgment problems and, 55

Fixation as sign of stress, 65
Flags, boating traffic and, 50-51
Flexible tube snorkels, mouth-to-snorkel rescue breathing and, 100
Floats
   boating traffic and, 50-51
   surface rescue and, 106-108
Food and Drug Administration, 10-11
Food poisoning, 151
Foot cramps, 148
Four-person carry, surface rescue and, 116
Fractures, first aid for, 147
Freeflow, regulators and, 39-40
Freeflow equipment, oxygen administration and, 139
Freeze-up of regulators, 40, 42
Frenzl maneuver, ear squeezes and, 54, 123
Freshwater, environmental hazards and, 46, 47
Function, assessment of, decompression illness and, 134-135

G

Gas toxicity, first aid for, 151-152
Gear; *see* Equipment
Gear squeeze, 124-125
Gear tow, surface rescue and, 102
Geographic currents, 48-49
Goggles, plastic, air evacuation and, 167
Good Samaritan law, accident management and, 170-171
Grates, trapping, river diving and, 47
Great barracuda, 150
Groupers, 150
Gulf Stream, 47
Gut squeeze, 126

H

Hand, burns to, first aid for, 148
Hand signals, recreational diving, 68, 69, 167
Handicapped Scuba Association (HSA), 11
Hangover, dehydration and, 43
Hard-breathing, regulator with too high a demand setting and, 40
Hearing, assessment of, decompression illness and, 134
Heart ailments as contraindication to diving, 11
Heart attack, first aid for, 153
Heart disease as contraindication to diving, 8-9
Heart murmur as contraindication to diving, 11
Heat exhaustion, 43
Heat stroke, 43-44
Heaving lines, surface rescue and, 108-109
Heimlich maneuver, airway obstruction and, 142
Helicopter, evacuation by, 166-167

Hemoglobin, carbon monoxide poisoning and, 151
Henry's law, 130
High blood pressure; see Hypertension
Hood squeeze, 125
Horizontally oriented diver, 70
Horse collar BC, spinal injury and, 110
Hose failure, regulators and, 40-41
Hot weather, environmental hazards and, 42-44
HSA; see Handicapped Scuba Association
Hypercapnia, 52, 53, 93
Hypertension, 11
Hyperthermia, 43-44
Hyperventilation, 51, 52-53
Hypothermia, 42, 71
Hypoventilation, 51, 52, 68
Hypoxia, 78
  asthmatic attack and, 8
  hyperventilation and, 53

I

Ice diving, 42, 50, 51
Independent emergency ascent, 78-80
  emergency buoyant, 79, 80
  emergency swimming, 79, 80
  redundant scuba, 79
Independent rescue procedures, emergency ascent and, 78
Infections, 9, 146, 148
Inflatable boat, surface rescue and, 114
Inflatable buoys, surface rescue and, 108
Inflatable floats, surface rescue and, 159
Inflatable motor boats, surface rescue and, 105
Inhalations, forceful, lung squeeze and, 124
Insurance, accident management and, 171
In-water distress
  signs of, 67-70
  at surface, 67-68, 69, 71-72
In-water rescue breathing, 98
Isolation as sign of stress, 64-65

J

Jaw, broken, as contraindication to diving, 9
J-bend snorkel, mouth-to-snorkel rescue breathing and, 100
Jellyfish, 150
Judgment problems, 55-59
J-valve cylinders, reserve air, 21

K

Kayaks, surface rescue and, 106
Kelp, entanglement and, 45
Knives, entanglement and, 45

L

Ladder carry, surface rescue and, 113
Ladders
  falls from, 147, 148
  surface rescue and, 117
Land pick-up, air evacuation and, 166-167
Leader in buddy system, 25
Leaks
  in exposure suits, 36
  regulators and, 39
Least flow, tidal currents and, 48
Leg cramps, 35, 147-148
Legal aspects of diving accidents, 169-171
Liability insurance, accident management and, 171
Life support, decompression illness and, 141-144
Lifejackets, surface rescue and, 106
Lifts, surface rescue and, 112-114
Lights, underwater, silt and mud and, 44
Line roll-up, getting victim aboard boat and, 111, 112
Line-pull signals, 27
Lionfish, 149
Lipoid pneumonia, 151
Litter basket, boat-to-boat transfer and, 166, 167
Liveboating, 46, 48
Local authorities, notification of, aftermath of diving rescue and, 168
Location information, accident management and, 163
Lock-up of regulators, 40
Longshore currents, 48, 49
Low-head dams, 47, 48
Lung overexpansion injuries, 122, 126-129
Lung overpressure injuries, 128
Lung squeeze, 124
Lungs, lung expansion injuries and, 128

M

Maintenance, preventive, of dive gear, 14-15
Marine life problems, first aid for, 149-151
Marine VHF radio, emergency communication and, 17
Mask
  air evacuation and, 167
  loss of, 35
  monitoring of, during towing and assisting, 103
  nonrebreather, 140
  oxygen administration and, 139, 140
  partial rebreather, 140
  Pocket, 139
Mask squeeze, 124-125
MAYDAY, 164
Mediastinal emphysema, decompression illness and, 127, 128

Medical examination, diving, accident prevention and, 5, 6-7
Medications, 9, 159
Menstrual cramps, 148
Mental illness as contraindication to diving, 12
Middle ear squeeze, 122-123
Minimal Impact Diving Skills, 44, 45, 53, 149
Moray eels, 150
Motion sickness, 10, 52, 121
    first aid for, 152
Motor boats, 105
Mouthpiece, loss of, 39
Mouth-to-mouth rescue breathing, 98, 99, 100
Mouth-to-snorkel rescue breathing, 99-100
Movement problems, underwater distress and, 70
Mud, visibility and, 44-45
Multiple person shore carries, surface rescue and, 115-117
Multiple scuba cylinders as alternate air source, 23-24

N

Nasal cannula, oxygen administration and, 139
Nasal spray, sinus squeeze and, 124
National Association of Cave Divers, 50
National Park Service, 16
National Safety Council, 170
National Speleological Society-Cave Diving Section, 50
NAUI, notification of, aftermath of diving rescue and, 168
NAUI Advanced Scuba Rescue Diver course, 12, 144
NAUI Dive Tables, 15, 16, 24-25, 28, 41, 46
NAUI Medical Form, 5, 6-7
NAUI Professional Liability Insurance, 171
NAUI Scuba Rescue Diver course, 12, 144
Nausea, 52, 121
Near drowning, first aid for, 152, 153
Neck injury; see Spinal cord injury
Negligence, avoiding, accident management and, 170-171
Nematocysts, jellyfish and, 150
Neurological examination, decompression illness and, 31, 87, 133-136
Neurotoxins, allergic reactions and, 150-151
Neutral buoyancy, 38, 88
Nicotine as contraindication to diving, 10-11
Niggles, decompression sickness and, 131, 132, 136
911, accident management and, 165
Nitrogen, residual, NAUI Dive Tables and, 41
Nitrogen narcosis, 10, 38, 44
Nitrox, 152
Nonprescription drugs, 9-10, 159

Nonrebreather mask, oxygen administration and, 140
Nose, broken, as contraindication to diving, 9
Notifications, aftermath of diving rescue and, 168-169

O

Obesity, decompression illness and, 130
Observation as response to stress, 66
Obsessive behavior as sign of stress, 65
Obstructions, underwater, 46-47
Oceans, environmental hazards and, 47-49
Octopus regulator, 22, 39, 42, 82, 83
Octopuses, 150
OK signal, 87
One-rescuer CPR, decompression illness and, 142-143
Outer ear squeeze, 123
Outfalls, rivers and, 46
Out-of-air emergencies, 21-31
    controlling diver in, 77
    dealing with panicked flight in, 77-78
    monitoring ascent in, 78
Overbreathing, multiple scuba cylinders and, 24
Overexertion, 51, 52
Overhead environmental hazards, 49-50
Overheating, 42-44
Over-the-counter medications, 9-10, 159
Over-weighting, 38, 68
Oxygen, administration of
    decompression illness and, 137-140
    equipment for, 15
Oxygen kits, 159
Oxygen toxicity, 44, 144, 151-152
Oxygen-augmented rescue breathing, 139, 141

P

Pack strap carry, surface rescue and, 114
Paddle boards, surface rescue and, 107-108, 111-112
Paddle craft, surface rescue and, 105-106
Pain, barotrauma and, 122
Panic
    approaching diver in, 94
    defense and escape from, 95-96
    out-of-air emergencies and, 77-78
    stress and; see Stress
    surface rescue and, 93-96
Paralysis as contraindication to diving, 11
Paramedic shears in removal of exposure suits, 117
Parbuckling, getting victim aboard boat and, 111
Partial pneumothorax, rib fractures and, 147
Partial rebreather mask, oxygen administration and, 140

Passivity as sign of stress, 64-65
Peer pressure, judgment problems and, 56
Periodicals, diving, 13-14, 59
Personal dive gear, accident prevention and, 14-15
Personal flotation device (PFD), surface rescue and, 106
Personal risk, rescue and, 72, 73
Personal water craft, surface rescue and, 105
PFD; see Personal flotation device
Physical disabilities as contraindication to diving, 11-12
Planning and preparation
   accident prevention and, 13-17
   buddy system and, 24-27
Plastic goggles, air evacuation and, 167
Pneumonia
   as contraindication to diving, 9
   lipoid, 151
Pneumothorax
   decompression illness and, 127-129
   rib fractures and, 147
Pocket Mask
   oxygen administration and, 139, 141, 159
   rescue breathing and, 100
Poisoning
   carbon monoxide, 151
   fish, 151
Pollution, visibility and, 45
Pony bottle, 23, 24, 31, 79, 81
Portugese man-of-war, 150
Power boats, small, surface rescue and, 104-105
Precautionary decompression stop, 25, 28, 31, 52, 79
Predive preparation, 13-17
   buddy system and, 24-27
   coordinating activity in, 25-27
   mutual gear checks in, 25-27
   planning dive in, 24-25
   reviewing signals in, 27
Preexisting conditions, neurological examination and, 136
Pregnancy as contraindication to diving, 9
Preparation and planning; see Planning and preparation
Prescription medications, 9, 159
Pressure relief plug of submersible pressure gauge, 41
Preventive maintenance of dive gear, 14-15
Privacy, neurological examination and, 136
Proficiency, judgment problems and, 57-58
Psychological factors, judgment problems and, 55-56
Punctures in dry suits, 37

R

Radio, marine VHF, 17, 159, 164-165
Reactive airway disease; see Asthma
Rebreather mask, partial, oxygen administration and, 140
Recompression therapy, decompression illness and, 136, 137, 145
Recreational diving hand signals, 68, 69
Recreational drugs as contraindication to diving, 10-11
Redundant scuba, 22, 29-31, 39, 83
   emergency shared-air ascent and, 81
   independent emergency ascent and, 79
Reefs, entanglement and, 45
Refresher courses, diving fitness and, 13
Regulators, 21
   freeflow, 39-40
   freeze-up of, 40, 42
   hose failure and, 40-41
   leaks and, 39
   lock-up of, 40
   octopus, 22, 39, 42, 83
   problems with, 39-41
   submersible pressure gauge failure and, 40-41
   too high a demand setting and, 40
Relaxation
   in-water distress at surface and, 71
   as response to stress, 65, 66
Removal
   of diver to shore, surface rescue and, 114-115
   of exposure suit, surface rescue and, 117
   of rescued diver from water, 109-117
Repetitive dives, decompression sickness and, 131
Rescue, 72-73
   emergency ascent and, 84-89
   independent, emergency ascent and, 78
   of responsive diver in distress, 85-87
   risk assessment and, 84-85
   surface; see Towing, assisting, and surface rescue
Rescue breathing, 98-100
   in-water, 98
   mouth-to-mouth, 98, 99, 100
   mouth-to-snorkel, 99-100
   out of water, 141-142
   oxygen-augmented, 139, 141
   using Pocket Mask in, 100
Rescue can, surface rescue and, 107
Rescue craft, surface rescue and, 104-106
Rescuer's identity, accident management and, 163
Reserve air J-valve cylinders, 21
Residual nitrogen, NAUI Dive Tables and, 41
Respiratory infections as contraindication to diving, 9

Responsive diver
    approaching, 96-97
    in distress, rescue of, 85-87, 96-97
Reverse blocks, 125-126
Reverse sinus block, 124
Reverse squeezes, 53, 122
Rib fractures, first aid for, 147
Rip currents, 48, 49
Risk
    assumption of, accident management and, 171
    judgment problems and, 56
    rescue and, 72, 73
    surface rescue and, 93-97
River diving
    current and, 46
    environmental hazards and, 46-47
    obstructions and, 46-47
Rowboats, surface rescue and, 106
Run-off, visibility and, 45

S

Safety through education, 55, 84
Saltwater, buoyancy and, 46
Saltwater aspiration syndrome, 153
Saunas, decompression illness and, 130
Scuba, redundant; *see* Redundant scuba
Scuba Rescue Diver course, NAUI, 12, 144, 145
Sea lions, 150
Sea snakes, 150
Sea urchins, 149
Seal failure in drysuits, 37
Seals, 150
Seasickness; *see* Motion sickness
Seizures, 151-152
    as contraindication to diving, 8
    first aid for, 153
Self-awareness as response to stress, 65
Self-reliance and buddy system; *see* Buddy system
Self-rescue, in-water distress at surface and, 71
Sensation, assessment of, decompression illness and, 134
Senses, assessment of, decompression illness and, 134
Separation underwater, planning for, 27, 28
Shallow-water blackout, 51, 52-53, 152
Shared-air ascent, emergency, 80-83
Sharing air procedures, planning for, 28-31
Sharks, 150
Shipwrecks, 44, 45, 50
Shivering, 41
Shock
    decompression illness and, 140-144
    first aid for, 146
Shore, removal of diver to, surface rescue and, 114-115

Shore transport equipment, surface rescue and, 117
Signals
    boating traffic and, 50-51
    hand, recreational diving, 68, 69, 167
    OK, 87
    reviewing, in predive preparation, 27
Silent bubbles, decompression sickness and, 131
Silt, visibility and, 44-45
Sinus block, reverse, 124
Sinus infection as contraindication to diving, 9
Sinus squeeze, 124
Sinuses, 124
Skin bends, decompression sickness and, 131, 132, 136
Skindiving, hyperventilation before, 51
Skip-breathing, 51, 53, 68, 93
Slack water, tidal currents and, 48
Smoking as contraindication to diving, 10-11, 127
Sneezing, 51, 52, 126
Snorkel
    flexible tube, mouth-to-snorkel rescue breathing and, 100
    J-bend, mouth-to-snorkel rescue breathing and, 100
    monitoring of, during towing and assisting, 103
Snowballing effect, judgment problems and, 56
Soft rescue tube, surface rescue and, 106-107
Sources, 12, 59
Spas, decompression illness and, 130
SPG; *see* Submersible pressure gauge
Spinal cord injury, 11
    first aid for, 147
    removal of rescued diver from water and, 109-110
    towing and assisting and, 101, 102
    two-person carry and, 115-116
Splinting, first aid and, 147
Spontaneous pneumothorax, rib fractures and, 147
Springs, underground, thermoclines and, 46
Squeezes, 122-125
    ascent, 125-126
    chest, 124
    dry suit, 125
    ear, 54, 122-123
    equalization difficulties and, 53, 54
    gear, 124-125
    gut, 126
    hood, 125
    lung, 124
    mask, 124-125
    middle ear, 122-123
    reverse, 53, 122
    sinus, 124

Squeezes, cont'd.
 thoracic, 124
 tooth, 124
SSB radios, 164-165
Staggers, decompression sickness and, 132-133
Stalling as sign of stress, 64
Stingrays, 149
Stings, marine life problems and, 149-150
Stonefish, 149
Strength, assessment of, decompression illness and, 134-135
Stress
 debilitating, 63
 definition of, 62
 helping buddy with, 66-67
 recognizing and responding to, 62-73
 rescue and; see Rescue
 responding to, 65, 66, 70-72
 signs of, 64-65
 symptoms of, 63-64
Stretchers, surface rescue and, 117
Stroke
 first aid for, 153
 heat, 43-44
Subcutaneous emphysema, decompression illness and, 127, 128, 136
Submersible pressure gauge (SPG), 21, 40-41, 77
Substance abuse as contraindication to diving, 10-11
Sunburn, first aid for, 148-149
Sunglasses, air evacuation and, 167
Surf
 entries and exits in, 49
 removal of diver to shore and, surface rescue and, 115
Surface
 in-water distress at, 67-68, 69, 71-72
 panic at, 93-96
Surface rescue; see Towing, assisting, and surface rescue
Surface resting in cold water, in-water distress and, 71
Surfacing of unconscious victim, 87-89
Surfboards, getting victim aboard boat and, 111-112
Surfmats, surface rescue and, 107-108
Suspended material, visibility and, 45

T

Tactile signals, 27
Talking, excessive, as sign of stress, 64
Task loading, judgment problems and, 56, 57
TB; see Tuberculosis

Tears
 in exposure suits, 36
 in mouthpiece, 39
Telephone, cellular, emergency communication and, 17, 159, 165
Tension pneumothorax
 decompression illness and, 127-129
 rib fractures and, 147
Thaws, internal water movement and, 46
Thermoclines, freshwater and, 46
Thoracic squeeze, 124
Three-person carry, surface rescue and, 116
Thrill-seeking, judgment problems and, 56
Throw bags, surface rescue and, 108-109, 159
Tidal currents, 48
Tide tables, 48
Time, problems with, drysuits and, 38
Tiny tanks as alternate air source, 24
Tobacco as contraindication to diving, 10-11, 127
Tooth squeeze, 124
Towing, assisting, and surface rescue, 92-117
 auxiliary rescue equipment and, 104-109
 do-si-do tow and, 102
 gear tows and, 102
 removing rescued diver from water in, 109-117
 rescue breathing and, 98-100
 of responsive diver, 96-97
 risk at surface in, 93-97
 spinal injury and, 101, 102
 of unconscious diver, 97, 98
 underarm assisting and, 103, 104
 wheelbarrow assist and, 103
Traffic, boating, environmental hazards and, 50-51
Training
 diving fitness and, 12-13
 judgment problems and, 57-59
Training dive, 12
Transceivers, emergency communication and, 17
Transfer
 boat-to-boat, 165-166
 boat-to-shore, 166
 diver, 164-165
Trapping grates, river diving and, 47
Treatment information, accident management and, 163
Trim problems
 dry suits and, 38
 underwater distress and, 70, 86-87
Tropical fish, 149
Tuberculosis (TB), 8, 127
Turtles, 150
Two-person carry, surface rescue and, 115-116
Two-person chair carry, surface rescue and, 117
Two-rescuer CPR, decompression illness and, 143-144, 145

U

UHMS; *see* Undersea and Hyperbaric Medical Society
Unconscious diver
  surface rescue of, 97, 98
  surfacing, 87-89
Underarm assisting, surface rescue and, 103, 104
Underground springs, thermoclines and, 46
Undersea and Hyperbaric Medical Society (UHMS), 5
Underwater distress, signs of, 68-70
Underwater dive lights, silt and mud and, 44
Underwater environmental hazards, 44-46
Underwater light signals, 27
Underwater obstructions, 46-47
Underwater rescue, emergency ascent and, 84-89
Upper respiratory infections as contraindication to diving, 9
Upwellings, internal water movement and, 46
U.S. Coast Guard, 16, 72, 157, 162, 164, 166
U.S. Navy bases, 157

V

Valsalva maneuver, ear squeezes and, 54
Valve failure in drysuits, 37-38
Vertically oriented diver, 70
Victim information, accident management and, 162-163
Vinegar, sea urchin stings and, 149
Visibility, underwater, 41, 44-45
Vision, assessment of, decompression illness and, 134
Visualization as response to stress, 65, 66
Vomiting, 10, 52, 121, 126

W

Water bikes, surface rescue and, 105
Water jet-driven personal watercraft, surface rescue and, 104, 105
Watercraft, personal, surface rescue and, 104, 105
Weight belts, releasing, 26-27, 39, 71-72, 87, 88, 89
Weight systems, problems with, 38-39
Weirs, river diving and, 47
Wet suit hood, outer ear squeeze and, 123
Wet suits, problems with, 36-38, 117
Wheelbarrow assist, surface rescue and, 103
Witness information, accident management and, 163
Wounds, first aid for, 146-147
Wreck Diving Specialty Course, 50
Wreck penetration, overhead environmental hazards and, 44, 45, 50

X

Xiphoid process, CPR and, 144

Y

Yoga breathing, stress and, 65
Y-valve, regulator freeze-up and, 42